ADD and Me

Forty Years in a Fog

Ken Patterson

Jessica Kingsley Publishers
London and Philadelphia

First published in the United Kingdom in 2004
by Jessica Kingsley Publishers
116 Pentonville Road
London N1 9JB, England
and
400 Market Street, Suite 400
Philadelphia, PA 19106, USA

www.jkp.com

Copyright © Ken Patterson 2004

Library of Congress Cataloging in Publication Data
Patterson, Ken, 1962-
 ADD and me : forty years in a fog / Ken Patterson.-- 1st American pbk. ed.
   p. cm.
 ISBN 1-84310-777-5 (pbk.)
 1. Patterson, Ken, 1962---Health. 2. Attention-deficit-disordered adults--Biography. 3. Attention-deficit hyperactivity disorder--Patients--Biography. I. Title.
 RC394.A85P38 2004
 362.196'8589'0092--dc22

                                            2003027295

British Library Cataloguing in Publication Data
A CIP catalogue record for this book is available from the British Library

ISBN 1 84310 777 5

Printed and Bound in Great Britain by
Athenaeum Press, Gateshead, Tyne and Wear

Contents

1

Introduction:
The Fool on the Hill?

I'M NOT ALWAYS scatterbrained. Or am I? If I am, then this book might not make much sense to you. If I am not, then maybe some things will be cleared up for both of us. The fact that I'm not sure definitely means something's wrong, right? Or does it?

You opened this book because, for one reason or another, you want more insight into Attention Deficit Disorder, or ADD. You said to yourself, "What's going on with this guy?" That was about thirty seconds ago. I've been asking that question most of my life.

According to the experts, ADD is a disorder of the central nervous system characterized by disturbances in the areas of attention and impulsiveness. In addition to these general symptoms, some people demonstrate aspects of hyperactivity, so they are diagnosed with Attention Deficit Hyperactivity Disorder, or ADHD. I fall into the ADD category.

An entire set of characteristics stems from the disturbances brought on by ADD, including: impatience; moodiness; intolerance of noise and chaos; carelessness with details; shaky communication skills; a limited capacity for work and stress; a heightened propensity to become easily bored; and a tendency for disorganization.

Given the above symptoms, an ADDer is prone to obsessions from things as innocent as neglecting chores, to finishing a video game, to domination of somebody's life. These obsessions often lead to addictions with alcohol, drugs, gambling, or sex.

Many of these symptoms might apply to people without ADD, and only someone trained to recognize the differences can make an accurate diagnosis. Generally, a diagnosis is based on a professional's assessment of the intensity of the characteristics mentioned above, and whether or not these characteristics have affected an individual's life through a pattern of recurring behavior.

But before you settle into this text too much, thinking I'm the voice of wisdom on ADD, let me warn you. I'm not a doctor, or a mental health worker. I didn't even get my college degree in the health field. I received a B.A. in Creative Writing—and that was hard enough for me to get.

That's why you shouldn't consider this book somebody's weighty deductions on ADD after decades of research and study. And don't in any way assume this book is an ADD self-help guide. The book is merely an account of someone's life—a loose and fragmented one at that. Someone who supposedly has ADD. A life that is separate and unique when compared to most people's lives.

There are those who know more about ADD than I ever will. Reading long books about ADD is boring, and I just haven't put in enough time to accumulate as much information about the subject as others have. But I've read enough literature and talked to enough people in the know to realize that I may actually have this disorder. At least that's what a psychologist told me a few months prior to my fortieth birthday. I went to see the psychologist because I always knew I had trouble thinking, and I wanted to consult an expert to find out if there was anything wrong with me. The psychologist was the first person to suggest that I may have ADD. Notice that I said "suggest," because according to the experts there's no definitive test to determine whether or not someone has ADD. But read on, and judge for yourself whether or not I have ADD. Take an impromptu trip with a man who's always in a fog. But put on your fog lights. If you're a doctor or somebody who does know a lot about ADD, this book might be illuminating. If you're not, reading this book will be like staring into a strobe light in a dance club after drinking three or four beers.

But before we begin our trip, it's only fair to give you a few paragraphs of background. Bear with me. This is pretty mundane stuff.

After seeing the psychologist, I visited a psychiatrist. He agreed with the psychologist's diagnosis and prescribed two or three different medications that generally help people with ADD. After taking the drugs for a few months, I didn't notice any difference in my cognitive skills or in my ability to process information. In addition, the drugs didn't seem to agree with my body. I was always constipated, and I felt hotter than usual. I told the psychiatrist I didn't want to take the drugs any more.

The psychiatrist told me that I might be one of those few individuals who doesn't react well to medication and suggested an alternative method of treating my ADD. Per the psychiatrist's suggestion, I attended an ADD presentation at an Austin, Texas hospital where various experts gave talks on non-pharmaceutical approaches. I listened attentively—well, as attentively as someone with ADD can—to a chiropractor, an optometrist, a nutritionist, and an educational kinesiologist. They spouted their theories on what might be responsible for the out-of-whack mechanisms in the bodies of those afflicted with ADD. The optometrist suggested that vision therapy might be the answer to many ADDers' predicaments, and the chiropractor thought manipulating people's spines could help. I chose to follow the nutritionist's advice to try different nutritional supplements, and I scheduled an appointment with the educational kinesiologist to test the inner workings of my brain. Working with the kinesiologist was the most fun. We talked a lot about his stint in Vietnam as a foot soldier; the most important thing I learned from my new war-torn friend was never to set foot on his Texas ranch without an invitation.

After seeing all these experts in the field and reaching for my medical insurance card far too many times, I made this determination: nothing had helped. My thoughts ran in circles. Initially, I decided I had been misdiagnosed. Later on, I thought there was a possibility that I might actually have ADD. To this day, I still take nutritional supplements hoping they'll clear away the fog. That's the problem, you see: I just don't seem to think very well. And not thinking very well has led to an entire host of problems that affect every aspect of my life.

And now, let's take that trip I promised you. But hold on for the ride and try to keep your thoughts inside the book at all times.

2

The Long and Winding Road

SEPTEMBER 1974

A Rude Awakening

Tap! Tap! Tap! Tap! Tap! It's the dead of night and even though my childhood home is situated directly over California's San Andreas Fault, I can tell it's not another earthquake. Still, my eyes can't get any wider, and they're fixated on the bulging springs that support my brother Richard's bunk bed mattress above me. The bed frame knocks against the tiny house's wall, and Bullet and Bosco bark in the backyard.

Tap! Tap! Tap! Tap! Tap! The sound is too steady for it to be my brother merely shifting in the darkness. Any time he moves above me, I fear the worst. Usually someone would have been here by now. I should go for my mother or father. After all, this is something too scary for a twelve-year-old boy. I get out of my bed; I back away from the shaking.

The scene is like something from *The Exorcist*. The room is bathed in the blue glow of darkness meant for horror movies. My brother shakes convulsively atop a child's mattress. But Richard is not a child; he's in his twenties now. His eyes are even larger than mine, but they're pleading, and froth spills from the side of his mouth onto my mother's clean sheets. Richard is definitely having a diabetic reaction. I've been trained to look for the signs, but even a complete neophyte not privy to the signs of someone displaying the onset of a diabetic reaction could tell there's something wrong with my brother. I don't want this to be happening. I've always slept lightly, dreading what I'm witnessing now.

Does Richard need orange juice? Or was it sugar water? Either one will do. That's what I remember my father telling me. Or was it my mother? I can't remember. I'm sure we're out of orange juice. And I can't remember the ratio of sugar to water. Richard shakes a lot more now. He slides over the side of his mattress and down onto the floor. His head lands with a thump. If I didn't know better, I'd have thought this was a controlled slide. One of his legs sprawls on the top of my mattress. I step backward toward the opposite wall.

Richard's head strikes the floor violently, and his still pleading eyes look in my direction. These are the same eyes that are usually filled with assurance. The steadfast eyes that oversaw the loading of a twelve-gauge shotgun and ultimately targeted a mallard about to land on a marsh pond. These are normally Humphrey Bogart eyes, sunk into a large head and a compact body. Eyes accustomed to staring you down if you cross their path. But now they're just begging for help. The only problem is I need help myself, and I struggle to move away from the wall. But just as I'm finally about to go to the kitchen to search for something to give my brother, even if it's wrong, my mother rushes into the room and flicks on the overhead light. She's wearing her ratty pink robe and slippers, the slippers with stinky rubber soles. Her small, hunched-over body enters the now sickly, yellow stain pouring out from the dirty light fixture above. The image before me bespeaks of someone who is ill equipped for this heroic mission, but everything is going to be all right now. She has a glass of sugar water in her hand, and her mouth is set in its usual narrow slit. It's a mouth shaped by years of abuse brought on by five hardheaded boys and an alcoholic husband. My mother hovers over my brother, her hooked nose thrust out like the beak of a bird of prey. She grabs Richard's head with one hand and presses the glass to his lips with the other. He moves his head away from the glass. But my mother is persistent. She's been through this plenty of times before.

"Drink it, Richard," she says calmly but forcefully. "Drink it." It's going to be all right. She gets some liquid down his throat, and he slowly shows signs of coherence. I'm saved. That's right. Not just Richard, but me.

This was one of the first moments in my life where I had to act. When I had to recognize a situation for what it was and do what was expected of me. And this was what I dwelled on in that tiny bedroom some twenty years ago. I didn't save my brother; I tried to figure out *how* to save my brother. It was the process that threw me then, and it's the process that still throws me today. Ultimately, it comes down to the same question again and again. *What do I do? I just don't know what to do.*

3

Helter Skelter

JANUARY 1995

All Engines Stop

The more nervous test-taker sits in the first row of a classroom. He has about five pencils, all sharpened and waiting. He anticipates the test prompter's "Begin" even as he eyes the clock to determine that "Put down your pencils" time. When it comes to taking tests, I take being nervous to a new level. I'll show up with six pencils and make sure I have two pencil sharpeners. I'll not only eye the clock in anticipation of a test's beginning, but I'll set both alarms on my watch to remind me of the time it's supposed to end. As soon as the test is under way, I'll rush through each question, getting faster with every one. I'm always afraid I'll run out of time before I run out of questions. I've always been very nervous taking tests. I take great care to ensure that I won't fail anything since failing is something I'm too good at.

Even so, I feel more confident taking some tests than others. Civil servant tests, for example, aren't as bad as college exams. I think they are designed for people who never graduated from high school—or at least for those who hold a G.E.D. (General Education Diploma) like I do. I feel I have a better than average chance at passing them.

It was a crisp early morning on a junior college campus. It was the day of the Hillsborough Police Department's entry-level test for the position of police officer. We were potential future crime fighters yearning to wear a badge. We filled every row. Everyone had an imaginary Superman *S* on his chest. We were ready to forge ahead into the seedier side of affluent Hillsborough.

The room was very quiet; testing rooms always are. People whispered quietly amongst themselves; nobody wanted to jinx his chances by filling the room with noisy karma.

Opposite me, a burly off-duty police officer sat with a stopwatch. He wore a T-shirt boasting the larger-than-life white word POLICE set against a blue background. The officer crossed his muscular arms over his chest, and I wished I had biceps like his. I respected him more than he'd ever know, but he eyed me more than I thought he should. It made me nervous. I'm sure it was my fault. I've always had this annoying habit of maintaining eye contact with someone longer than I should. I think some people find this challenging. Usually I am not aware that I'm doing it, and my intentions are innocent. In fact, most of the time when I lock eyes with someone, I don't have any intentions at all. The wheels in my mind aren't even turning. But by the time I realize I've thrown down a figurative gauntlet, it's too late. A few threatening words are spoken, or a few confrontational stares have already headed my way. That day, Officer Burly had that Clint Eastwood squint going on when he looked at me, as if I were a suspect in a Dirty Harry movie. Sometimes his biceps twitched in unison with the classroom clock's second hand.

I looked at the bubbles on my scantron, not really interested in them. I read and reread the questions and directions. The test format was always the same. Scenarios meant to gauge my response. What would you do if? What can you deduce from this? Based on the preceding excerpt, what is the best answer? Try to memorize the following images. You will be tested on them later without the luxury of reference.

And that's when it began. The stress. The confusion. More stress. My mind seizing up on me like an engine bereft of the proper amount of oil. And finally, the guessing. That's what the onset of confusion is like in my world. A total shutdown of logic and clear thought. The Hillsborough Police Officer Test no longer made sense to me. The words got jumbled. I knew what they were, but they just stood lifeless on the page. Their meaning was lost. I only knew symbols now. This word was *and*; that word was *to*. All together, the sentences and the intent behind the words were a mystery. Still, I darkened the bubbles on the scantron, making certain the number two grey inside them never extended beyond the tiny circles, double-checking that I'd darkened the intended bubbles two or three times. I always covered my bases. I figured that even when I was absolutely guessing, at least my guesses would apply to the right question. This type of arbitrary decision making in my life has somehow gotten me through. During times like these, few have realized that my clean-cut, coherent facade conceals a network of frayed wires within the intricate lacing of electronic highways inside my head.

When I was done that day, in that massive liberal arts classroom, I tilted my head in disgust at my state of confusion. I was frustrated beyond belief. I glanced surreptitiously around me at people who probably knew what every sentence meant, who knew that they weren't completely guessing, who were only perplexed by the test questions themselves. They knew that their minds worked. I was jealous. Envious of the normal. Still, I didn't have to pass by much. I just needed to pass, that's all.

The police officer in the T-shirt seemed to read my mind. His trained eye seemed to see into the frayed wiring in my head, and now, for a different reason, I made certain I didn't make eye contact with him. I was too embarrassed to look into the eyes of a success and too scared that he might learn my secret.

And then I heard it. "Pencils down." The solid, successful, important cop gathered our papers and authoritatively instructed us what to do next. He was all knowing to me. Omnipotent before us. In control of his world. I could be like him. Couldn't I? As I listened to what he had to say, something told me I never would be like him, or like most of those young people in that room. I realized I'd failed the test, even before it had been corrected. I knew I did not need to anxiously wait for the mail day after day, wait for that lovely slip of paper telling me I'd advanced to the next stage of the testing process. To reveal my S for all to see. The reason I knew I'd failed wasn't because I was doubtful of my efforts. I actually knew the answers to a lot of the questions. And come on, it was a civil servant test.

No, that wasn't it. In my frenetic state, I neglected to finish the test. In my haste to be perfect, my mind froze. I left at least fifty questions blank, fifty questions never even touched by one of those six perfectly sharpened pencils.

4

Ah, Look at All the Lonely People

I LIKED TO play with coins when I was a young boy. I'd line them up in order. Order has always been important to me. When one's life is often chaos and fog, order brings clarity.

Pennies would be foot soldiers; nickels were corporals or sergeants; dimes were lieutenants or captains; and quarters stood in the front as generals. All in rows. All in their place. Rank and position in the world preoccupied me. Sometimes I'd pick off a few of the enemy at a time, a few unlucky pennies who had wandered into an ambush, overwhelmed by a superior army. Other times, two sides of neatly arranged coins clashed. Then the order collapsed, and copper and silver lay there atop one another in an unruly mass. That's when the game usually ended.

But it wasn't just coins that intrigued me. Inanimate objects of any type held my attention. Ballpoint pens, pencils, erasers all became spaceships until I had whole fleets of school supplies floating around an imaginary universe. My dad brought home "steelies", marble-sized balls of steel from the machine shop, which I rolled into walls or off steps. I liked listening to the heavy miniature spheres move against other surfaces. Just looking at the steelies somehow brought joy. So solid, so perfect. So shiny and undisturbed. No blemishes or inconsistencies. So completely together and compact.

ADDers obsess over things. At least I do. Emotions seem to run higher. As a young child, I was calm, but I locked myself inside little worlds created to add excitement. Music was key to this excitement. At night, I listened to a transistor radio beneath my covers. Music hypnotized me there, in that makeshift tent. Songs like Paul McCartney's "Band on the Run" or Elton John's "Rocket Man" moved me more than anything else in my life, and they still do. Movies, too, were an escape from the mundane coins and inanimate objects. I particularly enjoyed Peter Sellers movies or James Bond movies. In these films, characters controlled their environments and manipulated them to their liking. They were set in exotic locations like Paris or some far-off island. They were stimulating. Any movie that especially stimulated me became forever a part of me. The more stimulating or moving the better. And sometimes I'd find myself home alone in front of the TV, an isolated boy yearning for what he didn't have in his life. Not just for what I lacked, but also for some reason, for what the world lacked. Sometimes I still get misty eyed over those movies.

Back then, I empathized to the point of extreme with characters wanting to be heard or to break out of their mediocrity. Movies such as *To Sir, with Love* or *Blackboard Jungle* especially touched a nerve. I loved the way the kids in these movies expressed their feelings and the fact that they had someone stable enough to vent to. Although there was a lot of venting in my home, I wasn't a participant. I was only an observer. Still, I felt the effects of what was going on, and I wanted to yell and carry on like everyone else. I wanted to be involved in the drama. My parents were vigilant about Richard's diabetic traumas. They fretted over my brother Danny when they found him drunk in his homemade fort in the backyard. He had passed out from drinking wine that he found on the railroad tracks. I wanted to be fretted over too, because of my constant state of disconnection to the conscious world. One of my other brothers, Stephen, came home from Vietnam and committed suicide because the war had messed him up. My parents mourned Stephen's passing, but I wanted someone to mourn my nearly non-existent life. I realized my family did not recognize my problems; my isolation did not merit their attention. Unfortunately, perhaps because I was the baby in the family, or because I was someone who was usually in his own world, I was left with nothing more than movies and the characters in them to act out my fantasies of confrontation. As a result, I constantly longed for another life, and I grieved over my bland existence.

Mostly, I was just too lonely. I was a small boy in a small house in an unincorporated area of the county. We lived near the railroad tracks where my brothers said hoboes enslaved children. I was immersed in a neighborhood where blue-collar fundamentals ruled the day, and white-collar philosophies were left to those who wore ties and slacks. A boy was supposed to go along with the status quo. Baseball in the street and make-believe in the fields were the norm. There wasn't much talk of dreams or what lay in the outer world. But there was always plenty of talk about how somebody might earn more money so he wouldn't have to work as hard.

No one noticed, or had the time to notice, if a boy had trouble understanding things or making friends. It was just understood that people did what they did. They were happy with what they had, and that was that. But I needed more. I had very few friends. And seldom would anyone in my family interact with me. My brothers had their own agendas, and my mother never played with me. My father usually worked or sat on a barstool down at the 300 Club. When my father was home, he tore apart an engine or some other part of a car with my brothers. In my desperate attempts to feel connected, I sometimes lingered on the periphery as a few sets of able hands dug into the innards of one of our wounded vehicles. Afterward, when the older males in the pack had their fill of digesting what lay before them, I moved in for my fair share of the kill. Sometimes I paused to look at a carburettor, a starter motor, or some other mysterious piece of discarded automobile technology. I wondered how it worked or where it fitted into the world. More often than not, I incorporated those car parts in my war games, not knowing until years later what the parts were for. I wanted my brothers or my father to include me in their repairs, but I knew, just as they did, that I had no mechanical aptitude. When I did try to get involved in repairing cars, I was on the receiving end of condescending smiles, or I observed the unspoken communication pass between those who were working. Attempts to bring me up to speed on combustible engines had long since ended. I continued to raise too many questions, and responded with too many blank looks when people explained how pistons worked or the reason why cars had coils. They lost time or patience when it came to trying to get through to me. Cars had to run *now*, and people had to go to work early tomorrow.

Still, I tried to get involved with the male bonding that took place during the times those engines were torn apart. I didn't want to be alone anymore. I recall one particular Saturday when I was playing in the front yard amongst the weeds and poplar leaves. I toyed with the idea of getting my hands dirty.

My father and my brother Mark were on either side of the family car, a '64 Buick Wildcat, which—appropriately enough, given its name—let out a growl any time we took the car out for a spin. It wasn't growling now, however, because a few days earlier the Wildcat had blown its top. The explosion took place as we waited for an exceedingly lengthy traffic light to change from red to green. All of a sudden, we'd heard a loud boom, as if someone had set off a stick of dynamite under the hood of our stealthy cat. Seconds after the explosion the car's hood went sailing into the sky, before ultimately coming down with a crash in the intersection ahead. It took a few minutes for us to regain our senses, and I remember that my ears rang for a while afterward. Luckily someone in a jeep nearby had a fire extinguisher handy, and the remaining flames were quickly snuffed out. Unfortunately, the damage had already been done, and a blackened bomb crater lay beneath the Wildcat's hood. It was into that crater that my brother Mark and my father now peered. Their tools were laid out neatly on two covers designed to protect the car's fenders, which miraculously had survived the blast.

Amazingly, much of the work needed to get the car back to normal had already been done, even if there were still some charred remnants. They bantered about possible reasons for the explosion, as they had since the day of the incident.

"It *must* have been a leaky fuel line," my father said, shaking his graying head. "It's a no-brainer." I thought I saw my father look in my direction when he said this; his trademark black-rimmed glasses were positioned just a tad below normal.

Mark just nodded in agreement. He endeavored to untangle a mass of colored wires purchased a few hours earlier. He was wearing his Chevron shirt, the one he wore to work when he pumped gas. The one he had worn to work when the cops took him away in shackles for smoking pot. Now he only smoked a pipe filled with rich tobacco, with a scent that always let me know he was home.

I looked up from the brick house I'd constructed in the front yard, acting as though I had things under control on my end; but I didn't. The windows in my house never stayed put. They'd loosen as soon as I moved them. Eventually one, then the other, would fall out of the house completely. I lay in the weeds and poplar leaves staring into the blackness inside the brick house, silently cursing those windows. The blackness made the house so cold and empty. I thought about trying one of the windows again, but I decided to leave the tiny white piece of stubborn plastic where it was. If I was lucky, maybe it would become lost under the crumbly poplar leaves for good.

I got up and brushed the rust-colored residue of the leaves from my button-down J. C. Penney's shirt and inched over to the pitiful two-rail fence that separated our front yard from the dirt-covered area where the Wildcat was parked. The two grimy mechanics were still hard at work trying to make sense of the mess that fate had left them.

I dug my hands deep into my pockets and pushed up my shoulders. When I was near the Wildcat, I could smell the telltale odor of whiskey and cigarettes coming from my father. Even now, a Lucky Strike dangled from two of his fingers, sending smoke rings into the cool air where they mingled with the few leaves remaining on the poplar tree.

I stared into the Buick's gaping black void where order had once reigned. The vibrant colors of the wires that my brother was sorting out were in stark contrast to the charcoaled flanks of the scorched engine compartment. Mark voiced his concern about something not being right, and my father chided him with, "Maybe you've got your wires crossed."

This time there was no doubt about it: my father looked at me when he said these words. His eyes paused on me a moment longer as he dug a piece of tobacco from his mouth and spat it in my direction. Mark quickly stifled a spontaneous chuckle as his gaze followed the discarded object past one of the Wildcat's fenders. Never saying a word, I merely smiled at my father, dug my hands a little deeper into my pockets, and turned around. I walked back the way I'd come. Past the insignificant fence. Past the pathetic plastic windows. And finally, past the empty brick house which I left to be consumed by the forces of nature.

Later in life I learned, or at least I came to believe, that what I really lacked were the skills of total comprehension that are a must when digging into an engine. There was always a mental block between me and participation in these repair projects. That fog prevented me from engaging in the more complex aspects of life. Because of my inabilities, I was unable to find companionship. People usually want to be around those who can relate with them on a particular subject. Often, I just couldn't.

But this is what I needed more than anything else. Interaction. Assimilation. And most of all, attention. Any attention. A way out of my isolation.

5

Time to Rock the Boat?

FEBRUARY 1974

See Me

"See me. Feel me. Touch me. Heal me." The verse, of course, is from *Tommy*,
The Who's modern-day version of a boy, Helen Keller, desperately trying to
break free from his deaf, dumb and blind existence. Although I wasn't deaf
and blind, I was certainly dumb one day in a sixth grade classroom.

I liked Mrs. Yencho's classroom. It had a long closet hallway you could
get lost in when the lights were off. I liked hanging my jacket on one of the
little hooks and putting my lunch in one of its many cubbyholes. I liked
gazing out the window at Garfield School's verdant lawn where I played
baseball until the sun went down. I also liked Mrs. Yencho; she was really
interested in her students and frequently drew happy faces on my papers.
Reading and writing intrigued me. I was ecstatic when I finished one of the
color-coded readers and I could advance to the next level. It made me feel
important. A young, literate achiever. I wanted to put my ideas down on
paper too, like the ones I saw in those readers. So what if I didn't know the
inner workings of a carburettor; I was going to be a writer. I set to work on a
story about a man who traveled to far-off places. When I got home from
school, I'd sometimes sit against one of the factory buildings near the
railroad tracks where the hoboes were said to camp. I'd watch the trains go by
and wonder where they were headed and what they saw. Wherever they
ended up, the traveler in my story would end up too. The monotonous perpe-
tuity of the sound of the trains' wheels was occasionally accompanied by a

rusty metal squeak or a quickly clunking jerk on a reluctant coupling. The grass in a field a few feet away moved with the train, and the tempting smell of licorice plants added to the sweetness I felt when pen touched paper. Of course when I started writing this story, I didn't have enough knowledge of the world to add any sense of realism to my scribblings, but it didn't matter. Writing was a means of escape, a way of purging myself of all the loneliness and restlessness I had inside. Ultimately, though, writing wasn't enough. I inevitably needed to experience more than my new-found hobby would allow; I needed to break out of my secluded bubble and have others experience me. But it wouldn't be a well thought-out plan that burst the bubble. In fact, it wouldn't be a plan at all.

I don't really remember when it began, that day in class, but I suddenly found myself rocking my heavy desk back and forth. The one that had that big lid you could slam when getting your books out of its obese metal belly.

I think Mrs. Yencho was trying to tell us something when the rocking began, and then I think she was telling me to stop what I was doing, but I didn't. It wasn't that I didn't hear her; it was just that I needed to do what I was doing. And I needed to continue doing it until I saw fit to stop. Boom! Boom! Boom! The desk started to rise and fall continually on the polished wood classroom floor. It was an enormous thing with one metal foot. My classmates looked on intently as if watching some sort of futuristic rodeo rider trying to tame his robotic beast.

As the rocking continued, Mrs. Yencho approached me. I think she was getting more vociferous, not necessarily because she was getting angrier, but because she needed to yell above the booming. I'm sure she must have been annoyed. What adult wouldn't have been? But I don't remember her being annoyed. I just remember her getting closer and closer to that desk. And before I could stop it—not that I would have—that weighty classroom dinosaur smashed down on Mrs. Yencho's feet. I'm certain she must have become a little angry then. But mostly, I realized that the desk had stopped rocking and the other children in the classroom were laughing, and I was smiling. They were noticing me. All of them. And I was important.

Later, in the principal's office waiting room, I sat there reflecting on what had happened and feared what Mr. Latherup might have to say to me. I thought about another kid in my class. A kid who repeatedly slammed his head against his desk. Poor square-headed Ronnie. My comrade in disruption. As with my senseless pounding of the floor with my desk, Ronnie didn't seem to have an agenda when he pummeled himself. He just seemed to be making noise for the sake of making noise.

When Mr. Latherup finally called me into his office, it wasn't to give me a spanking with that wooden paddle that looked like a small cricket bat; it was to ask why I'd done it. No matter how hard I tried, I couldn't give him a reason. But I was sorry. I saw a momentary smile cross Mr. Latherup's face and I knew everything would be okay. Still, I was worried. I couldn't help wondering if there was more to my acting out than just wanting to be noticed. What hidden demon prompted me to do these things? Why wasn't I able to keep myself in check? Moreover, even then with a child's limited capacity, I thought, "Will it happen again?"

6

Chalking Out of Line

JULY 1983

The British are Coming

The party at a local Brit's flat in Felixstowe, England, took place shortly after the Fourth of July. Dennis Clannihan, another GI with an Irish name, invited me to come along with him. Dennis and I shared a couple of rooms in a house around the corner.

I looked up to Dennis. I wasn't a buffed guy, and it had been my experience that most muscular guys hung around together. But that wasn't the only reason I liked Dennis. I think that because of the lack of attention I got as a child, I frequently sought out individuals who might be my friends. I had a need to make a lasting bond with whomever I thought worthy enough to be a part of my world. I also needed strong, together, clear-headed people like Dennis to act as guides and teachers. Early in my life I learned to latch on to people who could help me. I was always the person who didn't fully understand what the teacher said to do, or how to do it, the person who always had to nudge his classmate for information. Because I lacked the ability to figure things out on my own and overcome obstacles in life, a helper was a must while I was stationed in England; Dennis became this helper. If I needed help with learning how to play my guitar, for example, Dennis would bring his upstairs and show me how to play. When I had questions about the proper way to lift weights or do other kinds of exercises, Dennis would pump iron with me or tell me the best way to do sit-ups.

Dennis even helped me with making the transition from American life to English life a little easier. By July, he'd been in England a lot longer than I had. He knew the ropes. Not only did he help me adjust to England, he gave me a great deal of insight into the English lifestyle. Oddly, he hated everything about the country. I liked England then, and I still do. But Dennis's hatred of everything British turned into a show. One day I woke up in my top-floor room to the noise of Dennis rolling a bowling ball down the stairs to his room. He often did things like that just to tear apart that lovely old English house and get a rise from its English tenants.

Dennis's behavior didn't come without consequences, however. Another day, I was walking with him on Felixstowe's beach boardwalk when a bunch of Brits jumped him. I don't know why they jumped him, but I knew that I didn't need to come to my friend's aid. I just felt sorry for them as Dennis beat up his attackers. I didn't condone most of Dennis's behavior, but I admired the fact that he got away with it. He had a strange charisma that I'd never had. My inability to make many friends easily, or give off an aura like Dennis's, always kept me back from the kinds of social interactions I longed for. Just as I yearned for friends and attention as a child, I longed to find playmates as an adult. This desire was magnified by the fact that I was a long way from home and in another country. So when Dennis hung an American flag on the railing of our balcony on the Fourth of July, I hung one up too. When Dennis went to a party full of drunken British loyalists, I wanted to go too.

There was a lot of yelling that night, and it seemed that everyone in Felixstowe had been invited. I followed Dennis; I was the proud sidekick of a real all-American boy. He was an American abroad, James Dean with muscles to back up his rebel attitude. I followed my adopted big brother right up those carpeted English stairs. And before long I was drinking. I drank a lot in the military. I considered it a rite of passage. After all, I was a GI representing my country, the best country in the world. All young GIs had a tradition of hanging out in bars and tying one on. It would have been odd if I didn't follow suit.

This English house was a duplicate of the one in which Dennis and I lived. We walked up to a landing at the top of the stairs and drifted toward a room full of hearty British men gathered around a chalkboard. They were well juiced and having a good time playing some kind of game. I wanted to play, too, but I just kept on drinking while Dennis left me and roamed through the house. I didn't pay too much attention to this because Dennis was at his best alone. If there ever was a master of his domain, it was Dennis.

A goofy smile crossed my face after each potent foreign beer numbed my brain and my judgment. I got more and more interested in the game. Nobody paid any attention to me, and they definitely didn't explain the game to me. I didn't care. I was drunk, and I wasn't alone in my room shoveling coal into that little grate or searching for another fifty pence to feed the electric meter. I was content. But I was not absolutely satisfied. I had to play that chalkboard game.

From what I could make out, the stout British men were writing down the first things that came to mind about England, mostly the things they liked about their country. Quintessentially English things like the Queen or fish and chips. Cricket and snooker. It wasn't a well-planned game, and it seemed to be a free-for-all. Someone would just jump in when a thought came to mind. I was smiling and laughing with them, eager for my turn. When I saw an opportunity, I grabbed a piece of chalk. The laughter became even more raucous when they saw this silly American step up to the chalkboard. In keeping with the impromptu method behind the game, I wrote down the first thing that came to mind. I wrote in big bold strokes as tall and clear as their words. I even made certain the words I put down were all in caps. All the while laughing with the others in the spirit of fun and male bonding.

There on the chalkboard in those British men's beloved country were the words FUCK ENGLAND. There was no doubt about it. There was no less doubt that I was whisked away by the biggest of the gang, dragged all the way down those carpeted stairs I had traversed only a few minutes earlier, and thrown out the door. Why had I written those words? I thought it was all in fun; the alcohol had loosened me up enough to think I could jest with my new acquaintances. But the inappropriate impulsive behavior was obviously wrong, drunk or sober. This time I would pay for it and I needed to accept my punishment. After all, you don't come to someone else's country, especially a country you like, and do something like that. I can see that now. It's always easy to see things like this later on. In my case, however, insight has been a luxury reserved for comfy chairs or beds when the lights have gone down, long after the damage is done.

Fortunately, Dennis saved my looks and my teeth that night. He was my guardian anti-English watchdog, and he came to my rescue just as that large British man was about to pound me with fists the size of cantaloupes. I guess something in Dennis's gaze told him not to defend the Union Jack that evening. Still, Dennis said that I should head back home. I heeded his advice.

It was a long walk home in the dark. It seemed darker to me than any night I had ever experienced. My mood was dark too. Everything was diminished. The wind, the musky seafront air. Even the North Sea waves lapping against the round rocks of Felixstowe's shoreline seemed quieter, as if they were whispering in the murky brown water, "Shh, here he comes now."

I was consumed by confusion and bewilderment at the way I had acted at the party. Events like this followed a pattern. They happened wherever I went. Unmistakable demonic faux pas that moved inside me. Palpable transgressions attached themselves to the air that I breathed and the layers of wrinkles in my mind. I stood on the shore gazing out at the tremendous North Sea. Far from where I stood on the beach, a large ship lay upside down. It shouldn't have been there, I thought. Just as I shouldn't have been where I was standing.

7

What's Driving Me?

THE SMALL OBJECTS that fascinated me as a small boy did not energize me as much when I reached my teens, but I still needed the same kind of stimulation. Something to hold my attention. Of course, girls are always a draw for teenage boys, but I didn't have much luck with them. Instead, I fell in love with cars and motorcycles. I still couldn't repair either very well, but I could drive them. Finally, I found something I could do well.

The problem was that I wasn't satisfied just to get from point A to point B. I had to take diversions through mud or slippery grass. I loved to up-end my truck so that it would drive on two wheels. I did donuts (360 degree spins) until the smell of rubber made my pal, Jake, and me sick. But illegal experimentation of this nature comes with a price. And I began to pay for speed and irresponsible driving.

My growing hatred for the police equaled my growing number of moving violations. I would grind my teeth or swear under my breath at the many little colored rectangles of paper that I kept in a neat stack in my bedroom. But I marveled at the violations' differences. Speeding tickets were different from illegal u-turn tickets, and city police tickets were different from sheriff's citations. Each ticket had a different vibe. Some were written with an obviously upset hand, while others were written by someone who had taken his time, as if he had entered a penmanship contest. Each ticket conjured up a unique California location and a story to go with it.

As with rocking the desk back and forth in Mrs. Yencho's class, I couldn't control myself when it came to driving recklessly in vehicles, any vehicles. I've always been obsessive, and I craved driving. I loved the motion. It both relaxed and exhilarated me to be in a moving car—especially if that car was doing ninety. When I experimented with the different kinds of motion, I was too wrapped up in what I was doing to look for cops. Too focused. In fact, it was one of the few times that I could remain absolutely focused. And it was lucky for me that I did, because there were a lot of near misses with things like telephone poles and ditches. To add to the exhilaration of movement, I had a captive audience in my friend, Jake. He laughed at the things I did with a vehicle. He said "Oh" when we almost smashed into something, or "Man" when we did. Jake has always been a tough, no-nonsense guy like his Dutch father, who emigrated to the United States to escape Nazi oppression. And just like his dad—and the rest of his family—Jake has always believed in self-reliance and humor to get him through life. Mostly, Jake likes to observe how the rest of the world goes about its business and then find comedy in the little idiosyncrasies and anachronisms that are taken for granted by others. My friend of over twenty years is a closet Seinfeld like me, and when we're together, we become stronger in our ability not to take life so seriously, but to point out how ridiculous life can be sometimes. To some, Jake might come across as a hard-nosed big guy who has no empathy for people, but to me, I know him to be a very kind and just guy. A person I would literally trust if my life depended on it.

After a while, both Jake and I became expert at spotting cops, and the amount of violations I received decreased. We knew Atherton had black and whites. So did Redwood City; it also had a helicopter and four-wheel-drive SUVs. Palo Alto's patrol cars were white. We could even spot cop cars without the lights on top. We knew where all the traps were. And all the best fast food restaurants. Sometimes we'd stay out until one in the morning pursuing our passion for what we called The Cruise. We knew every curve and straightaway from Palo Alto to Redwood City. Every dip in the road. Every wet patch of mud or loose gravel. Every unincorporated field.

Again, my illogical run-ins with authority came to a head. I got pulled over far too much, often for things that were wrong with my car. There wasn't much I could do about that since I still wasn't very good at repairing cars and didn't have much money to have someone else do it for me.

One particular night, an Atherton police officer lit me up for a burned-out tail-light. I'd had enough. I sat there, my mind racing even though my car stood stock-still. I couldn't get a hold on what to do, but I knew I couldn't get another ticket. And even though I'd been told that I had to comply with whatever a police officer asked of me, my mind couldn't get a grip on reason like this. A mixture of confusion and fear took hold of me. One of the warning lights on my dash that had been lit up for the past two days drew me into its brilliance, a fire-engine red that wouldn't go away. The police officer was almost to the driver-side door. The idiot light bore into my brain and seemed to further ignite the already fried circuitry inside. Since I couldn't come up with a rational solution to my problem, I took the ADDer's irrational, unconscious route: when in doubt, let impulse take over. I told Jake that I wasn't going to go along with the program. To the clear thinker this probably wouldn't make sense, but to the ADDer, once you give in to impulse, you have to see it through—no matter where it might take you.

We sat there frozen in the police car's spotlight as the officer peered into the car, and when he asked me to roll down my window, I balked. I told Jake I wasn't going to roll down the window. Sensing my obvious reluctance to do as he had asked, the officer tapped on the window with his baton and said, "Roll it down." There was an insistence in that baton's tap that caused me to jump a little. Still, I didn't respond. The officer then told me he would break the glass if I didn't do as he asked. I asked Jake if I should roll down the window. He abruptly turned his head toward me and said yes. I rolled the window down and the officer told me to step out of the vehicle. I did. He explained why he had pulled me over and told me to sign a fix-it ticket for the burned-out tail-light. I took the pen he gave me and then balked again. I said no, I wouldn't sign the ticket, and he said if I didn't, he'd take me to jail. I asked Jake if I should sign the ticket, and he said yes. I signed the ticket.

We had many adventures in vehicles. Whether it was slamming into a telephone pole one night after sliding across a slick stretch of grass, or racing a mysterious Lincoln Continental around the streets of Menlo Park with my '68 Olds, Jake and I were always looking for the next challenge. One of my more impulsive and irrational moments happened in broad daylight when Jake and I decided to skip school for some dirt bike shenanigans.

As with most of our cruises with vehicles, the drive to some California foothills was at first completely innocent and without incident. It was only when we saw a police jeep at the base of the steep hill we were parked on that the trouble began. We didn't even know it was a police jeep at first. From our vantage point atop the hill beneath a dense grouping of oak trees, the jeep looked like somebody's recreational toy out for a little exploration. But something made us doubt our initial impression. After the four-wheeler non-chalantly passed a fence separating this non-developed area from a wealthy neighborhood overlooking the San Francisco Bay, it not only stopped at the base of our hill, but began climbing it.

Even then, we just sat on our bikes making small talk with our motorcycle helmets looped over our handlebars—that is, until we saw a set of blue and red lights stuck in the jeep's grill. They weren't lit, but they were a telltale sign that a cop was seated behind the jeep's tinted glass. At first, we didn't know what to do. Were we doing something wrong? We'd often suspected that dirt biking wasn't allowed in the area, but there was certainly no definite evidence of that. Nonetheless, if we weren't supposed to be in the hills, I certainly couldn't risk another citation. The jeep sped up; it was halfway between the base of the hill and us. Without any more hesitation, I strapped my scratched helmet onto my head and sped even higher up the hill. As soon as Jake noticed what I was doing, he did the same and followed close behind me.

Before long, there was another sound in the hills, a sound different from the powerful jeep's American-built motor or the familiar whine of our Japanese dirt bikes. But the steady thrumming I heard wasn't altogether foreign. After all, I'd seen enough war movies to know that what followed us now was a helicopter. I also knew I had to let loose all the two-stroke power that bike had to offer if I was to escape an airship on my tail. This wasn't as easy as it may appear to the uninitiated. Trying to dodge jutting rocks, duck overhanging tree branches, and manage uneven ground can cause even the most experienced dirt biker to take a spill. And I wasn't just continuing my day's excursion as my whims guided me; I was running from the law.

No matter what I did, however, I couldn't seem to shake the helicopter. It stayed just a few feet behind me. In fact, one time when I turned to see where it was, I was nearly struck in the head by one of the helicopter's landing bars. I was sure I wouldn't be able to escape, the way things were progressing. But thank God for oak trees. Because no matter how fast or agile a helicopter may be, it can't move through a grove of trees the way a motorcycle can. And the trees were truly thick now, and getting thicker all the time. I finally saw what I was yearning for: a patch of trees so thick that not only would I gain some distance from my airborne pursuer, but I'd completely hide myself from it. To make things even more to my advantage, I knew every trail and tree. I also knew a downhill slope was coming ahead.

It was only when Jake and I couldn't spot the helicopter any longer that we decided to loop back to the gate separating the unincorporated area from the wealthy neighborhood. By the time we reached the gate, we could see that the jeep was now parked on the hill where we had been parked just a few minutes earlier. Apparently, its driver didn't see us, or just thought (and appropriately so) that he wouldn't be able to catch us since we were so far away. For some reason, the helicopter was nowhere in sight. We speculated that its pilot had decided to follow a hunch and investigate another bunch of hills where we could have gone.

Again, we were two unencumbered teens free to pursue other avenues of mischief. But why had I decided to run? Surely, impulse and a sound lack of judgment had ruled the day once again. It was obvious that I'd been acting out some boilerplate scene from a two-bit movie. People always ran from the cops on TV. But was it worth it? In real life, running from the law is just stupid. Whenever I ran from anything it was stupid. I'm sure things would have been a lot easier if we had merely waited for the jeep. Unfortunately, my mind just shut down that day in the hills, the way it did when my brother Richard was having a diabetic reaction. The bottom line is that when I have trouble thinking about what to do, my mind runs—even if there is nowhere to run to.

Things like the motorcycle incident happened a lot in my teen years. I now know that I was more than just another rebellious teenager. I was finally able to explore another world. A world that left behind the isolation of my Eighth Avenue home.

My attention latched onto anything that would accept me, and some things that didn't. Speed accepted me. So did music. In high school I would skip classes just to play Beatles records on the little turntable my mother had given me as a child to play TV theme songs. I would listen to bands like Led Zeppelin and Bad Company over and over again on my car radio; I never went anywhere without music. I tried my hand at guitar since I wanted to be a rock star. But I couldn't give this instrument the dedication required to master its wonderful strings and wood. Still, I sang and I wrote song after song with a few simple chords. People would listen to me, but I didn't know how to become a rock star, so I never pursued this venue as fervently as I should have. Even so, I imagined myself on stage with thousands of fans screaming for more. Young women flocking after me. I drove amongst the massive redwoods, singing through my nose with Bob Dylan and screeching along with Robert Plant.

I was a lonely, long-haired boy with dormant dreams. Things were going on around me everywhere, and I didn't know how to get involved. One dream I had was to date a girl in my English Composition class. It was one of the few classes I attended on a regular basis in high school. I liked to write, and I liked Danielle Morrison. She was a rich girl who always sat on the other side of the classroom as Mr. Fuchs gave lectures on the craft of writing. I watched Danielle. And I watched her some more. In fact, I wouldn't take my eyes off her when I was in class. She was lovely. I was obsessed with lovely. From her long, silky, Scandinavian hair to her full, altogether too-soft lips. Sometimes Danielle watched me back. My watching never seemed to bother her, but sometimes she giggled with a friend at the intensity of my stare.

I wanted to be a part of her life. To walk with her and not be alone. To watch her some more, somewhere else. Alone on a California beach. I found her phone number in a school directory and called just to hear her voice. It was as soft and sweet as I had expected it to be. She always said hello when I phoned her, and I always hung up immediately. I found out where she lived, and Jake and I passed her lavish mansion night after night in my Toyota truck until we had soaked the seats with sweat and littered the floor with donut wrappers and Cokes from Seven-Eleven. We called Danielle the Easter Egg because Jake and I had followed the Morrison family station wagon to church one Easter morning.

One night, a Lincoln shot out of a driveway at a house next-door to Danielle's. Jake and I suspected that the driver's intent was to stop us. The massive, black luxury car completely cut off my little Toyota truck. I had no choice but to put it in reverse and back up until my tires smoked, and the tiny foreign pick-up swung around like some stunt driver's truck in a TV police drama. Jake and I stayed away from Danielle's house for a while after that.

The Easter Egg fiasco came to a head when a detective showed up at Jake's house. He had traced a phone call to Jake's home and came to question him about it. It had been my idea to place the call from Jake's house. The detective—given the name K101 by Jake and me because of a radio station bumper sticker on his Nova cop car's bumper—said he also had a note. The note spoke of my love for the Easter Egg. Danielle's family was concerned since it wasn't signed and because they knew about the phone calls and the mysterious truck driving by their house. K101 passed the note to Jake's father, believing that his son had written it and was harassing the Morrison's daughter.

"Have you ever seen this note?" K101 asked.

"No," Jake's father quickly answered in his heavy Dutch accent, and just as quickly, he passed the note to his wife. She said nothing and passed it to

Jake. Then Jake passed the note to me. I passed it back to K101. The entire note-passing event was shorter than the time it took for K101 to read the incriminating document's exceedingly poor penmanship and grammar. After the note got back to him, K101 said that I should leave Danielle alone. So I left her alone.

I returned to Santiago Avenue ten years later for one last pass by Danielle's house. It was shortly after I got out of the military. I had been away from California for so long that I yearned to see my old haunts. I stopped in the middle of the quiet little street in Atherton and gazed out at an empty lot. That single-story mansion with its many trees and bushes was gone. All that was left was a pile of dirt and a couple of sleepy bulldozers. Danielle was gone forever, but never quite forgotten. I drove on.

8

So I Sing This Song of Love for Julia

JUNE 1990

Oils Well that Ends Well

One time I had a sister. Well, not a blood sister. She worked at a florist shop, Wong Sum, where we drove vans together, delivering flowers to mothers and lovers, Christians and atheists. Julia was a taller version of Danielle; her nose was slightly more elongated than the Easter Egg's and her heritage was Italian, not Scandinavian. But both girls had blonde hair.

Julia and I played Scrabble once in a little park with one picnic table. She was too kind. I was too obsessed with finding a person who would embody all the virtues and tenderness I'd never had in a sibling. I wrote Julia a song and recorded it on tape. I imagined my adopted sister, in her room at night, hugging a portable cassette deck close to her body as my deepest feelings for her came out. I bought Julia a long T-shirt with a big-eyed puppy on it. I baked her banana bread that took three hours. I went on deliveries with her and watched her carry roses to happy customers or place wreaths before open caskets. I engraved her immaculate white shirts and well-pressed jeans in my memory.

The attention was too much for Julia. Another obsession gone awry. Ultimately, I scared her off. I lost my sister and my job on the same day because of this obsession.

I still recall the day I was summoned to the florist shop's office. It was a day like any other, and I hadn't expected the visit with Mr. McDonald. I thought it would be business as usual. A quick check of my van or the big truck with the lift gate on it and then out onto the road with a load of flowers or plants pre-tagged for deliveries.

But as I parted the swinging doors which led from the delivery loading dock to the large bay of computers where people sat ready to take floral orders, I had time to think about why I had been asked to McDonald's office. I'd seen him watching me for weeks from the periphery, hands on his hips. He was a tall, commanding man, the kind of man someone follows into battle when the odds are against him. But mostly he stayed behind the scenes, seldom coming down from his second-floor office. When he did, it was just to rub elbows a little with some of the bosses who were in charge of the various departments at Wong Sum, a casual inspection to make sure everybody was toeing the line. Seldom did this tie-wearing, rigid man in charge speak with the worker ants, let alone size them up the way he was doing with me. But he was eyeing me, and I thought I knew why. It was no secret that I had an obsession with Julia. It caused me some discomfort that people thought I had gone over the edge with another employee. But it didn't really matter to me in the long run because there was a principle involved and an adopted family member to win back.

What was happening between Julia and me did matter to McDonald, however, and his initial scrutiny became more intense, more readable. He took to moving his head to and fro when he saw me, as if to cast off some great burden stuck within the confines of his neck. One of his hands would frequently rub against his mouth until it opened, and he'd move his jaw from side to side. All the while he was doing these things with his body, I knew he was pondering my fate. He was like a poker player in a long hand wondering if he should keep holding his cards or throw them down on the table.

So on that day of McDonald's summons, when I left the familiarity of the loading dock and stepped into the unfamiliar beehive of activity where Wong Sum's order takers pushed their posies, I knew why I was being called forth.

I climbed a narrow staircase to reach the president's office. When I knocked on McDonald's tiny office door and heard him call me in with a voice meant more for a judicial bench than a place of business, I stepped inside like a man about to be sentenced.

He gestured toward a chair in front of his cramped desk and gave me another scrutinizing stare, as if not wanting to speak, only wanting to figure out what made me tick.

There was a ticking sound somewhere, a heavy tick-tock that I couldn't locate. Below us was the muffled thump-thump of the carts drivers used to roll their flowers and plants along the uneven wooden floor of the loading dock. There were things all around me that I could both hear and see. My heightened senses were trying to draw these things into my mixed-up head, but the thick black and white stripes on McDonald's tie were ultimately what I chose to focus on.

He pushed forward in his chair, his powerful body causing the old leather upholstery to let out a short, painful screech. "So it's true then?" he said, folding his arms across the desk.

I paused. Another thump-thumping cart rolled below us. I began to open my mouth as if to say something, but he beat me to the punch.

"We can't have this going on, Ken. It's just not fair to Julia."

There was a knock on the door, and without looking up, McDonald let out a bellowing, "Not now," which caused the person knocking to go away, but he never took his eyes from mine. Mine somehow managed to tear themselves away from that black and white tie.

"I'm not trying to interfere with her work."

"Oh, but you are. Do you know that she came to see me?"

My eyes raced back down to the tie and then just as quickly back to his eyes again. I tried to imagine her white shirt and well-pressed jeans in the chair where I now sat. Listening to the tick-tock, the thump-thump, taking in that yin-yang tie.

"She was crying, Mr. Patterson." He rolled up his sleeves and shifted a tad closer to me, a few important looking papers crumpling with the move. Once again he scrutinized me, and then made that now familiar movement with his head which emitted two tense pops from somewhere at the base of his neck.

I wanted to tell him about the Scrabble game in the park with Julia, about the banana bread that had taken three hours to bake, about her agreeing to be my sister, but I couldn't get the words out. The finality of those two pops and McDonald's relentless stare acted like a sort of freeze ray, something that had stunned me, the way those Star Trek phasers used to stun Klingons.

I knew McDonald didn't want to hear about principles and banana bread. He wanted to run a tight ship; he wanted to protect Julia from people like me. In his eyes, I was a virus that had worked its way into his pretty little flower shop, and it was keeping one of his busy bees from making her rounds.

McDonald gave a quick wave of his hands and head and said, "I don't think there's anything more to talk about, do you?"

His actions reminded me of my response on that day when Julia's father had made a surprise visit to the loading dock. The thin, aging landscaper had approached me after one of my deliveries. He'd picked a time when nobody else was around—nobody, that is, except Julia, who played at sweeping the loading dock. Julia's father had poked a finger in my chest and stood inches from my face before crossing his arms and eyeing me in somewhat the way McDonald had. Her father seemed to want to threaten me further, but he could tell that she didn't want that. There was a worried look on her face, as if she thought her father might hit me. I saw Julia's look and it bothered me. In my eyes, her father had come down uninvited and not needed. We could work this out ourselves. I told him between clenched teeth that it wasn't his place to interfere, and that he could find me after work if he still wanted to. He reluctantly walked away. I knew he didn't want to hurt his daughter with an unnecessary show of anger. There had to be other avenues for working this out. Julia looked at me and then held onto the broom a moment before slumping against a wall in the shadows, and I went on with my work.

All this was going through my mind when McDonald gave me the axe. I hardly heard him after he'd thrown his hands in the air. Who cared about this two-bit job anyway?

Even after I was fired and told to stay away, I still visited the florist shop. And I drove by Julia's house just as I had driven by Danielle's house. At least this time I had known Julia, rather than just stared at her from across a room, an outlying stranger.

I tried to call Julia at home, and I wrote her lengthy letters. I reminded Julia that she said she was my sister. But no matter how hard I tried, Julia told me that she didn't want to talk to me anymore. I followed her to Sonoma State University. I secretly left her gifts: an expensive camera, a micro cassette recorder, and a fine oriental carpet. I wrote her volumes of poetry she never received. She cried. I drifted into an obsessive coma, not aware of the world anymore, focused only on rekindling my sister's love for me. In desperation, I used a tractor-trailer from a job to move a twenty-foot-long sign with her name on it. I deposited it on a hill alongside the freeway I knew she drove to college every day. Later, I left the excerpts of some of my favorite songs on her family's answering machine. I played them over the phone from the law firm where I worked. The constraining tie I was forced to wear seemed even tighter with each verse sung.

A year went by and I still didn't hear from Julia. But I heard from others who urged me to stop trying to contact her. I just couldn't understand why she refused to be my sister. My frustration ultimately turned to revenge. One day I removed the bolt from Julia's sleek Mustang's oil pan. It is something that I am deeply ashamed of now. It was something childish and petty, but at the time I was in a rage.

I realize that if ADD motivated my actions, they make sense. Impaired thinking doesn't only make it difficult to figure out math problems or take civil servant tests. A simple algebraic equation can give me so much trouble, and sometimes, no matter how much I try, its solution just eludes my mental capabilities. ADD muddles my thinking in social situations too. My inadequate ability to say or do the right things often devastates my relationships with people.

Fortunately, I do see the light eventually. Julia's father told me to stop trying to contact Julia. So did Julia's mother. So did her boyfriend. So did a Lutheran pastor. So did a fellow employee of Julia's. So did Jake (in a friendly way). So did the police. So did a district attorney. And it took this last person's request, her reasoning, for me to understand that I needed to leave Julia alone. The possible consequences outweighed my obsession. So, just as John Lennon sang farewell to his mother Julia on The Beatles' famed *White Album*, I sing this song of love for Julia.

Rash and Carrie

SEPTEMBER 1979

Cleopatra Lost

Not all my relationships with women were so estranged, so chaotic. Some started out wonderfully. Perfectly normal and acceptable. Reciprocal instead of unattainable. And even though these relationships have been few and far between, they have been magical and intense. That's how it was with Carrie.

I was seventeen when I first saw Carrie. On Halloween, my date and I picked up Carrie at her house in my Toyota truck. Carrie walked toward us in her Cleopatra costume, and I knew I was interested in more than her asp. It was truly love at first sight, something I didn't feel for the girl I was seeing.

Carrie wedged in the truck with Debbie and me, and the staring between us was intense. An instant chemistry. In a couple of days, Carrie replaced Debbie as my steady girlfriend. At first, I didn't see Carrie much. I had dropped out of high school and worked until I got my G.E.D. I had just quit another job to begin college. It was difficult to find time for my new flame, but when I did see Carrie, I wanted to be with her all the time. My life couldn't get better, or so I thought.

Carrie decided to join the California Conservation Corps, or CCC, and I decided to join with her. So just like that, one day on campus, I literally threw away my textbooks and joined the CCC, impulsively leaving my formal education behind.

Soon, I had a new uniform with a California bear patch on my shoulder. I worked harder than ever, building trails, clearing rivers of debris, and renovating houses. We did whatever this state-run organization decided its corps members should be doing. Best of all, I shared a small curtain-partitioned room with Carrie. Well, not at first. At first, I bunked with the other young men on the other side of the scenic La Honda camp's single dormitory in the redwoods. But I yearned to share a bed with Carrie, so I broke CCC rules and moved into her room. I tacked a Beatles *Let it Be* poster on the wall above our bed. The Fab Four smiled approvingly at my fabulous new life, and I smiled more than I'd ever smiled before, finally feeling a part of something with a future.

At night, we snuggled and groped, and I did my best to learn all I could about the female anatomy. But because of Carrie's devout Christian upbringing, she wouldn't let me have sex with her. Incredibly, I respected her wish even though I pleaded for more.

In the morning, CCCers started out with exercises then ate a hearty breakfast that went along with their rent-free rooms. Large blue vans would drive groups of us off to various locations to work on our supervised projects. I seldom went with Carrie, and I became jealous of the other, mostly male, corps members who would go along with her. I thought of them working so close to my future wife. I guess I was insecure and didn't want to lose her. I'd sneak around at night to spy on Carrie when she went out, expecting to rush into a room and find her on the verge of having sex with someone else. The only thing she did was have an innocent conversation with another CCC member. She caught me a few times lurking outside her new friends' rooms, and my unfounded jealousy began to bother her. This jealousy consumed me and it became a new obsession. The outcome was inevitable.

Around this time, I found a friend in a man everyone called Strawberry because of his long red hair. I liked Strawberry because he was always smiling. I learned it was because he was always high on acid. But he was fun to be around and his antics took my mind off my jealousy. We would run through the forest at night with flashlights or lie on a hill gazing at the stars. Once we went to a Cheap Trick concert in Oakland, but when Strawberry peed on my truck after the concert in a drunken haze, I got mad at him. Still, I liked him too much for the peeing incident to sever our friendship. I knew he was just fooling around.

I'd spar with another friend who shared the room on the other side of the partition that separated him and his girlfriend from Carrie and me. Mike had a six-degree black belt in Tae Kwon Do. In an all-brick room across from the dining hall, he would show me some martial arts moves. I'd end up bruised and embarrassed afterward. But I wasn't the only one. One time Mike put a former marine who'd joined the CCC in his place when the marine challenged him. The marine looked tough, a pack of cigarettes rolled up in one sleeve, a tattoo with an angry-looking eagle on one arm. He pushed Mike, saying, "That karate shit is nothing," and Mike threw a round-house kick to the marine's head. The stunned marine staggered back a little and looked as though he might be thinking about throwing a punch when Mike hit him in the face with an elbow and then a back fist. The marine fell onto the floor and didn't move, so Mike and I went to get something to eat.

Even these distractions didn't curb my jealousy. But I tried to keep it together, sometimes driving Carrie through the mountains on my motorcycle to show her how thrilling I could be around the curves. I wrote her songs and clung to her, never wanting her to leave me, but my grip was too tight.

One night I not only put the squeeze on Carrie, but also on a new corps member. He'd come to visit me, inquiring about the hot girl with the curly brown hair, wondering if she was easy. The girl, of course, was Carrie. I threw out punches, never allowing him to catch his breath. Following the flurry, I put the new guy in a headlock and tried to strangle the life out of him. A very large woman in charge of security in the women's living quarters brought me to my senses. Later, the new corps member apologized for being so brash. He said he just didn't know that Carrie was my girlfriend. Carrie witnessed the new path my jealousy had taken and it further aggravated our already teetering relationship. Undeterred by this fact, I asked her to marry me, and that's when she decided it was time to break off the relationship.

Soon after that, she and most of the other corps members were called off en masse to a disaster in the San Joaquin Valley. A flood had ravaged a community, and the corps went there to build sandbag walls to curb the flash flood.

For some reason, I was scheduled for a break from work, and I had it good. A cushy life without tin cup water breaks and blisters on my hands. But I missed Carrie too much to stay in the camp without her. So I drove hundreds of miles and passed through one CCC camp after another to find her. CCCers had come from all over the state to help with the flood control, so it was a difficult task. Finally, after pulling into a gas station to top off my Toyota's tank, I spotted my grimy girlfriend in a CCC van also being filled with gas. It was an extremely fortuitous meeting. Even with our relationship troubles, Carrie was impressed. She blushed as other CCCers in the van pointed me out to her. They were laughing at my persistence, obviously teasing Carrie. She was smiling, but I sensed a concerned look in her eyes.

For the next few days, I shoveled sand into bags and hoisted them with the other CCCers. The long makeshift sandbag walls kept flood water from further ravaging San Joaquin homes, and I felt good about what we accomplished.

At night, covered with dirt and mud, completely exhausted from the nonstop disaster work, I'd lie on a cot next to Carrie. I smiled at her smudged face, and we linked hands between the cots. As I lay there that way, I remember thinking that I could go on filling sandbags forever, as long as I was near my true love. But that wondrous reunion didn't last, no matter how hard I tried to keep the two of us together. When we got back to the camp, Carrie ended our relationship a second and final time, and she said that she was leaving the corps. I pleaded for her to stay, tried every tactic a seventeen-year-old could think of, but nothing worked. Instead of just waiting there for her to leave first, however, I was the one who left the camp that we'd lived in for those long six months.

I knew I'd lost Carrie for good. I raced down the hill in my truck. In darkness and tears, I sped into the California foothills, unaware of the hairpin turns or redwoods caught in the truck's headlights. I had no idea where I was going or what I'd do when I got there. A future didn't seem necessary anymore. Not without Carrie. Of course, given my emotional state, I was very lucky to make it safely down that hill at all. But I made it without a hitch, as if the innate desire to go on existing guided my hand that night.

A few days later, one of the proverbial walking wounded, I entered an Air Force recruiter's office. I needed to get away for a while, run off somewhere that was new and far away from Redwood City. Far away from the city in which love had rejected me so cruelly. Incredibly, a couple of months later, Carrie and a mutual friend of ours drove me to the AFEES testing center in Oakland, where the Air Force conducted test after test to determine where best to place me. Based on my aptitude tests, they decided I was suited for three Air Force careers: aircraft mechanic, parachute rigger, and security police officer. I chose to be an aircraft mechanic because I thought it would be the most lucrative career when I re-entered civilian life.

Then, before I knew what type of a commitment I had really made, I flew to Texas for basic training. From then on, I remembered Carrie and the CCC as my last link to an innocence and freedom I'd never know again.

10

California Dreaming

IN 1979, MY teeth were crooked, my nose had a deviated septum, and my hair always got in my eyes. My life rarely rolled along smoothly, but while I was waiting for my Air Force enlistment to begin, I was free to do what I wanted. I could dissect *Sergeant Pepper's Lonely Hearts Club Band* in the afternoon, and lose myself in The Beatles' floating harmonies. I could hop on my motorcycle and race through redwood shadows on my way to the Pacific Ocean. I could strum my guitar and lose track of time in my own poetic lyrics. Jake and I could wander over to Woolworth's for a Texas dog, sit on a red leather stool and watch Stanford Shopping Center's customers lug away expensive booty. I could sit in the woods and listen to water roll past the sword ferns. Mostly, I could just dream. But summer slipped away in those last days of enchanted drifting, and my life was snatched away before another California fall began. For olive green was coming for me. The military grim reaper would smother me in his drab cloak of conformity.

1 1

Just ADDapt

AUGUST 1980

Ruby Slippers: Don't Leave Home Without Them

The first night in a military open barracks bed did not drive away my ADD fog, but it parted the mist enough to allow in the day's yelling and bellowing and to keep me asking why, more than I ever had before. I wanted to go home. Unfortunately, the Air Force had issued me a standard pair of black lace-up boots instead of the magic ruby slippers I desperately needed.

I don't think I slept that first night. I felt the fineness of my newly shaven scalp and listened to the whispers and sighs of those around me. I doubt any of my buzz-cut roommates slept well that night. There was the unmistakable smell of khaki and the presence of so many strangers. The idea that we'd left so much behind must have played through their minds; I know it played through mine. I kept thinking about having to stand so still in formation and not being able to leave the base. I was a prisoner of my own making. I had handed over my freedom to some crotchety old men for a firm mattress and a few meals.

As the days followed, I discovered that my concept of military life hadn't even scratched the surface. Having the lights turned on at five a.m. on the dot along with a loudspeaker playing reveille gave a new meaning to harassment. As soon as that amplified trumpet played, I knew the harassment would continue throughout the day, a torment that I wanted to avoid as each minute passed. Most knew that it was all a game: folding your underwear into precise measurements, scrubbing the floor with a toothbrush, or standing still while someone yelled in your face. But I had trouble thinking of boot camp that way. I'd always thought of a game as being fun. This so-called game wasn't as fun as fanning out a handful of cards or moving a token around a colorful game board. In this game, we were the cards, crumpled and mishandled in a deck that was shuffled repeatedly throughout the day. And we were the tokens who were never allowed to linger in one space.

Tyrannical referees controlled this game. They didn't only run alongside the players, but got in to play. And sometimes we were more than cards or tokens; we were balls. When the drill sergeants moved us down field, they yelled and directed us toward the goal; they definitely made certain we didn't roll out of bounds. And yes, I rolled along with the rest, and I tried to stay in play. At least for a while. After all, I thought I had no other choice. I'd signed up for this, and a signature bound me to these preprogrammed banshees with their persuasive screaming.

I tolerated the name-calling and the inane drills designed to break our wills. I even put up with a drill instructor when he asked, "Who is this whore?" after seeing a picture of Carrie during a shakedown which allowed him and his other brutes to sift through our personal items. I put up with it all, as if caught up in some sort of mind-manipulating madhouse.

But not everything was so tormenting. We marched with chants. A kind of military singing that I liked. It was the closest I got to music in basic training except for when we sang at church. Our drill instructor had a chant for everything. One of my favorites was the one he had us repeat when we jogged past the women's barracks:

> If all of the women were bricks in a pile
> And I was the mason, I'd lay 'em out in style.
> Hey, hey, all you women.
> Look up, all you women.
> Cause we are the Air Force.
> The mighty, mighty Air Force.

Basic training was mostly hell. I had a whole list of likes and dislikes when it came to its daily grind. For example, I liked standing at a chow hall table until it was full before sitting down, a basic training rule. It stands to reason I would like this, given my love of order and organization. But I didn't like people telling me when I could go to breakfast. I liked standing at attention in nice, straight lines. But I didn't like people telling me to do it. I liked placing my things in a clean, orderly locker. But I didn't like someone telling how to fold my underwear. I liked shooting the rifle they gave us while at the base's firing range. But I didn't like it when I inadvertently pointed my rifle in the wrong direction and caught a truckload of flak for doing so. There were people issuing us all sorts of military gear; I liked that. I liked being given things. But I didn't like it when I was told to stick out my arm for a mandatory air-gun vaccination.

I admired the precision and order of basic training. After all, I was a man who lived for the kind of exactitude the military demanded, but it stung to the core when someone told me I was screwing up. It wasn't my fault that I couldn't remember all the rules of basic training and keep them straight in my mind. I especially despised the forms we had to carry around in our pockets, so that when we did something wrong, a drill instructor—any drill instructor—could ask us to hand one over and write down the offense committed. These forms, no doubt, were probably handed in to some other source, to record our failures while we were being pushed to our limits. I lost track of how many of these forms I was asked to surrender. They could be asked for at the drop of a hat. There was the time I forget to take off my hat when entering the chow hall, for example, and another time when I forgot to put the hat back on when I exited. Once I was asked for one of those little forms because I hadn't stayed on a line on the ground that led from one building to another. Another time I handed over a form because one of the back pockets on my pants was unbuttoned.

Ultimately, even though I had occasional respites from the onslaught of military ritual, the mental mind games took their toll on me. The only time I truly found escape from the madness was when we were allowed to go to church. All the military conditioning of basic training was put on hold there and, for a while, I could regain a small of amount of sanity. Nobody saluted at church; nobody asked me for those annoying little offense forms. And just as every airman's way of worship was recognized, so were his or her spiritual needs. Church at Lackland gave me an opportunity to recharge my soul, to tap into what was really important. It reminded me that all that temporal stuff like uniforms and barracks, rules and yelling, were only a small part of the universe. With this new perspective, albeit temporary, I found solace. But there was more than the idea of the greatness of spiritual issues at church; there were commonplace comforts that reminded me of what it had been like before the military. There was singing in church: loud, joyous singing. And there was music. Granted, it wasn't the rock and roll I normally liked, but it was music nonetheless. There wasn't music back in the barracks, unless you counted that annoying prerecorded trumpet at five a.m. when we were rudely roused out of bed. There was also peace at church when we prayed. And lots of silence. A rare thing on a military base. And when I bowed my head like the others beside me in the hard wooden pews, I didn't always try to communicate with a higher power. Sometimes, I just let the fragrance from the flowers that were near the pulpit or the reassuring words of my faith's chaplain fill me with a new appreciation of the fact that there were things out there that even the mighty American military had no power over. When I did pray, I asked God to help me get through basic training, to be able to cope with the routine when church let out and we returned to our barracks. I asked God to help me deal with the fog, so I could figure out how to make a bed the way my sergeant wanted, and to make it in time for inspection. I asked God to help me understand what was being told to me. I had to get some kind of help if I was to get through my ordeal. But church didn't last long. And when services were over, we formed our straight lines and marched back to the barracks. Basic training was a place where people with afflictions of any sort weren't given special treatment. You toed the line and did what you were told, when you were told to do it, or you suffered the consequences. Not meeting the mark in that perfect environment was a recipe for disaster for many airmen without ADD, let alone someone with it.

Some recruits broke down during those arduous weeks in San Antonio, Texas. I witnessed one big guy named Al get chewed out by the insufferable Sgt. Wolf, our ever-present drill instructor, for something we all heard about.

The circumstances leading up to Al's tongue-lashing were fairly innocent as far as basic was concerned. Al had been standing in line with the rest of us during an inspection when Sgt. Wolf noticed some extra dust in his locker and some left-over soap residue in his soap dish. Al was ordered to accompany Wolf into his tiny office, which was located just off the open barrack's bay where we all slept. The rest of us were to remain at attention until Wolf and Al returned. From my vantage point, I could clearly see Al through Wolf's open office door. Al stood erect with his hands at his sides. He must have been at least six feet three inches. But now he seemed smaller to me, a big man made little by another's abuse. Al faced Wolf, who was seated behind his desk. I couldn't see my drill sergeant, but I could hear him. Angry words flew from his mouth like a knife thrower's knives meant for one particular target; and I could tell the words cut deep into Al. His face was red, and he trembled slightly, but he did his best to exercise the good military discipline instilled in him. Still the words kept coming, profane words such as "son of a bitch" and "goddammit," and demeaning words such as "foul-up" and "piss-poor performance." The strain was building up in Al. Incredibly, I saw this young, tough guy start to break. A tear rolled down a cheek and one of his hands wasn't as flat as it used to be against his side. Still, he planted himself there in that office on that hot Texas day and took all Wolf had to offer. Like a good little toy soldier, he stood his ground. Like his father before him, who'd been a decorated marine in Vietnam, he displayed the good military bearing that Al knew was expected of him. But even the best soldier has his limits, and sometimes he acts in a way that not even he is capable of comprehending. When the yelling and berating had finally ended, Al did an excellently executed about-face, then a right-face, and then a strong and sure-footed exit from Wolf's office. I was glad it was all over, even though I wasn't the one who'd been in that office. I hated yelling. I'd heard enough of it at home, and I'd definitely heard enough of it in basic training. And I hated seeing someone being abused the way Al had been abused. I thought the big man would go back to his bunk and stand there until Wolf dismissed us and then the scene would be done. But it didn't happen that way; it didn't happen that way at all. Al passed his bunk, then the airman's next to his, then the next five airmen's before reaching the tall metal exit door. Without even the slightest hesitation or a single word, Al then lifted one of his enormous feet and literally kicked the door off its hinges. Like some big kid who'd thrown a tantrum and had decided to run away from home, Al ran down the stairs, teary-eyed and broken, with the rest of us slack-jawed, but still at attention, craning our necks to see what had happened. A moment later, Sgt. Wolf exited his office with a surprised look and his trademark drill sergeant's hat in hand and asked what had happened. When we told him what we'd witnessed, he calmly, but assertively put on his hat and followed in Al's wake. We stood at attention for at least a half an hour, then we heard someone come up the barrack's stairwell. Sgt. Wolf appeared carrying a limp and unconscious Al over his shoulder. When he'd slung Al onto his bunk, Wolf authoritatively dismissed us and went back about his business.

The rest of the week went without incident. There were no more people like Al running off in despair, and even Al himself seemed to have returned to his old controlled self. There were still tongue-lashings, however, and airmen were still being pushed to the limits; this had not changed, nor would it. I tried to do my best, but even the prayers in church didn't help. I still couldn't seem to make my bed in time or get my locker in shape for inspection. I didn't know how to sew, and I had difficulty shining my boots the way Sgt. Wolf wanted. I tried to do these things like everybody else, but my old pal the fog wasn't allowing any clear, helpful information in my already over taxed mind. If it wasn't for a fellow GI who helped me with these things, I would have never have gotten anything done in time. William was a self-proclaimed Cherokee Indian from Alabama who hardly ever spoke or showed intense emotions. Basic training didn't get to him the way it got to the rest of us. He merely went about his business as if waiting for the time when the tasks demanded of him would all be over so he could move on to the next stage of military life. William was so quiet and introverted, in fact, that had it not been for my pressing him for help, he might never have helped me at all. He had a good heart, though. I could tell. Perhaps this is the only real reason he helped me in the end. He was the kind of person who sensed that I was in trouble, and he'd briefly help me make my bed or help me to sew an insignia onto my uniform. His help sometimes caused him to be late in taking care of his own needs, and once he got chewed out when he couldn't make up his own bed in time because he was helping me make mine. He just took the yelling, though. Even Sgt. Wolf seemed to realize that his yelling had no real effect on William. With William's noble stance and commanding but stoic presence, I tried to imagine him as a warrior preparing for battle or a man who lived solely off the land and was about to bring down some majestic buck. I'd never known an Native American before, and I thought it was cool to be bunking right beside one now. I never really learned anything about William or his people, however. William didn't say much, but he sure did show me a lot.

Even William couldn't help me with all the aggravation I was feeling. It was true that I got a little better at making my bed and sewing and doing all the other things Sgt. Wolf expected of me, but I got no better at handling the strain of basic training. The more that people yelled at me or berated me, the more I secretly rebelled inside. And the more I rebelled, the closer I got to breaking down completely—the way Al had. And that's exactly what happened. It was toward the end of basic training when something finally snapped in me. Another drill sergeant, a mean woman who sometimes filled in for Sgt. Wolf, had called me into Sgt. Wolf's office one day. She had come upon me near my bunk while I was still trying to get my boots as shiny as William's. He'd shown me how to use a lighter's flame with my shoe polish to get the gloss I needed. My shirt was lying on my bunk when Sgt. Walker found me.

"Why aren't you wearing your shirt, airman?" she bellowed.

I continued to polish one of my boots, making sure I made small circular motions with the cotton ball.

"I asked you a question, airman," Walker bellowed again, her drill sergeant's hat a few inches from my face. "Look at me when I talk to you."

I looked up into her angry eyes without stopping the cotton ball, and said, "I didn't want to get wax on my uniform."

"I didn't want to get wax on my uniform, *ma'am*," she corrected me. "Put that damned boot down right now and see me in my office, Patterson," she said, eyeing the name on my shirt.

I did as I was instructed, but something was different in the way I did it. I wasn't acting like my usual basic training robot self. Still, not all my military decorum had vanished. I walked into Sgt. Wolf's office with sharply executed left- and right- faces, and I stood at full attention, just the way Al had. Walker sat behind Wolf's desk.

"Is there something wrong with you, Patterson?"

I stared at the opposite wall. There was a picture of Wolf and some of his buddies in 'Nam. Wolf looked different, dirtier, and he had an M-16 resting on his shoulder.

"I'm talking to you, dammit! I said, 'Is there something wrong with you?'"

"I didn't want to get my shirt dirty."

"You will say ma'am when you address me. Do you understand me?!"

"I didn't want to get my shirt dirty, ma'am."

In the picture, Wolf was smiling. I'd never seen him smile before. There was a careless freedom about the way the former marine and his buddies beamed out of that picture. Something that reminded me of another time and place. Of rock music and motorcycles, and of long hair and setting your own hours.

Walker was standing now. "Your behavior is unacceptable, Patterson."

I don't know if it was the picture, or just something in me that had surfaced after those many weeks, but an independence was growing in me, and I couldn't break the feeling.

"The next time I ask you a question and you ignore me, I will crucify you. Do you understand me?" Walker had come around the desk. She was tilting her head from side to side with each statement. "The next time you see me, you will stand at attention. You will not sit, idly polishing your boot, or look away from me. And you will always say ma'am when you address me. Do you understand me?!"

"Do you think Sgt. Wolf kept his boots polished in Vietnam?"

"What the hell are you talking about, Patterson?! And what did I just tell you about addressing me without the proper respect?! God damn you, Patterson, are you listening to me?!"

"No, I'm not, ma'am." With that said, I broke my fixed stance that the military called "Attention" and assumed a more casual posture, something that made more sense, something that felt natural.

Walker let out with a rage that rivaled Wolf's when Al had been in that office of his just a few days earlier. There was name-calling and attempts to belittle me. Orders to do this and orders to do that. The sergeant screamed until the veins in her neck bulged and spittle flew in my direction. But I didn't care. I really didn't want to hear any more, so I just threw up my hands in frustration and left the office. Without a left-face, without a right-face, without an about-face. Without any face whatsoever, save the one with the mixture of anger and pure disgust I felt for the military, basic training, and especially all the yelling and berating.

Walker continued to yell at me though—even as I kept walking toward my locker to gather the few personal items I was allowed to have in it. The fuming sergeant reached the locker at the same time I did. She ordered me to go downstairs and report to Sgt. Wolf, who was working out of another office that day. This time I heard her clearly. "Fine," I said, as I crammed all my things into my duffel bag: the perfectly folded underwear; the slime-free soap dish; my impeccably clean toothbrush and toothbrush holder; a few shavings-free razors; and every other thing I owned. No longer was I concerned about how the things appeared to anyone else. I rapidly thrust every last item from that locker into that canvas bag and threw the bag over my shoulder before making my way to the stairs. There was no anger when I opened the door, however—the same door that Al had kicked off its hinges only a few days earlier—just a sense of relief. And pride. I was proud that I had finally broken the hold that the drill sergeants had on me. And I swore that no one would control me like that again. Even as Walker continued to yell at me as I was leaving, I no longer cared. She could yell at the others, at her dog, at any subordinate creature she felt like yelling at, but she wouldn't yell at me anymore. I was going home.

For some reason, something in my mind took over that day. Something absolutely against protocol and never tolerated: rebellion. Something with momentum that couldn't be stopped.

When I finally did reach Sgt. Wolf's downstairs office, it was with a swagger, not a rigid walk on a marked out line on the floor. It was a swagger that told people I was going back to a normal life, or at least a life that would seem less demanding and more sane.

I walked into Sgt. Wolf's office with just as much arrogance and lack of military bearing as I had upstairs. I flung my duffel bag at my feet and slumped in a plastic chair before him, like a man preparing himself for the arrival of a bus that was hours away.

Sgt. Wolf sat behind a large wooden desk, and he looked surprised. But he didn't yell at me or leap over that desk and throw me into a wall. That big Vietnam vet just put his hands behind his head and leaned back in his chair. He asked me what was going on, as if chatting to another sergeant on his own level, a man who had earned the privilege of entering his office the way I had.

I responded, just as casually, "I've had enough and I want to go home."

Again, to my surprise, Wolf just smiled. It was the same sort of smile I'd seen in that photo in his upstairs office. I then realized that this was all a game and there were two Wolfs: the one who acted for the recruits, and the one who just wanted to kick back and pal around with people while he told twenty-year-old war stories.

"You don't want to go home," he said.

I told him again that I did. He said no, I didn't. Then he just looked at me for moment before adding that I was going to be a good soldier.

"I won't be a good soldier," I said. "I won't be a good soldier just like my brother wasn't a good soldier. When they sent him to basic training, he went AWOL. I remember when he showed up early in the morning at our house. I was just a little kid then, but I could tell he didn't like the military, and now I understand why. My father told him to go back to basic training, and he did. He just didn't know what else to do, I guess. And my brother didn't want to go to Vietnam, but he did. And when he got home, he put a shotgun to his head and blew his brains out. My mother and I found him sprawled across his rented room. I won't be a good soldier, and I won't play your games anymore."

It was then that Wolf's smile disappeared. "You don't know anything about Vietnam, and maybe you shouldn't mention it again. Not around me at least. Okay?"

I heard a group of men running by outside yelling out a chant like those that Sgt. Wolf made up, and then the chanting slowly faded as I looked into Wolf's eyes and saw something there I didn't understand. It was the same kind of look my brother, Stephen, had after he got home from Vietnam.

Then Wolf's smile returned, and he said, "Why don't you go on back upstairs, Patterson. Everything's gonna be all right."

For some odd reason that's all it took to get me to do what he wanted, an appealing request, not an order or a berating yell. Maybe all I wanted was for someone to ask me something for a change. Or maybe I couldn't think of anything else to do, just like my brother, Stephen. Then Wolf came around and handed me my duffel bag and said to go put my things away. Something in me wanted to ask more about Vietnam, about what my brother experienced, but I knew it wouldn't be a good idea. So I did just as he told me, as if all the things I'd done a few minutes earlier hadn't happened.

I don't know what Wolf did that day. It must have been more than just the fact that he'd been nice to me. Maybe it was some technique he'd used before to deal with malcontents, or maybe it was just the fact that his easy-going demeanor gave me the confidence I needed to get through the rest of boot camp. Whatever he did, it worked.

After eight weeks in San Antonio, I graduated from basic training. As I stood there in my dress blues swatting the gnats away with the rest of my fellow trainees on the parade ground, I grinned inside proudly at my amazing accomplishment. Somehow I'd made it. I'd graduated. Now I would be moving on to the next phase in the Air Force's plan for me, and something had definitely changed in me.

I was eighteen, and I was wearing a uniform, not unlike the uniforms I'd seen in all those war movies I'd watched on TV as a lonely boy. And I was accepted by an elite club, a very old club, whose importance no one could dispute. I felt all of this and much more, but most of all I felt happy to be leaving Lackland Air Force Base. I hoped I'd never see it again. Of course, I would see Lackland again, some fifteen or so years later, from the freeway, flying by at about seventy. A bunch of inconspicuous, low-cut buildings behind a barbed wire fence where inside, a new bunch of eighteen-year-olds were sweating and crying and wishing they were home—as they are most likely doing even at this moment.

1 2

Last Call

JUNE 1977

Cutting Edge Diplomacy

In 1977, all the boys but me were out of the house. My parents were divorced, and I was living with my father, who I hardly ever saw. He worked all day and drank all night. Dad gave me money to buy food, and I was left unsupervised most of the time. But when Daddy Donald did come home, he would taunt me with his alcohol-laden breath. If he thought I was being a smart ass, he would remind me that he was The Kid—a phrase he liked to use a lot—and you don't mess with The Kid. Sometimes when he said this he would fake a punch or give me a little push as I washed dishes or waited for him to go to bed.

His drunken antics never made me laugh, only grit my teeth. I just had to tolerate them. I tried to make sense of them, turning on my radar in the fog. Sending out waves that would bounce back at the source. But the only things I could identify from my dad's drinking escapades were vague reminders of the times he'd promised to go camping with me and either never showed up or finally came home drunk, and then went to bed to sleep it off. Although I don't think my father's irresponsibility affected me as much as it might have some people, I get a fuzzy sense of disappointment to this day, and I rarely crack a smile when witnessing some drunk's behavior.

One particular night, I'd had enough of his foolishness. I'd just finished washing and drying the dishes when my father came into the kitchen with his usual stagger, potent breath, and drunken taunts. I tried to ignore him while I put silverware in a kitchen drawer. But the gibing persisted, and this night it invoked a demon inside me. A demon who wanted my father to go away.

Outside were normal homes with responsible parents and a warmth that helped kids get through the day. In those other houses, most children probably weren't lonely. But in the house on Eighth Avenue, there was a teenager who had lived too long with loneliness. A teenager who, not by choice, had learned to cope with an empty house. A teenager who now wanted nothing more than to be left alone. My family had, without realizing it, conditioned me that way.

And then it happened, in an instant. Without any planning on my part, I wheeled around on this drunk, this intruder into my dreary domain. I held a chef's knife pointed in anger at my father. I have to hand it to my dad; he didn't back away in fear or beg for forgiveness. Instead, he said, "So, you're pulling a knife on your old man, huh?"

"Get the fuck away from me," was all I said. I sidled toward the kitchen door and then backed out with the knife still in my hand.

I was barefoot and it was the middle of the night, but without thinking, I shoved the knife, handle first, into one of my back pockets and jumped onto my orange Kawasaki dirt bike. I pointed the bike into the darkness and sped away, anywhere, as long as it was away from that house. Away from the loneliness and the drunken clown in the kitchen.

The bike and I ended up on Fifth Avenue, and I was still unclear about what I was doing. When I got into those states, I just needed to go somewhere, and my mind was blank, as if everything just shut down, the same kind of shutdown I experienced whenever any strong emotion took over. It was then that a California Highway Patrol officer saw me heading in the opposite direction and swung his cruiser around with lights and siren flashing.

I'm sure I uttered some obscenity before pulling my bike over. Great. This is all I need, I thought. I remember getting off the bike and quickly walking back toward the cop to ask him what I'd done wrong this time. But instead of casually walking up to meet me, he bent down and pulled out his revolver, thrusting it into the V created by his open driver-side door.

"Put your hands up and turn around!" he yelled.

But I kept coming toward him. What? What was going on? I'd never seen a cop pull a gun on me. He was serious, so I nervously turned around and stayed that way. A few moments later, he came up behind me, yanked out the chef's knife, and backed away to place it on the hood of his car. Then I felt him frisk me for other weapons. When he found I wasn't carrying anything else, he told me to put my arms down and turn around. It's funny, when I think about it now. The cops have changed since then. Now I'm sure I would be lying prone on the street in cuffs. But this chippy just told me to turn around and asked me what I was planning to do with the knife.

I said, in about as manner of fact a voice as I could, that I was going to kill my father with it. Of course, I don't think I would have really ever used the knife. When push has come to shove in the altercations I've had in my life, I've never been able to hurt anyone beyond the first few punches or initial headlock. Gouging out eyes or drawing blood just isn't in me.

Still, I didn't get the knife back. And, incredibly, I didn't go to jail that night. I think the officer wrote out an FYI card on me, in case something really did happen.

The next day, I was back home alone, calm, raking leaves in my front yard. The same cop who had pulled me over slowly came to a stop a few feet from where I stood and rolled down his window. "Are you trying to make up for last night?"

"Yeah, right. My dad should be the one out here raking these. He's the one who deserves to be punished."

"How is your dad, by the way?"

I stopped raking leaves and eyed the trooper for a moment, recalling how different he seemed now without a gun in his hand and a potential threat before him. "Oh him," I said, leaning on the rake. "He's okay." I tried to sound demented and rolled my eyes around as if my dad wasn't really okay. The cop smiled, but he seemed more intent on listening to a radio call as he craned his head to hear it better.

"He's always better when he's had a chance to sleep it off," I added, starting to rake again.

"That's good to hear," the sunglasses-wearing chippie said. "Hey, if you ever need anything—you know, just to talk or something, why don't you give me a call," he said, holding out his card.

I let go of the rake with one hand and took the card with the other. As I eyed the small official-looking card, I ran my hand over the embossed words, California Highway Patrol, and an embossed gold star which gleamed in the morning sunlight. A few seconds later, I attempted a smile and stuck the card in my shirt pocket.

The cop craned his head again to hear the radio and then nodded my way as he said, "You take care, okay." I nodded back, and the cop slowly drove away.

1 3

Which Way to Wichita?

OCTOBER 1980

Screwdrivers

The Air Force decided to send me to Wichita Falls, Texas, to learn to repair airplanes. Wichita Falls was remote, and northern Texas was cold in October. This was an old town with scary-looking mannequins in antiquated buildings. I hardly ever saw anyone walking around, downtown when, on occasion, I went there.

Mostly, I visited the Airmen's Club on Sheppard Air Force Base's flat, windblown acres. There was usually some band in the club playing way too loud. Later, I learned that most of the Air Force base clubs were that way. My choices for clubs within walking distance were the club on Sheppard or a club just past the base gates called The Stayin' Alive. The commander told us to stay away from The Stayin' Alive, so I drank on base.

I discovered screwdrivers and drank them to excess. The drinks became another obsession that made military life more tolerable, but they were more than that. Drinking was a rite of passage in the military, so I didn't seem out of place when I returned to the club every night to sit alone and relish the new freedom of being away from Lackland. We still marched to school, but it was just a formality. And we were each assigned duties to keep the dorm-like environments tidy. I had to make sure the sinks in the latrine sparkled each morning.

Incredibly, I didn't have much of a problem learning what the teachers required. And everything went by without a hitch. Sometimes I visited a recent divorcee who lived in a brick building on the other side of base. I tried to get her into bed, but I hadn't acquired enough skills with women to do that yet. But at least I had a woman to talk to.

I became friends with an airman from Tennessee. The Tennessean had a southern drawl. I never came across people like him in California and I liked the difference. It was good to have a pal. Once we got a room in Wichita Falls' only big hotel in town just for the heck of it. We were pretty high up, so we looked out of a big window at the flat prairies, which seemed to spread out forever. And I remember that we jumped on our beds a lot. I don't think either of us had ever been in a luxury hotel room before.

I also met an airman from New York, but the only impact he really had on me was toward the end of my stay at Sheppard when he borrowed ninety dollars, promising to pay me back when he got to his next base. I tried to call him from McChord, my next base, after letters didn't get me anywhere. When I asked the New Yorker for the money, he said we had a bad line. I was so disgusted, I hung up.

One night while poring over textbooks at Sheppard in my windowless room, I heard over the radio that John Lennon had died. It was the first time I really cried at the thought of losing someone. I couldn't believe that some wacko had shot such a great man. This was during the same time I continued to mourn the loss of my relationship with Carrie. I'd been calling and writing her since joining the military, but she never called or wrote back. I'd pursue her for years this way. I don't think I've ever quite forgotten the way she made me feel.

I tried to lose myself and the fog in drink. Binge after binge. No socializing in the club. No epiphanies or productivity. Just the same lonely airman on the same barstool, in the same corner of the airmen's club, listening to whatever band happened to be booked that evening. Most of the time I'd just go back to my room and lie in bed. More often than not, I'd imagine Carrie someday back in my life and how happy I'd be then. Mostly, my binges ended the same way. I never got so drunk that I couldn't get back to that military bunk bed and that quiet room on the third floor of my Sheppard dormitory. But one night, I tried to out-drink the fog. If I couldn't make it go away, maybe I could replace it with a drunken haze.

On this particular night, I dined alone at the bar, and I was overcome by the usual screwdriver main course. The liquid dinner was a particularly long one, probably due to John Lennon's murder, and it left me passed out in a latrine. Sometime in the night, I awoke to stagger off to my bed, a young man now surrounded by two fogs, in a world with one less Beatle.

A few days later, for only the second time in my early military career, I was in my dress blues attending another Air Force graduation. I was clean and pretty on the outside, but cobwebby and disheveled on the inside. Still, I felt proud again. After all, I was graduating, and I was literally moving up in the ranks. But this time, while standing there on the parade ground by the statuesque airplanes that would never fly again, I had at least two more questions: Why did I always feel so alone in the world? And why had John Lennon been killed?

There was only one fog the day of graduation, the same one I brought from California, from my childhood that seemed so far away now. Soon after graduation, the fog flew with me to Washington and my next base.

1 4

Sins of the Father

NO ONE EVER gave me an official talk on the birds and the bees. No school ever taught me what goes where, or how a woman becomes pregnant, but I learned these things. I picked them up from friends or overheard people talking about them, where various inferences were left for me to decode. But the one place I picked up more information on sex than anywhere else was at 628 Eighth Avenue, my childhood home.

I stumbled upon a magazine my brother Mark had stuffed under his mattress. The black and white images in it were a real eye-opener. They were the first stills I'd ever seen of men and woman having sex, and not just mild, artfully done sex, but full-blown porn with all its graphically illustrated hedonism. That's where I got my first taste of a stimulus so great and consuming that I've yet to shake free of its addictive influence.

While my brother's magazine may have given me the visual images I needed to fill the cracks that my imagination couldn't, my father's thick novels gave me the text. Hidden under dad's clothing, or sometimes out in the open, I found the smoke-and-bathroom-stenched paperbacks and flipped quickly through the pages. My foggy brain wasn't interested in the book's plot or characters. And most of the very adult content the book had to offer was just too difficult to decipher. So I became expert at sifting through an author's painstakingly planned out fiction for keywords such as breast, pussy, vagina, buttocks, etc., until I discovered a few steamy pages that would hold my attention. And after I read these smutty rendezvous between various consenting adults, I'm sure that I could have passed any test given me on the subject matter. I don't know if I should thank authors such as Harold

Robbins (who my father seemed to love) for this indoctrination into the carnal, or despise them for sexually aging me so much sooner than I should have been at the impressionable age of twelve.

But I do know books like these gave me an appetite for sex that I couldn't appease. I experimented with anything that simulated the female anatomy, and I mean *anything*. Some of these things just didn't survive. And the vibrator I found close to some of those books in one of my father's dresser drawers was a blessing. Vibration became a close friend. Now vibration pales in comparison to some of the avenues I've explored over the years. Like driving, sex gave me a quick fix and helped me to focus. Both of these stimulants required not thinking, just doing. That's always helpful to someone in a fog when he's trying to obtain clarity and conclusion. Doing sometimes helps me to overcome mental blocks and heightens focus.

In exceptionally foggy times when it's imperative that I seek illumination as soon as possible, having sex, or participating in some other physical activity, will sometimes make me less prone to aggression, and even a quickie will set my occasional emotional instability back on track. In fact, sex seems to be one of the best cures for ADD, in my mind. Of course, I can only speak for myself when it comes to sex, since I don't know if sex helps ADDers across the board. Still, as I pointed out at the beginning of this book, if other ADDers are anything like me, they are definitely more susceptible to all the addictions the world has to offer. I know I'm just not equipped with the same defenses as those without ADD to ward off addictive temptations.

I think it's important to add here that while I've been prone to the same urges as other males when it comes to sex, there is a difference. With me, sex has always been like a drug, not just a testosterone-driven necessity. While it's true that my lonely childhood drove me to be close to women, that's not the core of what drove me. To me, the experience of having sex is literally like taking some drug a doctor has prescribed. It's almost as if somewhere in my foggy mind some force is continually coaxing me back to another sexual scenario and the clarity that comes with it. And like heroin to an addict who has just shot up, this sex brings me a sense of coherence and calm that is impossible to find elsewhere.

But even though sex has been helpful to me, it has also been a hindrance. As with any addiction, my addiction to sex has forced me to seek more frequent fixes. In addition, when simplistic sex acts weren't enough, I sought more complex ones to suit my ever-growing needs. These needs were, and still are, as present and meddlesome as those proverbial kids from the bad side of town.

I've come to realize that not only have my sexual experimentations been destructive in my life, but in my father's as well. My father was vulnerable to sexual addiction, even though I don't think he was affected by ADD. But I'm sure there must have been a reason for his addictive tendencies. My mother knew all too well of my father's sexual addiction. And since our walls on Eighth Avenue were thin, and my room was close to my parents, I knew the power it had over my parents' lives too. In the grunts and demands my father made. In the incessant squeaking of old bedsprings. And many times, as I sought to satiate my own seemingly insatiable urges, I would hear my mother's angry voice and her insistent no. I'm sure she hoped I didn't hear the stage whispers coming from my parents' small marital chamber, as my father pushed his desires relentlessly on his wife and I tried to make sense of the inappropriateness that sometimes occurs in a family home at night.

1 5

First and Whoremost

If This Van's a Rockin', Don't Bother Knockin'

I'd seen them plenty of times, and it didn't take me long to figure out why they were walking along El Camino. Call it intuition, or call it desperation. But I knew those squirrelly women with too much make-up were out there making a living off the predictable male sex drive. And I was going to get laid, even if it meant losing a few of the meager dollars I managed to scrape together every two weeks.

I passed prostitutes several times in my Mail Courier Service van, trying to get up the nerve to solicit one. I had hoped that I'd acquire the necessary skills to convince some girl my age to take off her clothes for me, but I just couldn't figure out how to do that. So, as I was prone to do later in my life when the need built up, I chose the most direct route to get what I wanted: good old American cash. I'm sure it's been many a boy's best friend in times like those. MCS was my first job since I quit high school. I picked up and delivered mail for the companies that paid for the service. The job gave me flexibility, wheels, and a little respectability. The only thing the job didn't give me was a girl.

So I cruised El Camino when I finished work for the day, usually late in the afternoon when the mail van was now as empty as I was. I'd become one pulsating nerve ending with a sole purpose. But day after day, I just couldn't bring myself to pull over and get what I needed. How would I approach one of those working women? I'd seen scenes on TV where a guy would just pull up to a prostitute and the deal would go down, but I wasn't a smooth actor with a script, I was a lonely teenager who didn't know how to talk to girls. There was a breakdown in my communication skills when it came to talking to anybody. I never knew how to approach a subject or find the right words. Things were jumbled in my head, and when I did finally spit out the words, they came out wrong. They weren't just the nervous ramblings of other teenagers; they were truly mixed-up messages—odd thought formulations that caused the listener to question whether I was all there. Even worse, sometimes I'd throw out absolutely inappropriate comments that were totally unacceptable in social situations. It's not that these comments were vulgar in any way; it's just that they were weird, nonsensical or offensive words, conjured up at the spur of the moment, that told people I wasn't altogether in keeping with popular opinions.

Still, all inadequate communications aside, I couldn't let the fog keep me from my goal. I simply had to know what it was like to be with a girl. I had to see her in the flesh and not in some magazine that had been crammed under my mattress, or my brother's, for six months. Then I saw the one I wanted: a bony woman with black hair. I'd seen her before many times, and she'd seen me, only I was usually driving too fast for us to make eye contact. Not this time, though. My desire to see a real naked woman, to feel skin instead of paper, must have caused me to ease off the van's gas pedal. I found myself inching along when this thin woman in the black suede miniskirt and red high heels turned a corner up ahead. She had a Burger King drink in her hand and, even though she was sucking on it, I knew she was trying to hold off a laugh. It must have been the way I looked at her. I looked at her the way a man lost on a deserted island might have looked at his first glimpse of a ship on the horizon. And like that man on the island, I somehow knew my rescue would be close at hand now that I had finally managed to pull my van to the curb where the girl in the mini stood.

She walked up to the passenger-side window and bent down to peer in at me, revealing a tiny bit of her black bra as she did. Then she took one last draw on the straw in her cup before saying, "Are you looking for a date?"

I considered the question for a moment. Was I looking for a date? Was she kidding? I didn't want to date her; I wanted to screw her, to explore her as no one had ever done before. Nonetheless, I knew from the way she emphasized the word "date" that it meant "screw." We went over some specifics so there was no ambiguity whatsoever.

We went through a little song and dance about whether I was a cop or not and what I was looking for. I was sure by the tone of her voice that this daylight siren had gone through this many times before. She got in the van and directed me to the other side of the tracks. A pair of train tracks ran parallel to El Camino from San Jose to South San Francisco. El Camino Real Blvd. is a six-lane road running north and south, and it is cluttered with the typical chain stores one would expect to find in the suburbs. But the whore took me away from the glamour of mainstream America onto Old County Road, a quiet strip with mundane warehouses and a smattering of semi-trailers left along the curb by truckers for indefinite periods. And it was in this non-flattering environment that my longing was finally about to be fulfilled by the thing I most needed: a willing woman.

There were no satin sheets or fanfare that day, not even a bed or the backseat of a car in which to relish my first time.

The prostitute left the passenger seat and snuck into the back. She peeked through the windows looking for savvy cops. I gave her my money, probably a twenty-dollar bill. She directed me to the bare steel van floor and pulled up her skirt. And she did these things automatically, habitually, never ceasing to scan the area for police.

I undid my pants and eagerly awaited the experience I'd dreamt of for so long. Throbbing with anticipation and gratitude, I lay there on that cold floor among the dirty smudges and scrapes, the aftermath of innumerable shoes and mail trays, metal clasps, and other paraphernalia used in the process of moving mail from one place to another. My back hurt from the metal ridges on the floor by the time the bony courtesan lowered herself onto my erect penis. I became aware of something new in the van, a souvenir which would mark my deflowering more than the sex itself for all the years to follow. It was the woman's stench, so hideously pungent that it almost caused me to vomit as I approached an orgasm. I climaxed as quickly as the time it took for the van's shocks to raise and lower six or seven times.

Then it was all over. The transaction, the nervousness, the stench, the sex, the mystery, and the sin. All in about ten minutes. She yanked down her skirt. I pulled my pants over my still-throbbing penis, and we drove back to El Camino.

When I dropped her off she continued to look over her shoulder furtively for the police, while she eyed potential new clients.

I never even knew her name. Only the stench, a glimpse of hair and flesh, and the feeling of being a part of her for a few moments. Where so many had been before.

I drove away slowly, sickened by the thought of her still on my body, dripping over it like some toxin. The van rolled along without purpose, and I wondered about what had just happened to me. We both crept away to finish our day's work in the pure California sun. She headed south toward San Jose, twenty dollars richer, and I headed north toward San Francisco, one step closer to being a man.

Choices and Higher Voices

JANUARY 1981

Losing Sight of the Yellow Brick Road

McChord Air Force Base is in a beautiful part of Washington, just a few miles from Mt. Rainier. The base was favored by those who wanted a place to spend their last days in the Air Force before retiring. Consequently, a lot of older men and women who had served their country dutifully over the years were stationed at McChord.

For me, the base was merely an assignment for the next phase of my training. A place where I was to apply all that theory learned at Sheppard, on the C-130—a stocky aircraft affectionately dubbed the Herky Pig because of its bulbous radar housing on the nose of the plane.

Life at McChord was more flexible than life at Lackland and Sheppard since I was now being trained for what the Air Force had hired me. Much of the harsh drilling and initiation to military life in boot camp and tech. school was over. I quickly became accustomed to the easy-going atmosphere of McChord. Like a college dormitory, there were only two airmen to a room. In addition, the hands-on training environment of the airfield gave me added freedom. We learned everything about what made the Herky Pig tick: from the many switches and gauges in the cockpit to the hydraulics in the innards of the aircraft. To my surprise, I actually digested the material passed on to me by the crusty old sergeants—or so I thought.

So I settled into life there at McChord in the confidence that I was becoming an aircraft mechanic. I lived at the Castle, a large brick building that not only billeted many of the airmen stationed at McChord, but also housed the administration offices. I shared a room with Terry, a gregarious airman who liked to party. Terry was a rocker to the core with blond hair and a square face that tensed up when it tried to mimic some legendary rock star's on-stage expression. My roommate loved to ask questions like, "Who do you think is a better drummer, Bonham or Moon?" Sometimes, I'd find him with his guitar, struggling to learn a classic with his head banging to the sounds of a heavy metal band in the background. One time we drove to nearby Seattle to see Molly Hatchet, a hard-driving band with a powerful singer at the helm who sounded like he had a few battling badgers stuck in his throat when he sang. The band was best known for the song "Flirtin' With Disaster." Terry used to link this phrase to someone who had decided to enlist in the Air Force. "That's all anybody is doing when he signs up," he'd say.

But as much as I liked spending time with Terry, there was someplace I liked more: the third floor, the floor above ours. My favorite part of the Castle. This was where the female airmen, or WACS, lived, and when I visited the third floor I couldn't have been happier.

I spent a lot of time upstairs pursuing my highly focused hobby of figuring out the opposite sex. For some reason, every woman I met at the Castle had some kind of turmoil in her life to explore. It was much better than TV. I met a young woman in the chow hall on the Castle's ground floor, for example, who opened my eyes to the fact that there were other people in the world like me who obsessed over things. Terry told me that this woman, Lisa, had the hots for me. She was a woman who had trouble controlling her sexual appetites, and given my lack of judgment—and my own obsession—I pursued her. It was tough finding time alone with Lisa, though, since she had a friend who followed her everywhere. A chaperone who made sure her friend didn't give her body away too easily. But the chaperone wasn't always there, and one day I was alone with her charge. We ended up playing cards. Apparently, I still needed to work on my tactics.

I met another woman who had recently divorced. The relationship smacked of one I'd had with a divorcée at Sheppard. Stacy was a thin, quiet girl with no noticeable emotions whatsoever. I'd met her in the Sheppard chow hall as she fumbled with a square of peach cobbler. I leaned over my table and told her that Wednesday's cherry cobbler had a better crust. This comment brought out the only smile I was to see on Stacy's face the rest of the time we saw each other. Her barracks was on the other side of Sheppard's sprawling grounds, and I had to walk on the snow-and ice-covered walkways just to visit her. It wasn't worth it once I did finally complete my journey. Stacy brooded over the snow, brooded over the large, ugly glasses she had to wear, but mostly she brooded over the past. She held her former husband responsible for her present state of unhappiness. Even though I knew of Stacy's past, I didn't know much about her. She didn't talk much and mainly just wanted to sit with me and stare blankly into space, searching for the right words to describe the way she felt. Usually, she didn't find those words. Usually, she didn't say much of anything, and we'd just sit there pondering the world together in our own silent ways. Ultimately, the silence and Stacy's introverted behavior were too much for me to take, and I merely stopped making the lengthy trip over that frozen ground between the places we lived.

Janet, McChord's third-floor divorcée, was a lot like Stacy—with the one exception that she'd smile at least twice a day if I thought of something clever to say. But as with Stacy, we sat around a lot, each of us trying to break free of some mental cloak covering our minds: me of the fog, and Janet of thoughts of a man she once knew swirling around up there somewhere in her head. I decided that Janet and I were very compatible because of the confusion we both felt about life. Even so, due to my frequent inability to fully understand what someone else was going through, I had a hard time connecting with Janet. When I did get the opportunity to calm her down from one of her emotional side trips, I'd persuade her to seize the moment, to just forget the past for a while and take advantage of the present. Then, we'd lie in bed, and I would cop a feel before Janet changed her mind. But either I wasn't convincing enough with my moves, or the memories of her past were just too consuming, because mostly she cried when I tried to touch her and told me how sad she was. I don't think I was a very good listener, but she must have thought so.

Terry and I took a few more trips to Seattle, and I kept thinking how much the city reminded me of San Francisco. With all the city's pizzazz and eclectic artist types, we at least had an escape from military predictability. But even Seattle wasn't enough to keep our minds off military life. The sticker on the mini fridge in our room that read "The Air Force, A Great Waste of Life" (someone had crossed out the *y* in the word *way*, and replaced it with *ste*) began to ring true to us. I think we were just bored. By now we were used to the routine of things like saluting and making sure the buttons on our back pockets were buttoned. All we really had to focus on was learning a few more tricks so that we could both become aircraft mechanics and move on to the next stage of our Air Force careers. To help ease the boredom, one afternoon we took my truck to Tacoma and found a whore on the main drag in town. We drove her to a run-down hotel room and took turns with her. I waited in the dingy bathroom while Terry went first, then I had what guys usually call "sloppy seconds." At least I wasn't in a van this time, and this woman smelled okay. And she was pretty. But what pleased me most of all was the necklace dangling between the prostitute's breasts with the name Carrie on it. I kept smiling all the way through my turn at bat with her. She probably thought I was just some young kid who was happy to be getting laid, but it was more than that for me. I imagined I was in that room with my first love back in the redwoods of La Honda, and for about ten minutes anyway the Air Force didn't matter anymore.

Even though military life was starting to get to me a little, and what the mini fridge sticker said rang partially true, at least life was stable. I thought that I had a prosperous career in aircraft mechanics to look forward to, and there was always the Castle's third floor. I even had another stripe on my arm by then. A few days later, I took Janet to the movies on base. We watched one of the funniest movies I'd ever seen: *Airplane*. It seemed only too appropriate given my chosen, or should I say Air Force chosen, profession. It took me a while to realize that whenever the prop-driven airplane on the screen flew, it did so with the accompanying sound of jets, not propellers. Much later, after seeing the movie again, I noticed that this incongruous flaw was exceedingly obvious, but back then at McChord, my old friend the fog kept me from catching this. When you eat, sleep, and drink airplane mechanics with an airplane as unique as a prop plane, the propeller/jet gag should have been as telltale as a car propelled by rocket thrust.

Still, I was somewhat surprised because, in general, the fog didn't seem as prevalent at McChord. Or so I thought. Not very long after seeing the movie, there was a sign the fog had never gone. It was an event that changed the direction of my life forever.

It occurred on a brisk afternoon when Senior Master Sergeant (SMSgt.) Petty pulled me off the C-130 I was working on and into the office of Lt. Kennedy, the officer in charge of training. I had no idea why I was asked to accompany SMSgt. Petty, and I went along happily. But when we got into that very orderly officer's office, there was no mincing of words. Petty said I just wasn't cutting it as a mechanic. I was shocked to say the least. I thought I was doing okay. Once again I wasn't as aware of what was happening in my world as I thought.

But dwelling on my shortcomings would have to come later because Lt. Kennedy's response to SMSgt. Petty's observation was just as straightforward, and it demanded a decision then and there on my part. Kennedy gave me three options. Just like that. No "What do you think, Airman Patterson?" No wasted "I'm sorry." Just the options. As if no rebuttal or discussion was necessary.

I was told that I could wait for another class to begin and enter it in the hopes that I'd pick up what I needed the second time around. I could get out on an honorable discharge (since according to Lt. Kennedy, the Air Force hadn't fulfilled my needs). Or I could pick another Air Force career. This last option required another long and intensive training program and most likely another tech school.

It took just about as much time for me to decide which of the three choices I would select as it had for my superiors to tell me that I was basically a failure and needed redirection.

Of course, the first option Kennedy had offered was out of the question. Secretly, even before I started tech school, I had a feeling the airplane mechanic thing wouldn't pan out. After the Air Force people in Oakland had given me aptitude tests, I'd told them I wasn't very mechanically inclined. But they said the test scores didn't lie. I was mechanic material. Maybe I should have told them about the time I tried to repair my motorcycle and got so frustrated that I threw a screwdriver. And that the screwdriver ricocheted off the driveway and imbedded itself into the gas tank. That may have given the test-givers more insight into my abilities as a mechanic. So why try being a mechanic again?

The second option was out of the question too. If someone had told me that I could be given a free pass earlier in my Air Force life, I might have taken it. But not now. I had invested too much time in the military, and after all, I had another option. I told Petty and Kennedy I would choose another career. They said okay, and I was yanked out of the C-130 training program. Suddenly, my path had been blocked by an impenetrable object, and I had no alternative but to choose another direction.

The same old feelings of incompletion and instability resurfaced. Somewhere, in the back of my mind, it made sense. I was a high school drop-out and a young man in a constant fog. Why should I have been given the privilege of working on such expensive and important pieces of machinery? Something so important for the defense of my country. But even in my downtrodden state, I had hope. I could start again. I still had one more chance.

I worked in the Castle administration office while I was in my transition stage. Where else could they put me? The Air Force doesn't like to have its people wasting time. That would be a great *waste* of life, after all. That slogan in my room glared at me more than ever now.

My days in the office passed without much excitement. I did tasks meant for the simple minded, like filling out forms and issuing parking stickers. No sensitive airplane parts to screw up here. No lives to put at risk because of some dumb mistake. At least that heavy responsibility had been taken away. I felt comfortable in the administration office. No real challenge. And I was good at my new job. I made friends with a very nice sergeant who showed me the ropes and even told his superior that I should stay where I was. Sgt. White invited me to his house for dinner once. At his home and at work, White always made me feel comfortable with his smiles and jokes. This wasn't the strict and disciplined military life I had known before. It was a cakewalk.

I walked by the flight line sometimes and stood there at its edge. I thought I'd never again to be allowed the luxury of getting near one of those green miracles. Stay back, foggy, my fellow trainees probably would have said. Their world wasn't mine anymore. Even their uniforms were different. They still wore the olive greens, the uniform of people who got dirty, up to their elbows in the grease and oil of complex technologies. My uniform was the pretty blue of one who passed his days in obscurity. An airman only in name. Someone in the most remote part of the military backbone. A paper-pusher. And every time I heard an airplane roar overhead I sulked.

Maybe I should've gotten out of the military. But I trudged forward, looking out of the windows of the Castle, whiting out things that weren't typed correctly, getting Sgt. White's coffee. And in my spare time, I looked through a thick book of new careers. Of course, now I learned that I couldn't choose any career that required more tech education. That might be a waste of taxpayer money. I might fail again. I didn't know what to do. What should a failure, one who so often lacks the ability to comprehend things, do? I arbitrarily chose carpentry. It seemed to be a hands-on field. And Jesus was a carpenter. In my mind, that made the work righteous.

So I submitted the proper paperwork, and all I had to do was wait. Then, about a month later, I was brought into the administrative officer's office with Sgt. White. The officer told me that Bill White's request that I stay in the office had been denied. My own request to begin carpentry training was also denied. Instead, this officer told me that higher powers had reassigned me to the motor pool at Ellsworth Air Force Base, SD. What? Where? Why? I wanted to ask. But all I did was stand at attention. When the officer said I was dismissed, I saluted. Then I did a smart left-face and left the office.

Bill felt sorry for me and said the Air Force should have kept me in that office. I was too good at what I did. But, as his boss had told us, it was Air Force needs that determined my ultimate assignment, not his or my own. Even though Lt. Kennedy had promised me I could choose my own career path.

Everyone was assigned a code in the Air Force. My aircraft mechanic code had been AFSC (Air Force Specialty Code) 43132, Aircraft Maintenance Specialist. The codes were commonplace. Most people knew what most of the AFSCs were. My new official title would be AFSC 60350, Vehicle Dispatcher/Operator Specialist. I often had to explain what a 60350 did. The typical response would be "Oh, really." It meant "You got screwed."

But a 60350 was still very new to me back at the Castle, so I did my best to learn what a Vehicle Dispatcher/Operator Specialist did for a living. How bad could it be? The title had the word *Specialist* in it. But most of the Air Force titles had some word like that in them. I think it made the younger airmen feel better to know that they were specialists at what they did, especially if their specialties were mundane or unimportant.

So I looked in the big book of careers again, this time under AFSC 60350. At the time, things didn't look very bad. Apparently, as its name implied, one of a 60350's duties was operating vehicles, an old obsession of mine. I learned later that this was the main task in a 60350's job. Simply driving. Not dispatching. Only a few people did that. Dispatchers had to think fast and juggle a lot of things at once. Mostly decisions about who should drive certain vehicles to certain places, and which vehicles should be driven. And dispatchers had to be the motor pool supervisor's favorites. I've seldom been a favorite, given the fog's propensity to distance me from others.

I visited McChord's motor pool—even though I never knew it existed until that day—since that's where 60350s worked. Every base had a motor pool. Maybe it should have been obvious to me that the military's vehicles had to originate somewhere. But I'd been so wrapped up in aircraft mechanics prior to this epiphany that the idea had not occurred to me. A motor pool was just what the name implied, a place for motors. Motors attached to chassis. And chassis attached to wheels. And seats on top of them with 60350s behind the wheels.

When I got a first-hand look at a motor pool, I knew that the other airmen's impressions had been right: I *had* been screwed. Based on what I saw, the motor pool was insignificant. It was a dirty, cold place, full of disenchanted faces. It smelled of diesel fuel and depression. I soon learned that this assessment wasn't far off, and I was headed to a place where the disenchanted belonged.

Bye School

I'VE NEVER BEEN completely at home in any school or classroom environment. The fog hovered in my mind early on, and it seldom lifted. I tried to make my way through a subject the way a blind man might attempt to find his way through a broken plate of Braille. I lost interest in junior high school. My best friends had disowned me by then. For some reason—I'll never know why—the few guys I played baseball with said I was gay and stopped interacting with me. I assured them that I liked girls. I had never shown the least bit of interest in pursuing boys, but it didn't matter. I think my friends felt they were just too cool to hang around with me. They were about to enter junior high, and I didn't fit into their world.

But the fact that I had lost touch with my baseball pals shouldn't have affected me in the classroom; by then, I was very used to being alone. School didn't appeal to me. Subjects became more and more difficult to understand. Information would go in, some of it would stay, but more often than not, it was all a blur of numbers and data drifting around in my mind and not taking root. Somehow, I was able to pass the tests, so no one ever knew what was really going on inside my mind. This is how a lot of people perceive me as an adult, too. A seemingly intelligent individual who is capable of performing most tasks. Later, these same people see past the facade and become truly privy to what's beneath my apparent competence.

Music and writing still intrigued me in the seventh and eighth grades. So at least I did relatively well in these subjects. I played third-string trumpet in my junior high school band. I even did a little marching with them. And I found a new friend in Bill Maloney, a compulsive liar, a guy who the girls liked. We played basketball a lot, and he liked the Beatles as much as I did. Sometimes we would mess around with his brother's Marshall amplifier and belt out the Fab Four's songs. Bill lived with his grandmother and a big arthritic German shepherd in a large house on Fifth Avenue. We both had dreams of being famous. Bill's personality was very outgoing, but he had outbursts when he didn't take his Ritalin. Unlike me, he had a tendency to be hyperactive.

When he got irritable, I'd politely excuse myself and go home. Bill called me years later, after I got out of the military, and said he'd struck it rich gambling. I had an urge to go see him, but I had a hunch his wealth was another one of his lies, so I never set up a meeting. And I never heard from him again.

Unlike my brother, I stayed in school during my junior high years. Danny always skipped school. When my father and I went looking for him, we'd usually find Danny smoking a cigarette behind the handball courts—unless he was out stealing something or looking for beer. I didn't start skipping school until high school.

Menlo Atherton High was a new world that didn't monitor my movements as much junior high's Hoover School. In the minds of my teachers, concern for my coming and going only came into play when roll was taken or assignments were handed out at the end of class.

Everything in high school was laid out on a large scale. No longer did I engage in familiar activities, such as playing chess with Mr. Beonerrude, my junior high school teacher, or a quick game of HORSE on the basketball court (a game every kid played where I lived). The personal touch was lacking in high school when it came to nurturing my intellectual growth in the classroom. I was either to understand what was being taught to me—with as little input from the teachers as possible—or not. I just became a number on another computerized printout sent out before the start of term. Consequently, I fell behind. I simply couldn't keep up with this sort of mass-instruction approach. So it was understandable that I lost interest and drifted into more interesting pursuits.

Not only did the pace and lack of one-on-one instruction affect me, but I found that the curriculum in most classes was just too complex to comprehend. In social studies class, for example, I sat at the back of the room trying to make sense of ideas that, as far as I was concerned, were beamed from another planet. The social studies teacher, Mr. Price, would show us slides of medieval sculpture. Sometimes I'd try to figure out what Price wanted us to know from his lecturing, but sculpture after sculpture passed over the screen, and the best I could do was marvel at the intricately chiseled lines in the stone faces staring back at me.

In our general math class, I just sat there trying to avoid Mr. Neubauer, a teacher with bad breath who used to circle the room filled with students attempting to grasp basic mathematic concepts. Most kids called for Mrs. McCovey, Mr. Neubauer's aide, to help them. She presented things better and at least her breath was tolerable. On the wall in front of us, a bigger-than-life chart monitored each student's progress. Following each name were gold stars. I didn't receive more than a couple of stars. I just figured that the class would end someday and we wouldn't have to hear the words "integers" or "whole numbers" anymore. Then a black kid named Blue motivated me to get my stars moving a little faster. Blue was a small kid with a big mouth and a bowler hat that had a feather in it. He came from East Palo Alto and had it in for white kids. Menlo Atherton High School had a history of racial problems between black and white kids. There were even a few riots. There was always talk about another one breaking out, and rumors floated around school about kids stocking up on weapons in their lockers.

Blue threw pretend punches in my face from the first day we were in that class together. He never said why he did it. He never said much of anything to me. I remained stoic; I tolerated this daily intimidation. I thought the punches were far enough away not to bother me, until one landed firmly on my cheek.

When it did, I flew out of my desk and chased Blue around the room, but he hid behind Mr. Neubauer. Blue didn't bother me after that day, but he'd lit a fire under me, a fire that rapidly made it all the way up to my brain. For some reason, Blue's behavior suddenly made me frustrated with class, and it gave me the incentive I needed to work harder. But Blue's punch did more than that; it gave me the power I needed to focus my attention on something. And with this focus and motivation, mathematics started to make sense to me. I decided my only way out of this class was to completely fill the chart on the wall with gold stars. And that's just what I did. Gold stars began to march after my name on the chart like a linear universe, and Mrs. McCovey couldn't believe it. I couldn't believe it either. I don't know how a boy's punch focused my powers of attention so finely, but I didn't care. I just wanted more gold stars, and I wanted to be as far away from Blue, or people like him, as I could.

Still, I didn't attend school as much as I should have. The idea of leaving it for something else appealed to me. I saw a world away from school that seemed less confusing. A world of people whose daily routines didn't rely on algebra or medieval statues; a world I understood a little better. Away from school, I might still have problems with the fog, but at least I found that most of the things I did were less trying. Out there were the things that really mattered. Things even more important than gold stars. There was my motor-cycle, for example. Racing around in the dirt was a whole lot more fun than sitting at a desk listening to the same old thing. Menlo Atherton locked its student parking lot after lunch and made it even easier for Jake and me to skip school. We simply couldn't get back in when we needed to. Of course, we made a habit of taking exceptionally long lunches. Since we had no place to park our bikes, we sped off in search of adventure, and we usually found it.

I didn't hate everything about school. I enjoyed putting words together in English and I liked the stories Mr. Fuchs would make us read. That is, when I could understand them. And, of course, English was the class that the Easter Egg was in. The chess club met in the English classroom at lunch, and sometimes I hung out to play a few games. It's just too bad there wasn't a chess class; I would never have missed it. My brother, Mark, had taught me how to play years before high school, and I wasn't that bad. But I kept to basic strategies. Never able to think too far ahead. Other more experienced players would see past my rudimentary approach to this complex game, and ultimately they toppled my king. I almost got into a fight with one of these more experienced players who made fun of my inept chess skills, but I thought better of engaging in the confrontation since my tormenter was on M.A.'s wrestling team and had a build to back up his learned moves.

Mr. Smith, our science teacher, also pointed out my weaknesses when it came to knowledge. He was a short, no-nonsense man who demanded our full dedication when it came to this extremely important fact-based pursuit. And Jake and I gave him none. As with the math class, the two of us merely took up space in Mr. Smith's class. We were just as non-responsive as the dead things in jars on the shelves. Our minds were as empty and clear as some of the glass beakers and test tubes. Smith always called on us, and he got fed up with our nonchalant attitude. One day, Smith had me stand up after yet again not knowing the answer to a question he'd posed. I turned red and asked for help from Jake, but he couldn't assist me. Some good soul, sensing my embarrassment, tried to come to my aid, but another student shot him down by saying, "Let the idiot answer for himself." To this day, I still recall the tone of that kid's command. He knew what I was really about. He knew I was not just some James Dean-like rebel, but I was a person who truly had a problem understanding things. And I couldn't rebuke him. I simply stood there for another minute or so, Smith holding the handle to the spit I was on, turning it a little more with each foggy moment. Smith gave Jake and me an ultimatum: if we didn't return to class with a completed homework assignment, then we needn't come back to class at all.

A few days later, after wood shop, and after Jake and I had finally completed the boxes that every kid made at M.A., we took a walk in the school's empty soccer field. Jake stood with his wooden box under one arm and asked, "Do you want to keep doing this?" I knew exactly what he meant. I said, "No." We never returned to any classes after that. It's some twenty-five years later now, and Jake still has his wooden box.

Heads Up

MARCH 1981

Back to Driving

I pointed the '54 Ford east for Rapid City. The truck's only flaw was a faulty heater, and I didn't find this out until the Rocky Mountains. But I had my heavy Air Force jacket with the big eagle on the back of it to keep me warm. Most airmen who passed through Wichita Falls had a jacket like this. They were bought from a downtown shop that had every kind of patch and Air Force insignia a true-blue American could hope for. In addition to the eagle with its talons open to rip into its prey, I had an American flag sewn onto one of the jacket's shoulders. I wore that jacket proudly and always made a point of flashing it in civilian faces, especially those who didn't live close to an Air Force base.

I slept in old hotels in even older towns on the way to Rapid City. One hotel had a creaky bed and a pitcher and basin just like the ones cowboys used to use. It was the only hotel in town, and it didn't even have a TV. The eeriness of the place scared me so much that I didn't get much sleep that night.

Once on the road again, I picked up Mormon broadcasts in Utah on the truck's antiquated radio. Then the Mormons faded as I got farther and farther away from Salt Lake City. I finally pulled into Ellsworth Air Force Base the next morning, and I got a cup of coffee in a rickety white administration building.

Eventually, a sergeant from the Sixty-First Transportation Squadron found me a room in another white building, a barracks that housed mostly airmen who worked in the motor pool. When airmen returned to the barracks later that evening, a torrent of stereo music passed through the walls like water through tissue. I soon learned that everyone in the barracks had bought a stereo to compete with his neighbor. Of course, as soon as I located the PX, I would add to the expensive boom-box- booming cacophony with my own Pioneer system, which I made certain was by far the loudest.

My barracks roommate, George, was from a Colorado coal-mining family. He talked a lot about mining, and how he'd probably return to it when he got out of the Air Force. The talk scared me more than that room in that desolate Utah town with the throwback decor. Somewhere, I'd heard that miners' lungs eventually turned black, and these hard workers died soon thereafter. I think I heard that in a movie called *The Coal Miner's Daughter*. George was a nice guy, so I hoped he'd find a different line of work when he got out of the Air Force.

Once I settled into my new base, I began doing what most of us in the motor pool did out there on that cold prairie: drive. Our main objective was to take pilots to their airplanes, mostly B-52s, C-141s, and a few C-5s, the Air Force's Goliath cargo plane. But sometimes, I'd take pilots to a few fighters that were passing through. Then I'd remember all those Air Force posters with helmeted warriors zooming flashy airborne predators toward the viewer. My Air Force recruiter had one of those posters in his office when I walked in to see him.

And now, there I was, wheeling my twenty-nine or forty-five passenger diesel bus around like a pro. I had my part to play too. And I did it unceasingly, in the snow or dead of night, accompanied by some of America's best. Sometimes I drove with only row after row of empty vinyl bus seats and my own thoughts to accompany me. I passed South Dakota's many prairie dogs, which stood at the edge of their mounds like diminutive spies recording the madness of buses and planes rumbling along in their barren world.

I'd drive along the frozen roads to the pilots' billet or from it to an airplane's wingtips. Each day I envied the pilots with their shiny brass and silver, envied their all-important grins and cocky posture, which contrasted with my directionless frustrated shuffle. Those peacetime heroes sat behind me like victorious Roman Caesars. It didn't do much for my already suffering self-esteem.

I thought that I could sense the pilots' stares at the back of my head as I taxied them out to those symbols of American might that I would never again be allowed too near. They seldom said more than a few words to me. But I'm sure they must have asked themselves why I ended up in such a menial position. Not that all airmen in the motor pool had dropped out of tech schools to become bus drivers. I think at least two of the many drivers in our squadron had come straight from basic training. Of all the rag-tag team there in the middle of nowhere, I felt sorriest for them. At least I'd had a chance at a more prestigious job.

Most of us were washouts from one school or another, though. And when enough failures had filled the motor pool's quota, other fallen angels would end up in the chow hall slopping food onto trays, or worse end up with the base security police holding M-16s all day or night so that undesirables wouldn't sneak past that bold red line that separated the airfield from the rest of the base.

Back at the motor pool, if we weren't driving buses, we might be wheeling a staff car to the Rapid City airport to pick up an officer who had been assigned to the base. And when we weren't doing that, we were washing and waxing vehicles, especially staff cars belonging to high-ranking officers. It seemed that there was no end to this chore since there were long periods in between shuttling people from one place or another, and our superiors didn't want us to be idle. Senior NCOs and officers in charge of the motor pool took their jobs very seriously. They were on us all the time to make sure everyone who needed a ride got it on time, and that every general's staff car was immaculate inside and out. During the day everything was by the book.

But sooner or later, even the vehicles wouldn't be enough to occupy our time. When we weren't doing some other mundane task like picking up trash in the snow, we would sit around eating our "box nasties" as we called them (boxes of cold sandwiches and potato chips meant for aircraft crews) and play cards. Or we'd arm wrestle, or look at dirty magazines, or just talk about what we would do when we got out of the Air Force. This preoccupied most of our time since the majority of us knew we'd been screwed. I often thought of all those who were thinking of joining the Air Force, or who had already done so and were in basic training. Of all those who would end up where we were. The many young men and women who would walk around with eyes on the ground thinking about how their lives could've been so much more.

Even though we were depressed and disenchanted, we bonded. Most of us were in the same boat. We understood what the other was going through, and we developed a comedic approach to what fate had dealt. We were all in a sort of therapy together there in that roomy converted aircraft hangar filled with vehicles and dispatch radios.

When we ended up at the motor pool, most of us had lost the sense of urgency and importance toward the Air Force mission that had been shoved down our throats. And many of us certainly had lost any sense of military decorum and morale. It was tough to motivate us, or to threaten us. Some welcomed early discharges for going against military regs, even if it meant getting a less than honorable discharge. Sergeants were always on at us to cut our hair or keep our uniforms pressed. And if we lagged when it came to our duties behind the wheel, harsh words were directed our way. I always wondered how those sergeants and officers ended up in the motor pool. Had they screwed up somewhere else too?

Airmen who were continually difficult to deal with went to the night shift, where a skeleton crew tried to keep warm until needed. Hard cases were easier to handle at night, and if nothing else, we were usually out of the base's high-ranking officers' view. I was sent to nights after I inadvertently filled a diesel bus with gasoline. Even with all my driving experience, I had never driven a diesel vehicle, and I didn't know the difference between gas and diesel. After being humiliated by a plethora of dumb jokes, a really pissed-off mechanic who had to repair the bus I damaged embarrassed me even more in front of my peers when he instructed me on the difference between gas and diesel engines. He also showed me the clearly visible diesel placards on the buses that my foggy mind had neglected to notice.

Because of this and other reasons, I was glad to leave the day shift. Too many people laughed behind my back following the tongue-lashing with the mechanic. The people on the night shift didn't seem to care as much about what I'd done since they hadn't been there to witness the onslaught of jokes unleashed on me, and they certainly hadn't been contaminated by the jesting day-shift atmosphere.

Mostly, I was left alone during those many hours before the sun finally rose each day. This allowed me to dwell even more on my predicament. If only I had been interested in reading back then.

Although I liked it, the night shift was a place of incessant loneliness and solitude, filled with the occasional jet engine firing in the distance and a ceaseless, whistling South Dakota wind. Sometimes, we'd wait in our long buses for an aircraft to arrive on a virtually deserted airfield. I had an endless supply of tapes for occasions like these, and bands such as Led Zeppelin and Yes would play hauntingly amongst the black empty seats. Sometimes a call would come over the bus's radio to check on my progress. Sometimes just to annoy the dispatch sergeant, I'd act as if the radio didn't work. Then I'd pick it up and sleepily inform the patient sergeant of my status.

Once, during a particularly boring night in the hangar, a few of us took out the Snow Cat that was to be used for rescues only, and we drove up and down some nearby snow banks. We laughed and held on tightly as the Snow Cat would fall over an especially steep pile of snow. We thought we were putting something over on those rigid day-shift NCOs and well-pressed officers. But the next morning when the higher ups discovered the tread marks in the snow, those of us on the night shift were admonished for this childish trek.

When the night shift finished, some of us would go over to the chow hall in the wee hours of the morning for an omelet. Then we'd go back to the barracks for some late night shouts and a little booming music.

If we woke up early enough, we'd go into Rapid City and try to find something interesting to do. After I sold my truck to a fireman on base, I bought a Rambler. One afternoon before an upcoming night shift, we drove it to a hilly park where life-sized cement dinosaurs looked down on South Dakota and Ellsworth Air Force Base. The prehistoric reptiles were more than anachronisms. They were alone like us, with no apparent purpose for being there.

I found out the Rambler's parking brake didn't work when we started walking toward the dinosaurs and somebody told me the car had started to roll away. I almost let it. That's how little I cared about anything anymore. But we stopped the car from rolling down the hill just in time since we knew it was a long walk back to base.

Unfortunately, events in the motor pool rolled along with destructive momentum. My Air Force file was being filled with nasty Letters of Reprimands and Article 15s. These were documents that told of my increasing insubordination and clash with authority. I had settled into my new life and surrendered to the fact that I was being used by a government force that needed peons like me to tend to the whims of an exceedingly more important Air Force purpose, but I resented a military that pushed its toy-soldier games on me, demanding that I still go through the motions of being an obedient little pawn.

I accepted the fact that I still had to serve my four years, but the higher ups knew I was never really an essential part of the force that would repel a Soviet attack. I was just another glorified taxi driver with a uniform. Someone who didn't quite warrant being discharged, but someone who didn't deserve a loftier military purpose.

With this unwritten understanding between me and the higher powers, I just wanted to be left alone. The way I had been left alone as a child in front of the TV with one of the steak and potato dinners I cooked for myself when I had gone to live with my father after my parents' divorce.

But unlike much of the civilian world, the military doesn't leave people alone. It thrives on invading one's privacy. Because of this, I became increasingly agitated and argumentative, not only with the NCOs and officers but with my fellow bus drivers too. My desire to be left alone got so bad that I wouldn't even sit in the cozy dispatch office with the other night shift people. Instead, I would sit in the empty drivers' lounge at the back of the hangar. I'd sleep, listen to my music, or seethe about my predicament, until the sergeant in charge needed me for something and called me on an intercom system. Then, disheveled and bleary eyed, I would grudgingly saunter over to the glowing dispatch office and take the keys to one of the blue buses or government issue Fords. Outside in the freezing night air, I ferried more essential personnel to their destinations.

Things went on like this until I entered my Christian phase. Men will seek God more fervently when they're feeling low, when they need guidance in life. A few guys I met on base were spreading the Good News like sweet jelly on toast, and I was a dry piece of bread ready to receive it. Not that I was an atheist before they came along, but I certainly wasn't practicing my religion.

One of my most vivid memories of being a Christian as a child was doing my damnedest to miss the Snoopy bus that took me and some other reticent kids to church. In another particularly vivid memory, a stern Sunday school teacher told me I'd go to hell if I didn't accept Jesus. This stuck with me the rest of my life, and because of the fear instilled in me by that teacher, I thought that someday I needed to get in touch with Jesus again.

So I started attending sermons and functions at a church in Rapid City where another airman named Randy Leacock and I would sing songs to the Lord. I was so good at singing that a few elderly women in the church set it up so I could solo occasionally. On a somewhat lower level, of course, this kind of performance in front of an audience fulfilled that rock star dream of mine. It didn't really matter that I was belting out Don Francisco songs, not to drug-influenced fans and bra-less young women, but to sober, God-fearing Christians.

When Randy and I weren't at church and he wasn't loading bombs onto B-52s, we'd go bowling or visit some hearty South Dakotans he knew. I thought I was happy then, that God was working in my life, but the fog made even that fact uncertain for me.

I came to the conclusion that if I wanted God to be true, after a while he would be. Therefore, I believed in God. Maybe my belief in God went beyond necessity. Maybe the reason I believed in God was truly divinely inspired.

Or maybe I was just too scared not to believe in God because of that Sunday school teacher who had scared the hell out of me, and I'd just found an outlet to help lift my spirits. Whatever the basis for my belief, I confessed it both in private and public places, and I thought my confession insured my place in heaven. Believing in God also helped to yank me out of that dull and taxing existence on base. And a fringe benefit to being a Christian was the fact that a lot of girls also attended church. For a short time, I even had a relationship with the preacher's daughter. I took Katie for rides on my brand new motorcycle; the two of us raced through the Black Hills to the ranch where she lived.

In return for the ride on my motorcycle, my young American cowgirl showed me her rodeo trophies and took me for bareback rides on one of her horses. There weren't very many girls in South Dakota. I was glad for the close proximity to a female, even though I never did reach home plate with her.

I was also glad that I'd discovered the Black Hills on my way to Katie's house. My roommate George and I visited Mount Rushmore, and I told him to watch me from one of the telescopes at a viewing area while I climbed to the top of the landmark. I wedged myself in a crevice just large enough to allow me to climb to the top of the chiseled presidents, and I ended up standing atop one of their heads. As I waved to George, I was not only a speck atop a gargantuan piece of granite in the Black Hills, but also a small man atop Teddy Roosevelt, a giant of a man in American history.

Another time, George and I visited Custer Park and walked out into the lush grass where buffalo roamed. The name of the park made me think of Custer's last stand, and I tried to imagine the fighting Seventh Cavalry up against so many Native Americans. I got so lost in these thoughts that I hardly paid attention to the large mounds of buffalo chips on the ground. It wasn't until I was about fifteen feet from a buffalo that I noticed it snorting in my direction. Seeing the massive black animal eyeing me in that vast open field, I had never felt so vulnerable. I learned to respect Native Americans a lot more that day, knowing that they took down these intimidating creatures with their primitive weapons long before white men shot them with their high-powered rifles from the safety of passing trains.

When my new Christian friends got to know me better, they asked me if I'd like to be a D.J. at a Christian radio station. I couldn't believe they'd asked me. I'd never had any experience working at a radio station, but they said they hadn't either, and it hadn't stopped them.

The station was old and small, way up on a hill overlooking Rapid City. My Christian friends showed me how to work a few levers on a control board and how to play records on the two turntables. I found neither task was beyond me.

When I wasn't working for the Air Force, I was left alone there at night, spinning the pristine discs and taking requests. The songs I sent out on Rapid City's airwaves were traditional numbers, mostly choirs or solo artists who just about lulled me to sleep. But I liked talking into the microphone when I introduced various artists, and I affected a smooth, late-night delivery by lowering and slowing down the tempo of my voice. At the end of the night I'd read from a huge Bible, which was repeatedly read from beginning to end throughout the lifespan of the radio station. I'd stumble with pronunciation of biblical cities or names, and I'm sure the listeners—if there really were any—laughed at my botching the names of all those well-known places and theological heroes.

When my Christian phase waned a little, and my superiors trusted me enough to send me back to the day shift, I took on a night job washing dishes at a country club. I worked with an old black guy who used to smile while I sang over the rattling plates and silverware in a deep stainless steel sink. He said I had a great voice, and he laughed when I'd really belt out a song that I loved.

I had a big Oldsmobile Delta 88 that I used to float across the prairie from the base to the country club, at least until the car died one day and I abandoned it beside the highway. I found that even an old beater like that Olds was better transportation in the snow than a motorcycle. Before getting the car, I used to creep along at about five miles an hour toward Box Elder and the trailer court just off base where George and I rented a mobile home.

When I laid the bike down and slid into an intersection on base one day, I gave up riding it until the following spring.

I remember having to run a plug from the mobile home into the 88's engine when it got to sixty below zero with the wind chill factor and stalactites hung over the front door. That South Dakota winter was just too much for a California boy like me.

But even the bitter winter and all the distractions that Air Force life and South Dakota had to offer didn't move the fog that I continued to try to blow out of my mind. And my lack of judgment in recognizing trouble almost got me blown out of the military.

A tough old sergeant from Tennessee had me on the mat about once every other week to keep me in line. He tried to get me to see the bigger picture, but I think even this wily lifer sensed that his heartfelt words weren't getting through.

I did want to better my life though. I wanted to feel I was worthy of staying in the Air Force, competent in something other than driving buses. So I requested to be trained to drive the tractor-trailers in the motor pool or the large wreckers. Those drivers got more prestige, but I guess my pleas to be trained on these vehicles fell on deaf ears. After all, I was a troublemaker, and why should I get the privilege of something so wonderful?

Besides, these vehicles were the best the motor pool had to offer, and I was the guy who'd filled one of the diesel buses with gasoline. They still hadn't forgotten about that. So I knew I had about as much of a chance of driving an expensive rig as I did working on another C-130.

My career opportunities took another blow on the chin, and I fell into another stupor. I moped around again. This only made things worse. I took to hanging out with a group of black airmen in the motor pool. For some reason I was fascinated with them. I began listening to R&B as well as the rock and Christian music that bored George to tears. Both the black guys and the white guys laughed at me at first, and the rednecks on base wouldn't let me get near a tractor-trailer or wrecker. Nonetheless, I empathized with the way the blacks were treated, and I thought they were ridden even more than troublemakers like me. At an early age, I had always drifted toward those who were given the short end of the stick, those as unfortunate as I was.

But I liked hanging out with the gang of black guys for another reason too. They were cool, and things didn't seem to get to them as much as they got to me. I tried to imitate their composed demeanor. They just played the game and took things in their stride. When I adopted their attitude, I didn't get into as much trouble. Life in the motor pool got a little easier and I learned not to take things so personally. My new friends of color just laughed off insults or derogatory comments, or they tried to one-up those who were trying to belittle them. My new friends accepted me as one of their own, even though they wondered why I had joined their ranks. But I still didn't play the game as well as they did, or for that matter, as well as anyone else in the motor pool.

Sometimes I got to drive a busload of security police far away from Ellsworth Air Force Base. I think NCOs liked sending me into the deserted prairie. At least they knew I was happy out there and couldn't get into any trouble. After leaving Ellsworth, I'd get the bus going as fast as I could on the down slope of one of the many hills on the main highway. The bus would slow up again when it crested another hill. Then I'd rev it up on the downhill to compensate for the weighty security police holding the bus back. This slow/fast scenario happened over and over again, and it was annoying, as annoying as my life was with its many ups and downs.

But I was used to the roller-coaster ride by now, and at least the fact that I got to drive so far away from base gave me the feeling I was fleeing the military. And no one governed me when I was out on the open road. It was as if I were a tour bus driver steering that barebones government workhorse to some exotic locale. It was quite a fantasy given South Dakota's lack of beaches, resorts, tourists, and just about every other frill.

Eventually, I'd pull the bus onto an unmarked dirt road and traverse a maze of other dirt roads deep into the prairie. Using memory and guess-work, I found a missile complex where I could drop off my precious Air Force soldiers. The drive back to the freeway was especially liberating; I was alone with my blaring stereo strapped to my driver's seat.

Sometimes I would pretend that Russian missiles were zeroing in on the American silos and I had to get out of the area fast. So I'd race through the dirt and gravel, past the jackrabbits and scrub brush, swinging the back of the bus around each curve and flying up the hills at breakneck speed. But my freedom never lasted. I'd find the freeway and Ellsworth. And then my confrontation with the military would begin again.

I was given many suggestions to help deal with such a restrictive life. Higher ups told me to walk a straight line and not question anything. My friends of color told me not to dwell on things so much, to just be cool. One of my new friends told me to smoke dope. But back then I was afraid of getting caught. Dogs sniffed the barracks periodically to find marijuana, and

I told an airman friend named Sam he'd end up in Leavenworth if he kept up his illegal puffing.

Christians told me to pray harder. God was the answer to everything. So I did pray harder, especially late at night, asking God for a sign, some reason why I was the way I was, and why the military was the way it was. I pressed the Creator for proof of his existence to help me feel better. To give me the clarity and intellect I'd always wanted in my life. I'll never forget one night. I was reading about Jesus telling His disciples that when they served people by giving them drink, they had served Him. I stopped reading that Bible passage and prayed even harder for a sign. For something obvious and other-worldly that would back up the Bible's two-dimensional pages that always left a sliver of doubt in my mind.

At exactly that moment, late in the evening, an unexpected knuckle tapped at the flimsy door of the mobile home. It was my airman friend, Sam. And I could tell by the missing stripes on his uniform shirt that something was wrong. When I asked him what had happened, he said that they'd caught him smoking marijuana. He had lost his rank and was being dishonorably discharged from the Air Force. I asked him if he'd like to come in or if there was anything I could do for him. He said he'd just come to say goodbye, but he could use a glass of water. I gave him one, and he went away. It then occurred to me that just before the knock on the door I had read that passage about Jesus instructing His disciples to serve people. Mention of giving His people drink was especially telling to me, an almost immediate and very direct answer to a prayer just a few minutes before.

I thrust open the door and looked for Sam, but he'd already gone. Still, this was all I needed, the sign I had been looking for. And it was one of the most peaceful and fulfilling times in my life. For once I had the clarity I had asked for. The event was all the more memorable because I had actually noticed something of importance that night, instead of missing it completely the way I usually did. And nobody had been there to help me—at least no human.

The clarity and peace I had that night didn't last long. The fog returned. I thought a change might help. Besides, South Dakota was beginning to bore me. So a year from the day I entered Ellsworth, I filled out a "dream sheet." This was an Air Force document that could only be filled out once a person's stay at a particular base had reached one year, a document that requested reassignment. I asked to be sent to one of eight bases, all in Europe. Most people told me that it was common for airmen to be sent to their least desired base on their "dream sheets," if indeed the Air Force honored the request at all. But I was in luck: I received reassignment orders, not immediately, but sooner than I'd expected. And I wasn't assigned to my last choice. They assigned me to the United Kingdom, my first choice. I was on my way to the home of The Beatles. A country known for its fog. So how could I go wrong? Fog or not, I had a new reason to be happy.

19

Driving on the Wrong Side of the Road

MAY 1982

Trucking and Toking

A sergeant picked me up from Heathrow in his Morris Mini. The quintessentially minuscule English car didn't even allow me a look over most of the hedgerows that bordered many of the just-as-minuscule roads left over from the Roman occupation of the country. The car whined like a bear cub as it raced toward RAF Bentwaters where I'd be stationed until January 1984.

The fact that the car was driving on the wrong side of the road freaked me out. Of course, the English later told me it was Americans who drove on the wrong side of the road. This information didn't help newly arriving Americans. During the weeks following my introduction to the U.K., I heard a story about some airmen who habitually reverted to driving on the side of the road they'd been accustomed to for so long in the U.S., especially if they had been drinking. The results were catastrophic.

I got to a point where I welcomed the reverse of the usual though. It fitted in with my normal reverse way of thinking. I liked all the green England had to offer too. South Dakota was mostly dreary brown. The Mini sped past quaint little pubs and houses and stopped in front of the red brick barracks that Sergeant Johnson said was my new home. I immediately liked it better than the white clapboard I'd been housed in for so long.

After the customary processing that was expected of a new arrival at a base, I got a look at the motor pool. The driver's lounge and dispatch office were located in a tiny shack on a squat little piece of land about a hundred yards or so from the airfield. American tank-killing A10s with enormous Gatling guns sticking out of their green noses buzzed frenetically on the Queen's soil.

Once settled into my new room, I learned that my roommate was a smoker so I yearned to find new digs, preferably off base. But that would have to wait until my motorcycle arrived from South Dakota. The red Kawasaki racing bike and I had fled Ellsworth together after I got my orders. Not more than a mile from Box Elder, South Dakota, I'd gotten a one hundred dollar speeding ticket issued by a trooper who said if I didn't pay it on the spot, I'd be taken to jail. I peeled off one of my travelers checks meant to sustain me in California before my trip to England. I think that kind of justice was literally highway robbery. I now doubt he could have actually justified taking me to jail that day, but I didn't want to call the cop's bluff. Anyway, I was loaded with cash and could afford to miss a measly hundred. After the trooper drove off, I continued toward California at the bike's top end, never slowing to less than a hundred all the way to the west coast. The trip in itself was an adventure, which included practically laying the motorcycle down on fresh, wet cow patties in Kansas, getting extremely sick after eating lunch in a New Mexico restaurant, and nearly flying over a guardrail after taking a turn too fast on a Southern California off-ramp. The bike needed a clutch repair in Needles, California, and I was lucky enough to find a Yamaha shop in the middle of nowhere that fixed it for free.

But now I was far from cacti and anything with needles on it, and I doubted I'd find any Mexican food nearby. But I would frequently dine on new fare I found very appealing: fish and chips. I thought it was novel that the greasy fish and thick wedges of potatoes were wrapped in newspapers. I could be well fed and well read at the same time.

When I finally retrieved my motorcycle from a shipping area in Felixstowe, I was elated. So elated that I immediately found a room in a house in Felixstowe, a cold resort town that looked out onto the North Sea. This was the same house where I met my friend Dennis Clannihan who had saved me on the Fourth of July.

I began to feel more and more like a civilian in England. I lived about thirty miles from Bentwaters, and when I got home and took off my uniform, the military simply faded away. The house I lived in was usually warm, save an especially cold period when, after getting a negative response from my landlady to turn up the heat, I burned the few pieces of well-used furniture in the room I rented.

When the weather in Felixstowe was fair, I enjoyed the beach boardwalk with its many attractions and tourists. It's hard to feel lonely in a resort town. In the boardwalk's arcade I held Donkey Kong's high score, and I even found a girlfriend. Shelly slapped my butt one day, while I was in an especially difficult level of Kong. Then she ran away. When she returned to slap my butt again, not even Donkey Kong was that important anymore. In about ten minutes, the time it took for us to climb a narrow staircase and walk back to my room, we were in bed together.

It had been raining that day when we met. The little windows in the room were open, allowing the North Sea air inside the house's tiny top-floor flat. We were both wet when we fell onto the mattress without a box spring or headboard. And while we were wet from the rain, it had been a dry spell for me when it came to sex. I devoured every inch of Shelly. I fed on her young, sexual desire, taking advantage of her pent-up longing. How long had she toyed around with the idea of luring some arcade junkie into a quiet place like this? She fed on my need just as much as I fed on hers. She gave herself to me as if she were a housewarming gift meant for new arrivals to England. Outside, England went about its mundane business with its usual composure, but inside that solitary room with Shelly, we lustily stripped away the placid British niceties.

When it was over, and we lay there in an embrace of English and American perspiration, my senses had been revived again. The fog lifted. I pondered ridiculously banal things about life, like the way a sergeant had instructed me how to tie down a load on a flatbed trailer using a certain knot; it was a knot I hadn't been able to comprehend up until that point. I considered the currency exchange rate and how I could better utilize my U.S. assets. I thought about ways I could mend a volatile relationship with a dispatcher on base. I reveled in my ability to feel Shelly's emotions as if they were my own. Even the clouds floating by my window seemed to have some kind of significance that was yet to be discovered.

Shelly was a bit younger than I was, but I enjoyed her coy behavior and beguiling smile. What I enjoyed most was the fact that someone was paying attention to me—unconditional attention—and that's all that mattered. Furthermore, I expended no effort to attract Shelly. This vivacious, dark-haired vixen lived around the corner from me in a simple house with her brother, mother, and truck-driver father. They were a close family, but Shelly didn't stay home often. She was virtually unsupervised; it was reminiscent of my upbringing at her age.

A week or so into our relationship, two of Shelly's friends tried to seduce me, but I resisted going to bed with them. Not because I didn't want to have sex, but because I thought I'd ruin the sure thing I had with Shelly. If I could go back in time, though, I'd risk losing my spunky girlfriend, since our relationship didn't last anyway. I became bored with her, something she took to heart. For some reason, the initial sparks that led the two of us into such a spontaneous relationship began to fizzle for me. Shelly nonetheless fought to keep me interested.

I hadn't seen her for a long time, and then one day she showed up at my door, not saying a word. She just smiled. Then she pushed me deeper into the room and made love to me. I performed, but I still wasn't very interested. Amazingly, even though I was getting sex—something I had longed for and loved most in life—things with Shelly already seemed old hat.

That day when she suddenly popped back in to my life, Shelly said that she had just come by to find out if what she suspected was true, that I was in fact bored with her. After the sex, Shelly left, as if to say, "Right, that confirms it. We're really through."

A few days later, I found a note from Shelly on my motorcycle stating she was breaking up with me. Winter came and the tourists left. Without them and Shelly, the town was a very lonely place. I had to get away from anything that reminded me of the warmth of better times.

Ipswich, a town bustling with life not far from Felixstowe, was an inevitable draw. I left my chilly room by the North Sea without even saying goodbye to Shelly. I didn't see her again until months later when I drove back to Felixstowe from my new house in Ipswich. I wish I hadn't found her. Leather-clad, smoking heavily, and wearing way too much make-up, she was hanging out by the sea wall with a bunch of friends I didn't know. This wasn't the Shelly I remembered. Something made her hard, and to this day I believe I was that something.

I think back to the carefree days we had together, the happy days, when Shelly consulted a psychic to find out if we'd be married. The time when we attended a festival in Felixstowe with marching bands and boys wearing tall white hats. The time we went to an open-air market where her mother had a stall, and Shelly smiled at her mother because I had shown up, and her mother smiled back, seeing the mischief in her daughter's eyes.

I never even let Shelly know I was there that day when I came back to find her. Instead, I simply rode away, saddened by the influence I had had over her. I hated the impulsivity that drove me to get involved with her. I should have just said no to her silly advances that day on the boardwalk, but I couldn't. I liked the attention too much, and as always sex stimulated me more than other things. It helped to make the fog go away for a short time.

While still living in Felixstowe, I met my new roommate in the Bentwaters chow hall where I sometimes ate its affordable meals. My soon-to-be roommate, David Carruba, worked in the chow hall. Incredibly, I later found out that he was one of those people who hadn't flunked out of any tech schools. He was very good with numbers. Since he had a few more stripes on his sleeve than the other airmen in the chow hall, Dave oversaw the day shift, managing people and food the way a civilian entrepreneur would manage a restaurant.

The day I met Sgt. Carruba, he was on a smoke break at another table when I overheard his conversation. He needed to find a roommate to share the expenses in a house he was looking at in Ipswich. I was so eager to find a roommate that I overlooked the fact that Dave smoked.

Dave had a nasal Boston accent; later, it really got on my nerves. He also talked a little too fast for me, but I was looking for a place in Ipswich too. And there were fringe benefits in having a cook as a roommate. Our English neighbors were on what the English called the "dole." They were out of work and living off the government, and they rarely had meat. So we'd throw them some of Uncle Sam's scraps now and then. I sold them a few cuts of beef, even though selling Air Force rations was definitely a no-no.

The brick house on Bulstrode Road was down by a wide canal where an old clipper ship was moored. It was a magnificent white and black vessel with five masts and forty-two square sails. Its stainless steel riggings and polished brass sparkled even when the sun was hidden by the ever-present overcast sky. Every time I walked by the clipper ship, I thought back to a time when England ruled the seas. When I went to the beach, I envisioned vast flotillas just off the coastline with seasoned sailors and cannons at the ready, the Union Jack flapping in the breeze. But it wasn't just ships and sailors and fanciful adventures that played through my head. It was around this time that a whole slew of creative images and ideas came to the fore. Because of this, I felt the need to put pen to paper once more. The round stones of Felixstowe's beach and that lovely old clipper prompted me to write a poem about Ipswich and the prevailing mood I was feeling from English living.

But it wasn't just poetry that held my attention. I had the urge to write a great yarn again. In my childhood, I'd spend lazy afternoons in that field by the railroad tracks. I'd find escape and pleasure in concocting some elaborate tale. In England, I began a lengthy project about a teenager who wanted to be a rock star. I fashioned the protagonist in this weighty work of fiction after myself since I once had the same dream of hitting the big time. Like my childhood attempts at fiction, the manuscript was crude, had many grammatical errors, and lacked the polish that only a veteran writer could bring to such a work. But I plugged on with the story. After my Air Force duties ended for the day, I added to the pages I'd accumulated in my little room by the sea wall.

When I wasn't imagining England's past or churning out what I thought surely would be the next bestseller, I carried on with the more mundane pursuits of a nineteen-year-old life such as chasing after women and filling up on junk food. One of the best fish and chip shops I've ever eaten in was just around the corner from my house on Bulstrode Road. I dined many a night on plaice, white rolls, and some sort of fizzy orange drink that I'd only seen in the U.K. I also feasted on candy at a nearby shop, which seemed to have every type of sweet in the world. Sometimes the candy was all I'd eat after a new kind of fog had invaded my brain.

This new fog was thanks to Dave, who survived on a daily diet not only of food, but also of speed and hashish. I was too scared to snort speed the way he did, especially since his hair began turning white only a short time after moving to Ipswich, but I did love smoking hash. Oily black chunks of it and moist Lebanese pieces speckled with orange opium. Dave showed me how to smoke it in tiny pipes with screens in them. Soon, I even had a pipe of my own.

The supply of hash in our house was endless, and I seldom had to buy any. And when there wasn't a stash, a rock singer friend of Dave's named Nicki brought some by. I liked listening to Nicki's stories about hanging around with guys like David Bowie and Jimi Page before they'd become famous. Nicki once told me that Bowie had another name back then and wanted to change it. He also told me that Bowie tried to mimic everything crusty guys like Nicki did. "Should I change my hair?" Nicki said one day, with an affected pretty-boy voice supposed to be Bowie's, which I'm sure he must have followed with "What a fucking pratt," or "wanker," two English put-downs that Nicki loved.

I liked Nicki because he was really streetwise. He wanted to be a famous rock star the way I had wanted to be. I used Nicki's rough image for the aging rock star in my book. My character's world came crashing to the ground because of his disenchanted view of life. At least he had succeeded in becoming a star. Nicki, on the other hand, hadn't and probably never would. He was getting on in years and the chance of his becoming famous was highly unlikely. Because of this, I think he was jealous of anyone who'd made it. But he was a down-to-earth guy who talked really fast as he rolled cigarettes laced with hash on the Air Force coffee table on loan to us from Bentwaters.

Dave was a master at making friends, but I'll never know why. He could be a real asshole sometimes, but he had a knack for making gab and a carelessness that his friends could relate to. It seemed as though Dave always had a few new friends over, many times people I'd never seen before. And they were always getting stoned or drunk together. I wondered when we were going to get busted, but for some reason we never did. At least I didn't. After leaving the U.K., I learned through the grapevine that Dave had lost his stripes and ended up in Leavenworth. Poor Dave. I wish I knew where he was now. Dave, who introduced me to hash and getting wasted the fun way. Dave, who introduced me to bands like Rush and Traffic. Dave, who helped me learn how to open up to people. A truly likeable asshole.

The two of us were really hooked on hashish. I've heard it's not addictive, but when we were out of it, the need to smoke got so bad that we'd resort to crawling around on our hands and knees on the carpet in hopes of finding a small piece of dope that had somehow missed the pipe. When we did locate something and tossed it into the pipe to light, more often than not the foreign object would turn out to be a piece of wood or something else unsmokable. This potent substance called hash decreased my ability to think even more than normal, but I wasn't the only one whose thinking had been compromised.

One night four of us from Bulstrode Road set out for a pub downtown. We reached one of the first crosswalks and saw a bobby van being filled with a rowdy bunch of locals bent on destruction. The traffic light turned green; we all tried to move at once across the street, tried to act normal.

It took us a long time to cross that street. One of us would step down and find he was out of sync with the others, so he'd step back up onto the curb. Then as soon as he'd stepped back up, another one of us would step down thinking he was in sync with first person that'd stepped off the curb. It went on like that for a very long time. The four of us tried our best to act as one and appear sober. Although we were doing our best not to attract attention, we were a ridiculous troupe of red-eyed clowns. Fortunately, none of the bobbies noticed us since they had their hands full thanks to a bunch of drunks who had started a fight in a nearby pub.

It didn't take long for this new hashish fog to bother me even more than the old fog, and I told Dave about my concerns. I said that I just wanted to be able to think clearly and to feel less moody. I was having trouble keeping track of when I needed to go to work—and why. I'd taken to lying on the couch for long periods with my headphones on to analyze repetitive guitar rifts. Days and dates were a blur, and I strained to focus on even the tiniest detail, like which way to loosen or tighten a bolt or screw on my motorcycle. I was also having more trouble with the big picture. The past, present, and future all seemed to blend together. All that really seemed to matter was the way the wind and rain felt when I needed to walk downtown, or how wonderful the sun looked behind a wall of English clouds, or where I'd find the next meal.

When I insisted to Dave that I really had to stop smoking dope, he only smiled and, in his most sincere Carruba address, said, "Why do you want to think clearly?" I answered that I just did, and he smirked and shrugged his shoulders. After that we went for a drive in the Daimler he'd bought. It had a wooden dashboard and a sunroof. We usually went for drives to help lessen the tension. Dave let the car's twelve cylinders open up on one of the narrow country roads until we found a pub we liked.

The hashish did help me to cope with the increasing friction I felt in with the Air Force. I'd smoke up and then get lost in the fine rock music coming from my stereo. At that time I mainly listened to Pink Floyd, especially *The Wall* album, which Dave hid from me after I had played it steadily for days on end. Smoking the hashish not only heightened the negative effects of the fog, but it also eroded my sense of responsibility. My hair and mustache got longer, my uniform was pressed less often, my boots seldom shined, and I smiled goofily at my superiors when I was on base, as if nothing they did would affect me. I'm sure they knew why I was acting that way. I know one guy did, but he was even more stoned than I was and just smiled back at me. Everybody called him Gonzo.

My job at Bentwaters was a lot different than the one I had at Ellsworth. Of course I still drove, but instead of ferrying pilots back and forth from their planes, I mainly drove a set route across expansive RAF Bentwaters, or from

Bentwaters to RAF Woodbridge, a base seven miles away. And I was no longer merely shuttling pilots. The bus routes were set up just like city bus routes, and aircraft mechanics, security police, any Air Force personnel and their dependants could just jump on a bus at a designated stop and get a ride.

It took a little getting used to driving on the other side of the road and manipulating a stick shift with my left hand, but before long it became second nature. The buses barely fitted on the tiny roads, but I mastered them too; so well, in fact, that I knew every pub that jutted out, every pole, tree, etc. I would always exceed the speed limit, driving as fast as the bus would allow. Those behind me in the bus would hold on until their knuckles turned white as I missed stationary objects by inches and rolled around roundabouts with ease. On base, of course, I had to go down to speeds as slow as fifteen miles per hour, and I had to stop at checkpoints before being allowed onto military installations so Air Force law enforcement officers could check passengers on board.

Occasionally, I taxied Air Force personnel to and from RAF Mildenhall, as they arrived in and departed from England, just as I had taxied Air Force personnel to and from the Rapid City Airport.

One officer I picked up at Mildenhall and drove to Bentwaters sent my commander a Letter of Recommendation for the "above and beyond the call of duty" attention I paid him. I was very proud of that letter. It was one of the few times I'd received praise like that. I've never forgotten it.

It wasn't long before my dream of being trained to drive tractor-trailers became a reality. I wasn't the most sparkling airman in the motor pool, but for the most part I played by the rules. I had too much rank for my superiors to continue to ignore my request to drive rigs. And the stigma that had surrounded me at Ellsworth because of the fueling travesty was unknown in England.

It was decided that Sgt. Brown and I would be sent to a tractor-trailer school in Mendlesham, where we'd learn to drive what the English called "lorries" or "articulated vehicles." I thought Brown had been in the military way too long not to be driving rigs by then. He was petrified to get behind the wheel, but his bosses kind of forced him into it. It looked so ridiculous for a man with his rank and time in the service to continue driving buses.

I liked the time away from base, but our sweater-and-tie-wearing civilian instructor was strict and thorough. With just the three of us in the tractor's cab, we'd tour the area around Mendlesham. Our heavy-accented teacher told us when to shift and when to turn, but mostly he kept telling me to slow down. We ground gears a lot, until we got the hang of shifting and double-clutching smoothly. But Sgt. Brown never seemed to get over his fear of wheeling around that monstrous English truck—even when he finally figured out that he had to match the engine's rpms to the gear he was shifting into.

"There's a roundabout coming up," Mr. Watersmead, our tractor-trailer teacher, would often say to me, his statement carrying the strongest suggestion to take some sort of action. Of course, I usually wouldn't take any action. Then, as we reached the roundbout, Watersmead would say, "Slow down!" and I'd feather the brakes a little as one of the trailer's rear set of dual tires came off the ground because of my excessive speed. Sometimes, the tires would run over a portion of the roundabout because I'd neglected to take my turn wide enough, and I'd barely miss hitting one of the short directional signs with an arrow on it. Then Mr. Watersmead would yell, "Is it your intention to run over every one of our directional arrows, Mr. Patterson?"

I wouldn't respond, of course. I was too busy trying to avoid the next obstacle in the road or a frightened English native trying to cross the street.

Mr. Watersmead would offer a plethora of commands and criticisms at that point, such as: "What are you doing, Mr. Patterson? Did you realize you were in fifth gear as you approached this residential area? You're on the wrong side of the road again! Slow down!"

In my peripheral vision, I could see Sgt. Brown cowering opposite me in the cab. I knew he was glad I was being yelled at and not him. Finally, when Mr. Watersmead had had enough, he would tell me in a very official tone, "Pull over to this curb, Mr. Patterson. Do you think you can manage *that.* Bloody hell, I don't know if the truck, or England, can take any more."

Then it was Sgt. Brown's turn and the yelling would start all over again with the same kinds of criticisms and comments about controlling the truck's speed and not grinding away "every last bit of gears in the truck's transmission."

When it was lunchtime our instructor had us pull into some pub's incredibly tiny car park, and we'd treat ourselves to a sandwich and a pint, and watch the locals playing darts or snooker. At those times, our teacher was very kind and calm, but when we'd get back on the road, even though he still displayed a sort of reserve, he would yell at us again sternly for making mistakes or ridicule our driving practices. Still, both Brown and I graduated from that trucking school, and it was one of the proudest times in my life. Something even better than my letter of recommendation. Anytime I could graduate from anything, I felt lucky. Even when someone handed me a diploma, I thought I still lacked the skills needed to do the job competently.

But I didn't care if I didn't know everything after Mendlesham. I was a trucker, and for me a trucker was a kind of American folk hero; a tough man who earned respect by wheeling one of those massive vehicles on the road as if only his type could do so. A trucker was also a man who had many adventures. And even though I was in the Air Force and those adventures would be limited, I had the basic skills needed to someday travel the old highways that traversed every state in the U.S., stopping in every truck stop and meeting the kinds of people that Kerouac's main character in *On The Road* would meet.

If nothing else, I had a new career, and it would lift me above the rest in the motor pool and fill me with pride. There weren't many trucks or truck drivers in the motor pool, so when I took the keys of a conventional Mac tractor or a GMC cab-over, I did so with a new swagger, with a confidence and elation that kept me going for some time. Since most of the tractors pulled flatbed trailers, I learned to use things like gigantic tarps, breaker bars, chains, and straps to secure my cargo. This new work kept me busy and gave me purpose. I felt I was really accomplishing something. The Air Force needed the freight I pulled. All kinds of things. Some things I recognized, and some I didn't. I felt like a kid again, loading strange mechanical things onto my truck that went into something, did something. Things that probably went into those jet engines. And sometimes I hauled the engines themselves.

And tires were loaded on those flatbeds. Big tires that might someday land in hostile territory. And auxiliary power units which the aircraft needed in order to power up. And I gave a piggyback ride to other vehicles like cranes needed for building. And I loaded other odds and ends of military hardware and took them to their destinations. In wartime, those at home could watch the planes and parts flying proudly into harm's way and glimpse all the U.S. military paraphernalia that people like me delivered to a needy war machine.

I had now become a necessary worker in the busy little American beehive, and it knew it. But when I went out on my trips, I worried about things going wrong. Now that I had status, I never wanted to lose it. I even slowed the trucks down to reduce the chance of accidents. Of course, this was not only by choice. It was a great deal more difficult to maneuver tractor-trailers on those tiny roads. I had loads that would shift and weight factors to consider when I took corners or geared down for a stop sign.

Brits would look up at me from their miniature cars and wonder if I was going to fit around a bend in the road or under one of their historic bridges. Sometimes I wasn't sure myself. It's lucky that I didn't destroy something major with all that truck and all that power.

There were times that I did get into jams though. It was the fog creeping in again, the way fog comes in every afternoon on the Pacific Ocean in California. Sometimes minor things went wrong. I wouldn't tighten a strap enough, or I would incorrectly position it. To my surprise and relief, however, I never lost a load. Sometimes, because of my inability to use numbers correctly, I would distribute freight in a dangerous manner. When the truck took a turn too fast, I'd almost lose the trailer as the load shifted too far to one side, or I had difficulty braking. Many times I would just guess about how to load something. I learned by trial and error if there wasn't anyone there to help me. Even if someone was there, I didn't ask for help because I wanted to appear to be in control of the situation. I always wanted superiors to have confidence in my ability to pull anything they asked me to.

This headstrong attitude—and the ever-present fog—led to some interesting occurrences. One time, on the way back from Mildenhall, I tossed a small box marked "Top Secret" in the fifth wheel's storage compartment. Then I turned up my boom box as loud as I could, the way I always did, and sped out onto the A45, a major freeway in the U.K., close to Ipswich. About halfway back to Bentwaters, a red Sixties-era Mustang convertible pulled up beside me in another lane. The driver was a high-ranking NCO in his dress blues. The sergeant waved a hand frantically to get my attention. He gestured with an index finger for me to pull over.

Confused and a little perturbed, I did so, shifting down all thirteen gears in the huge conventional Mac truck. I hopped out of the cab, and the sergeant ran up to me. He said that something had flown out of my trailer onto the motorway a way back and that he'd help me retrieve it.

We drove a lengthy distance to find an exit, then returned to find the package in the middle of the motorway. When there was a short lull in traffic flow, I dashed into the middle of the busy road and retrieved the somewhat crumpled cardboard box. I recognized it immediately as the one marked "Top Secret" I had tossed in the fifth wheel storage compartment.

The sergeant told me that the unsecured hatch to the compartment had come open and the box had shot out. After I thanked him, showing obvious embarrassment due to the screw-up, the sergeant introduced himself and told me that he was going to be the transportation commander's new senior

NCO in charge of Bentwaters' motor pool. I thought my esteemed career had come to an end. What were the chances of something like that happening right in front of my new boss? Incredibly, the Mustang man just slapped me on the back and told me to be more careful. Then he drove off toward his new base. I tossed the "Top Secret" box in to the cab this time and got in, turning my boom box back up to its maximum volume. I followed the NCO back to Bentwaters.

Another mishap took place when I was asked to haul a load of diapers back to Bentwaters PX, so all the military dependent babies could do their duty in the comfort of premium Pampers. It was the strangest load I had ever taken, and it seemed highly irregular, but what the heck, a load was a load.

It took a lot of tarping to secure the load. The diapers weren't in boxes; they were in loose packages stacked on pallets that towered behind me over the cab. Everything went smoothly until I got on the A45. Looking into one of my outside rearview mirrors, I noticed a strap flapping against the green canvas tarp. If the strap loosened much more, there'd be more than a box marked "Top Secret" on the road. This time there would be diapers, and lots of them. I had to pull over and tighten the ratchet that held the strap, so I frantically looked for an exit. There wasn't one; for miles there was simply no place to pull over.

I kept looking into the outside mirror to check the load, and I turned red and I panicked. What am I supposed to do? I thought. I don't know what to do. I was like a kid again, back in my diabetic brother's room as he shook convulsively in his bed. I hoped I could get out of this jam soon. An exit appeared. I looked down the road. I had discovered early on in England never to take for granted that there would be a place to turn around once I took an unfamiliar exit, but I had to tighten that strap.

Once off the A45, I put a breaker bar on the ratchet's handle and pulled with the scrawny Irish muscles that my dad had passed on to me. That strap might never come loose again, I thought to myself, and if it did, someone's jaw might break when the ratchet mechanism let go of its hold on the tough nylon and its handle flew up with an abrupt jolt. And I remember thinking that I'd probably be the one who got the brunt of that force since it would probably be me who released the ratchet. But I didn't dwell on this fact; the load was secure and I'd saved the day. I was the capable trucker with leather gloves on his hands and honest sweat staining his olive green T-shirt.

That truck was my truck, and I was like a captain at sea taking charge of his troubled vessel. But now I faced a bigger problem. In my haste and panic to pull onto the first exit I saw, I discovered just what I had feared the most. I was on a road that seemed to get narrower and narrower and led into a thick forest with low-lying branches. The truck simply wouldn't fit on the road ahead, and there was no place to turn around. And it was too difficult to back up the way I had come, so that I could get back on the A45. I was stuck. The captain had run aground so to speak. I was the skipper who had read the tides wrong, a fool, inept and in need of help.

I slumped down against one of the truck's big wheels and stared out past the deserted road into never-ending farmland, lands that Romans trod upon in full battledress many years before. My shirt with its two well-earned stripes hung over a fence that paralleled one of the farm's neat rows of rich earth. Even though I had gotten myself into such a perilous situation, I couldn't help but to see the humor in the situation.

A tiny car drove by, slowing as its British driver craned his neck to look at this young American invader and his huge foreign truck. I avoided the Brit's gaze as he drove on, finally disappearing into the dark Sherwood-like forest ahead.

There squatted what should have been one of the Air Force's best. One of its highly trained motor pool warriors stuck on a road with a load of diapers in the middle of nowhere. An example of the seemingly endless might the American military had to offer stranded on one of its crackerjack operations. I didn't know if I wanted to laugh or cry. Then I noticed a break in the metal rails of the fence bordering the nearest farm field. It was a gate, a way into the expansive farm fields. Surely, an American truck shouldn't drive onto that farmland, I thought. That would be ridiculous. Then I thought how much more ridiculous it would be when I had to radio back to base because I couldn't turn my truck around. That would never happen, I thought. I got up from that tire with its walnut-sized lug nuts and set out for the gate. I only hoped the gate wouldn't be locked. I was in luck; it swung open easily.

I fired up the Mac's engine, which I now had sense enough to fill with diesel, and with a victorious smile on my face I drove that truck, diapers and all, into that fertile English field. I was now like Captain Kirk in *Star Trek*, regaining command of my Enterprise when all had seemed lost.

I gripped the truck's very long gearshift, with its many numbers engraved in a strange pattern, and shoved it into reverse. That's when I noticed the truck wouldn't move. The motor worked okay, and the transmission had engaged the axles on the tractor, but the truck stayed put, going neither forward nor backward. I looked into the outside mirror, like an enlightened gypsy gazing into a crystal ball. The truck wasn't moving because it couldn't get any traction. One set of dual rear wheels just spun. The tractor was stuck in the mud. I started sweating again. I turned red and screamed expletives at the top of my lungs as I gunned the powerful Mac and tried to rock the tractor free. I've solved the problem. This isn't fair, I thought. It just isn't fair. But fair or not, the tires continued to spin.

The fog drifted in a little heavier, and once again I did nothing. Nothing, that is, except rest my head on the truck's enormous, black steering wheel. I had been so proud to place my hands on the helm of the Mac each time I wheeled past the watchful eyes of superiors and those still stuck in the motor pool lounge because they hadn't been trained to drive the big rigs. Then, thankfully, the fog parted slightly. Sheer determination burned a hole in that soup. I'd proven my worth at the new base and I wasn't going to be the butt of another motor pool joke. I would push that tractor out of that field if need be. It was going to move, dammit! I jumped down out of the cab and looked around for rocks, pebbles, anything I could find, and shoved them under the wet wheel, which had dug itself deeply into earth and manure. I kicked those firm dry objects as hard as I could with the same black, lace-up boots that had pounded Lackland Air Force's parade ground in the sweltering Texas heat when I was in basic training. I jumped into that cab, said a quick prayer, and gunned the motor. I deftly rocked the tractor back and forth. This was my last chance to save face. If the tractor didn't get free now, I knew—though I had sworn I wouldn't do it—I'd have to radio Bentwaters and live the life of the village idiot once again.

To my amazement and relief, the tractor grabbed the rocks and other debris just enough to allow me to back it out of the field. And I never slowed until that truck had whipped around to face the A45 motorway and freedom. I got out of the tractor one final time to close the gate and retrieve my shirt and dignity. I headed home, still some twenty miles from Bentwaters, but back on track. As usual, America was victorious. Its power reaffirmed in a foggy-brained tech school washout with a mission and a reason for holding his head up high as if nothing bad had ever happened.

I would travel back to Mildenhall many more times before my tour in England was over, since it was the base from which most of the other RAF bases got their supplies. Most of the time I would take tractor-trailers, but sometimes I'd drive one-and-a-half-ton trucks. They held heavy metal rails that had to be manually pulled out of their square holes in the truck bed so a forklift could drop a load onto the truck. Once, while loading one, I glanced over to another truck and saw an old friend from the group of blacks I used to hang out with in South Dakota. The meeting was odd. We were a little older now, with more rank and knowledge, in a far-off land. But what made the meeting even stranger was the fact that my friend interacted differently with me. Something in the way I carried myself told him that I wasn't the needy troublemaker I used to be.

"Patterson," a voice called from within the cavernous building where my truck was parked. When I looked down from the bed of my truck, I saw a thin black man coming toward me with a bold stride. The man had another stripe on his sleeve, and the darkness made it difficult to see clearly, but I knew by the cocky way he had called my name that it was my old friend, Boyd.

"Boyd. What are you doing here?"

"Driving, brother. Same as you."

"I see you're moving up in the world," I said, tapping one of his triceps.

"Damn straight, man. You too, huh?" he said, smiling.

"You ever see any of the old gang from Ellsworth?" I said, leaning against the back of my truck's cab.

"Nah. I'm the only one here." Boyd followed this statement with a familiar sucking sound he used to do back in the States, and he turned his head briefly to check out what was going on in another part of the loading area. Some men were lifting caskets onto another truck. I turned to look at the caskets too. Boyd looked back at me. He wasn't smiling anymore, but his look said "You're doing all right, Patterson. We're doing all right."

We talked a little longer. He never came right out and said it, but I knew he approved of how I'd turned out. I didn't quite know how I knew this. Maybe it was something about the way he looked at me. There were none of the old familiar but lighthearted put-downs or the patronizing smile that said "Man, what's up with you?" It's almost as if he now treated me as his equal. "I've got to go," he said and walked away.

That chance meeting with my old friend that day bolstered my spirits and indicated to me that I was on the right track in my life. It was an important turning point in a foggy-minded man's life. I never saw my friend again, but I hope he fared well. Since he had been crucial to my being accepted into that group at Ellsworth, I secretly thanked him for all he had done.

My prestige lessened somewhat when I went to the night shift and drove buses again. This time, however, I wasn't sent to the night shift because of my attitude. The motor pool simply needed someone to fill a bus route between Bentwaters and Woodbridge. So I raced my bus down those small English roads again. Instead of hauling aircraft parts or diapers, I hauled weary mechanics or bouncy teenage dependants going bowling in Bentwaters or going to the base's solitary movie theater.

I only got into trouble driving buses once when someone called the motor pool to complain about my excessive speed. Someone also complained because I frequently left a bus stop early. Late at night, there wouldn't be any passengers at a stop, and I was just too bored to stay until the time the bus was supposed to leave. But at one particular bus stop I left early for another reason.

It was my last stop at the edge of Woodbridge's airfield. The place was eerie, and people talked of it being haunted. Apparently, the base had been used as an emergency landing strip in WWII for war-torn planes coming in for a last ditch effort. Many pilots died on approach as their beat-up bombers went up in flames. There were tales of ghost pilots from these ill-fated landings still roaming the pitch-black airfield. This was also the same time that newspapers reported a strange incident. Woodbridge security police officers claimed to have witnessed a UFO sighting.

Needless to say, given my impressionable young mind, I kept my bus's door shut tight, and I frequently looked in the rearview mirror toward the empty, darkened seats as I anxiously waited for my departure time. If a tired mechanic at the end of his shift happened to bang on the door to be let in, I would jump and make sure he was who he said he was before I let him on board.

One such night, I waited nervously in the darkness. A man got on the bus, a pale man dressed in a worn leather bomber jacket with a soft, white collar. It looked like one of the jackets I'd seen in those old WWII movies. A red flag immediately went up since the man didn't say a word upon entering. What made this even weirder was the fact that he never said anything during our drive back to Bentwaters, not even when I tried to start a conversation.

I kept a constant vigil in the rearview mirror, watching my suspicious passenger who had taken a seat near the bus's emergency door at the back. He met my eyes in the mirror as we drove into England's ancient blackness. I no longer said anything, and my usually raucous boom box was silent.

The only time I didn't watch my mysterious guest was when I had to watch the road. I longed to see Bentwaters' friendly entrance shack where an armed military law enforcement officer would be waiting to greet me.

As the base's red brick buildings made their familiar appearances on my left, I knew it wouldn't be long now. And then there it was, the small shack with the government cop inside. It would soon be over. I would open the bus's door for the hired gun to enter the bus and check my passenger's credentials, so he knew I wasn't hauling an escaped mental patient or somebody more sinister. My fears would be eased. But shortly after I'd opened the door and put on the overhead light so the law enforcement officer could check the bus, I looked back and saw that my solitary passenger was gone. To make things worse, I knew he hadn't exited the bus via the back door because I hadn't heard the very loud and noticeable latch mechanism that sounded whenever the door was opened, or the familiar earsplitting buzzer that accompanied it.

In addition, all the bus's windows were closed and firmly latched. Anyway, they were small rectangular windows that would have been difficult for a child to pass through, let alone an adult. The passenger had simply vanished. I didn't say a word to the law enforcement officer, but I'm sure my mouth was agape.

Still, the officer made his rounds, checking between all the seats, making certain that no unauthorized personnel were about to enter the base. Then he said his goodbyes, gave me the okay to enter the base, and exited the bus. But the officer's security check didn't convince me that I was alone.

I traveled that last short drive to the motor pool overshadowed by a heightened fear. I was also completely dumbfounded, and I went straight to the motor pool's lounge to sit down on one of those abhorrent metal and vinyl chairs that made sure drivers never got too comfortable, never fell asleep when needed. I sat there staring into space the way my passenger had, until one of the other airmen who worked nights came in and saw me in that state. He asked me what was wrong, since he noticed I was completely drained of color. I ignored his question and continued to ponder my experience with the vanishing passenger. Then he said, "You look like you just saw a ghost."

A clichéd but appropriate thing to say, I thought. Had a joke been played on me? If so, how? There was no way off that bus when I stopped at the security shack, and I'd made no stops in between. Had I actually seen a ghost that night? An apparition that had been hanging around RAF Woodbridge since WWII after leaving its physical body in a war-ravaged plane? Later, when I had recovered enough to tell the tale, some laughed, but others said I wasn't the only one who'd experienced this rider's appearance. Motor pool folklore told of a ghost who would ride the bus to the gates of Bentwaters, then disappear, the same way my rider had. Always from Woodbridge to Bentwaters, never the other way round. After that night, I requested to be put back on days, or rather I begged to be put back on days. The begging was approved, and I went back to a welcome sun and corporeal passengers. Back to the heavy-handed guidance of authority, but also back to driving more rigs, since tractor-trailers were dispatched during the day.

20

An English Soap Opera

BACK IN IPSWICH, the routine with Dave got a little monotonous, and I started to feel alone again, even though the house was full of partiers most nights. Of course, this was nothing new. As usual in my life, I got bored with things quickly or unnecessarily.

I needed a new friend, and as luck would have it, I met one on base. John was a tough, easy-going, little, blond-haired guy who smiled a lot more than he needed to. He was from some rural town in Pennsylvania. John didn't say much owing to his John Wayne like male code that said men should remain quiet unless they had something worth saying. Ironically, he thought the fact that I said a lot was amusing, but he never put me down. He just laughed under his breath whenever I rambled on about some unimportant topic. John didn't seem like someone I could really depend on, but he was worth having around given my poor ability at making friends. We both rode our motorcycles great distances over the tiny roads which are well suited to such modes of travel. That's about all we did together. It was a perfect activity for one person who didn't talk a lot and another who did. Not much can be heard from someone wearing a motorcycle helmet on the open road.

Once we drove north, all the way to Nottingham. We drank pints in a pub called The Old Jerusalem, which claimed to be the oldest pub in England. It was situated below Nottingham Castle where tales of Robin Hood were still told. We'd ridden to see a fireman friend of John's father. He put us up for the night, then we rode back in the morning. John was a nice guy, but we drifted apart once I met Susan McAlister.

New Year's Eve, 1983, Susan was buying a hot dog (or banger, as they're called in England) at a banger stand down the street from a pub named Dukes, frequented by airmen. Susan and I were both drunk, standing there in the moderate night air waiting for the attendant to finish preparing our bangers. Susan smiled a lot, a happy drunken smile that showed off her full English dimples and the lovely skin that her countrywomen are known for. She was pretty and had a celebratory golden tassel wrapped around her head. I normally wouldn't have talked to her, but the alcohol made me bold.

I must have said all the right things because not long after having paid for and eaten our bangers, I carried Susan the long route home to her house. My shoulders ached, but I used the fireman carry. I don't know why I carried her, but it seemed like the right thing to do at the time.

After that night, we started dating, and then she moved in with Dave and me. It felt good not to be alone at night. It felt good just to look at Susan as she slept there next to me, her dark hair mingling with mine on our adjacent pillows. I soon learned that this young nineteen-year-old was as impulsive as I was about life. I should have guessed this by the way we met but, as I said before, there was alcohol involved that night, so I might not have been seeing the real her. Susan wanted to do adventurous and sensual things with me. Once she wanted to join me in taking a bath. I'd long since gotten used to the fact that I wouldn't take showers in England because of the fact that most people took baths and most houses didn't even have showers. Usually, I hated taking baths. A bath was a cumbersome ordeal and most of the time I just wanted to get in and out of the tub as quickly as possible. But Susan showed me how wonderful it could be when two people gently let the water roll over their bodies. She lathered up the two of us until we slipped against each other and the smell of lavender soap filled the softly lit bathroom. The warmth between us was worth the trouble of having to manage the confines of that small tub. From then on, baths took on a special meaning.

Impulsivity and sensuality went hand in hand when it came to Susan. It seemed to be something we had in common. I recall one night when we went looking for ghosts at Susan's request. She chose a church graveyard where spirits were known to have appeared. The headstones were cold and so was the night, with an eerie fog filtering around us, but we never did see any ghosts. And even though the only recognizable beings moving through the fog that night were our own corporeal selves, the mere fact that I discovered Susan stalking the graveyard when a wall of fog had cleared was all the evidence I needed to believe that supernatural entities walked the earth.

When Susan smiled, her cheeks were like small apples, firm and round, and she glowed. There was a radiance that emanated from her face even when she was sad. Her eyes were clear and bright, and hopeful—even though she often worried about her future. She said that she didn't know what to do with her life, that maybe she'd take some psychology classes. Maybe that would lead somewhere; but she didn't really have a clear plan about where. She thought people were interesting and often talked about the way they acted. If we saw a young woman pushing a "pram"—the word the English used for strollers—there was a story behind the scene. The woman had probably had a baby out of wedlock. "I feel sorry for her," Susan would say. "Her whole life is over, isn't it? Silly cow. I don't want to have a baby. I can't get pregnant."

There was the way Susan held her "ciggy"—her word for cigarette. It was the way a young movie star would hold it, high and tossed back behind her shoulder a little. She'd let it dangle back there for what seemed like hours as we sipped our cold glasses of Fosters at Dukes—our main hangout in downtown Ipswich. We'd talk about how a friend of hers liked head-banging bands like Status Quo, or how Susan liked U2—a band I hadn't heard of until I met her. But as many times as Susan would tell me what she thought, there were just as many times when she wouldn't speak a word. It was these times I liked best. I enjoyed watching her just looking at me or taking in her surroundings as if viewing them through an older, more sophisticated woman's eyes; as if knowing something that I didn't. It wasn't a pompous kind of knowing, just an insightful one. When I looked at her too long, Susan would break into an embarrassed little laugh and say, "What?" I'd just smile back and cause her to blush until those apple cheeks filled with a wonderful shade of red.

There were times when we'd dance through the streets of Ipswich with a friend of hers named Ruth, the one who liked head-banging music. Ruth would joke that she "fancied" me, and I'd smile back at her with Susan looking on as if she didn't care what anyone said or did. Susan took me to see other friends of hers who seemed as if they were right out of a Dickens novel. Her friends became my friends, and I soon had more of a social life. Susan's friends were a common sort of English crowd of people who dropped the *h* from the beginnings of words, and who always enjoyed a good strong laugh and a pint. They were people who always appeared to be on the make, con artists; but they really weren't. You just had to get to know them to realize that they were just individuals who wanted more in their lives. But some of

Susan's friends did have questionable intentions and pasts. She told me of an old boyfriend named Perry, for example, who had had run-ins with the law. Even so, I never worried about any of Susan's friends, not at that point anyway.

As much as I liked Susan's beaming, carefree way of living, there was another side to her, a side that worried about things; things having to do with more than her future. Sometimes, a sadness and hopelessness would come over her, and she'd enter a deep reflective state. I think she was mostly sad that she didn't have any pursuits other than partying and playing, that there had to be something else more worthwhile. Ironically enough, it was during times like these when I told Susan that a couple good drags on my hashish pipe might help—even though I knew I had to stop smoking hash myself.

Susan didn't really want to smoke hashish, and because of this I started spending more time with her and less with Dave. I don't think Dave liked her living in the house, probably because he was jealous. Although I knew he liked girls very much, I'd never seen him with a girlfriend the whole time I was in England.

Susan was my second true love, Carrie being the first. In fact, Susan replaced my obsession with Carrie for a while. One day, when Susan was out of my life, I'd think of Carrie again, but I've never truly forgotten either of these women.

Having Susan in my life made it full again, and more important. Simply knowing that a girl would stick around brought me untold happiness. Whether it was watching Susan freak out because she lost an earring, or going to "Woolies" with her to have a few photos taken in one of those drug store photo booths that print out tiny remembrances of one's youth, or visiting cities like Cambridge together to watch punters guide their boats down placid English waterways, all of it gave me a reason to get up in the morning.

I felt a sense of stability and considered future possibilities with my lovely Suffolk maiden—mostly marriage. For some reason, I think the fog has always prompted me to find someone to share my life with. Maybe because I've always felt so lost and a little bewildered when alone. And after all, two minds are better than one. Of course, if all of this wasn't reason enough to marry, there was always the fact that I loved her.

Susan introduced me to Janet, a friend who struggled with her reasoning skills. She was much less aware of her problem than I was of mine, but I could still relate to what she was experiencing. When Susan and I would visit Janet, it would be a somber affair with little to talk about. Susan would ask Janet how she was doing, and Janet would say she was doing okay. Then we'd have tea and sit on Janet's couch, as our host would recount what she had done that day. There were a lot of details left out of her stories, or she put in too much insignificant information. She also had a tendency to focus on one thing. An account of her day was always incomplete, as if only one part of it really mattered. When actually describing what she had done on a particular day, for example, she might not say what she'd done during the morning hours and shoot right up to the afternoon. "I went to Woolies at one and got some shampoo. It was near the hairnets." Then, we'd sit there not saying a word for a very long time before Janet would add something that related to what she had said earlier. Something like, "Susan, would you like to smell my shampoo?" Janet's living room was always dimly lit. A long shadow would often cut her face in half, so that I only really saw one side of her when she spoke. The rest of the house was always completely dark and quiet. I felt as though I was attending an impromptu funeral and I was to pay the utmost respect. I felt sorry for Janet, but I also felt sorry for myself when Susan and I would visit her. I've since learned that Janet was killed by an unknown assailant, and I couldn't help wondering if her not being all there had something to do with the murder. I often think back to her slow mannerisms and incomplete stories and that darkly lit room. When I do, I not only mourn Janet's death but my own shortcomings, and wonder if I'll ever escape the fog's clutches.

Everything went along well in my relationship with Susan. It was as if we were already married, and I had a wife who would be there for me when I got home from an important day of truck driving. Sometimes, Susan would even have dinner ready when I got home. Meals such as toad-in-the-hole or Yorkshire pudding. This made my life seem worthwhile and adult. But then things started happening. Little events would set me off and ruin my bliss. One night, while Susan and I were sitting with Dave talking about something or other, Dave began telling us what I thought were crude jokes. I didn't think this sort of thing was appropriate in front of my cherished girlfriend, so I told Dave to stop telling jokes. He just laughed at me and continued. It wasn't until the two of us stood up and squared off, and I put Dave's windpipe beneath the wooden arms of one of the Air Force chairs on loan to us, that he stopped telling the jokes. It was a wild scene, with me repeatedly yelling "Do you want to die?" and Susan beating me about the head, yelling at me to stop.

Things with Dave's friends began to bug me too. Nicki especially started to get on my nerves. He came to our house one day and treated himself to a peanut butter sandwich in the kitchen without even asking; I told him to leave. About thirty seconds later, while still venting my frustration with this sort of behavior to Susan, I heard a hissing sound. When I opened the front door, I discovered Nicki letting the air out of my motorcycle's front tire. I chased after him, and he ran away. When I found Nicki in the house talking to Dave a few hours later, I told him again to get out or I'd call the police. When Nicki didn't leave, I walked down to the red phone booth on the corner. Nicki followed, taunting me, "So you're really going to call the police, huh?" I just continued onward to the phone. "What a fucking pratt," he said to his guitarist friend.

But before I could enter the phone booth, Nicki's taunts became worse, and he said that he wanted to see some of the karate I knew, since I'd been taking karate with Susan's brother William.

Nicki threw a punch that landed on the side of my face before I could enter the phone booth and I turned on him, my teeth clenched. I was in the karate pose Nicki had probably wanted to see, and I was ready to fight, but I changed my mind and decided to have the police deal with this aging rocker. I backed carefully toward the phone booth and went inside, making sure I didn't let Nicki out of my sight. He continued to taunt me all the while—even when I lifted the telephone's receiver. I stood there for a moment, unsure of what to do, the loud buzz of the phone's dial tone in my ear. Finally, I chose to replace the receiver; I decided that Nicki was right. My calling the police was prattish. So I replaced the receiver, left the booth and headed home. But Nicki and the taunts followed me again, until I finally acted from reflex and put Nicki in a headlock. I walked him toward Bulstrode Road. I was so upset I even slammed his head into a red brick house like mine. Then I let him go and yelled at him to just leave me alone. He did. Amazingly, Nicki's lead guitarist never came to his friend's aid.

Shortly after that, Nicki apologized and we were friends again. But because of the stress of what had happened between us and the stress of dealing with Susan, I started to feel at odds with everything. I needed a vacation from my new life, so it was lucky that a new assignment came along. I was one of the motor pool airmen chosen to go to Italy for a temporary assignment.

I was eager to go on a trip away from Ipswich because Susan was moody. She talked of leaving. She said that she couldn't stay holed up in someone's house for free, eating his food and not paying for anything. There was talk of her enrolling in a nearby college. Susan's worst fear had been realized: she was pregnant. Her need to assert herself in life and establish a career was now accelerated because of the baby's future. Susan frantically went on about the fact that she had to begin some classes in something right away. To further complicate matters and aggravate Susan, we weren't entirely certain who the father was. She had left her old boyfriend, Perry Ripley, just prior to hooking up with me. But regardless of who the father was, I still wanted to marry Susan, and I told her so. Her mind was still firm in this area: she didn't want to get married to anyone, and she definitely didn't want to move to America as I suggested we could do. A lot of young girls in Ipswich tried to latch onto young Americans like me, so they could visit the land of the movie stars and move into some big house in someplace like California where the weather was a whole lot better. Susan preferred England. Her talk of leaving me was overwhelming. She said she just didn't want anyone, meaning any man, and that everything had just gotten fouled up in her life. She continued to live with me only because she didn't have anywhere else to go.

Before this new turn of events, everything seemed to be going along as I had anticipated. And now there was talk of Susan's leaving? I just couldn't fathom the idea of a life without her, but at the same time I needed to get away so that I could sort things out and so Susan could sort things out. Maybe she would get thoughts of leaving me out of her mind when I came back. Maybe she would decide that marriage was a good thing. I was sure she would think that when I returned.

My assignment to Italy was part of a mass deployment of American troops from England who would be participating in war games to support the conflict in the Falkland Islands. The deployment was supposed to last at least a month, a good long time to think over the situation with Susan.

Shortly after volunteering for this new assignment/getaway, a sergeant and I flew from Bentwaters to Aviano Air Force Base in a C-130. It was ironic since this was the craft that I had trained on as an aircraft mechanic. Now I was flying in one for the first time. My female sergeant friend and I sat in very uncomfortable parachute seats with the roar of the plane's mighty propellers on either side of us. Vehicles were secured to the floor in front of us and we could smell rubber and gasoline.

Sgt. Flemming, my watchdog while in Italy, was a thin, laid-back woman with blonde hair and a love of the ocean. She showed me a shell necklace she'd made herself, which she was sure to keep very concealed beneath her Air Force olive-green. She asked me to call her Sandy as soon as we got on the C-130, and it was clear that we would both be exempt from a lot of the military machismo while we were away from England—or so I thought. Sandy was originally from Los Angeles. She had wanted to be an actress but was unable to find steady work in the biz. After a lot of soul searching and the depletion of most of her assets, Sandy decided to make a break from her freewheeling lifestyle and lack of a career. She joined the Air Force. The idea was that she'd lay low for a while until she figured out what to do next. Of course, she had to go through the same rigorous mind games that I had been subjected to, but Sandy hadn't come out too bad. Somehow, she managed to maintain her carefree ways and the California hippy-like drawl that singled her out from the rest of the people in the motor pool. If it hadn't been for her uniform and compulsory salutes and so forth, I'd have envisioned Sandy in some commune smoking dope and planting a vegetable garden in the woods. She had completed her first tour of duty and had signed up for another simply because she still hadn't figured out what to do in civilian life. Now that she had four stripes on her sleeves, people hardly bothered her. In fact, I rarely saw her when I was back in the motor pool in England. Sandy had a way of just disappearing on people or blending into the environment. She was one of the only people in the military I ever identified with, and I envied her ability not to let the regimental atmosphere of the Air Force get to her.

Once in Italy, Sandy and I were issued a bus to drive Air Force personnel to and from the base. Most airmen who had flown in for war games were billeted on base or in run-down hotels near Aviano. But the war games were so huge and demanded so many personnel that Sgt. Flemming and I ended up in a ritzy chateau a good twenty minutes from Aviano. It was the only place close enough to base to allow us proximity to airmen needing transportation.

The chateau had wooden shutters on the windows overlooking the balconies, and maids were running around in fancy white hats and aprons. The estate was situated high on a hill, and one side of it looked out onto an expansive plain and Aviano in the distance. The back of the chateau stared up at towering green hills, and from my room's balcony I occasionally heard the faint sound of cowbells. It was clear that relaxation and solitude were essential to this Italian retreat.

Few people sat at the linen-topped tables in the chateau's restaurant and looked through its massive plate glass windows at the valley below. And few sat drinking the chateau's own brand of smooth red wine at the wooden tables lined up in rows on the veranda. To say that my sergeant friend and I were in the lap of luxury does not do justice to that chateau; we were not only in the lap of luxury, we lay cuddled atop luxury's beautiful breasts and amid her velvety green cleavage, taking drinks of her plentiful red ambrosia whenever it suited us.

I loved playing songs on the chateau's jukebox, especially "Puttin' on the Ritz." I'd let the song ring out through the spacious corridors and climb its old staircases toward Italian heaven where dancers like Fred Astaire and Ginger Rogers would have fitted right in, dressed in their finest, tapping along empty tile floors.

I hiked in the sparsely treed hills behind the chateau up to the tallest point. I lay in the grass and let the soothing Mediterranean wind blow over me. This was a time when I didn't worry about fog getting in the way. Responsibility took a vacation. I found a book on plants in town and set out looking for liberty cap mushrooms, hoping to pop a few in my mouth and let psilocybin have its way with me. My redheaded friend Strawberry, from my California conservation days, had told me about these so-called magic mushrooms, or "shrooms," as he liked to call them, but I was never brave enough to try any back then. I'd heard psilocybin was a strong hallucinogenic that would play with the mind the way LSD did, forever subjecting me to flashbacks in later life.

But even though I was well aware of the potential consequences of ingesting these innocent looking mushrooms with their powerful nectar, I was now ready for the challenge. I set out into the hills armed with my botanical book, looking in moist places for the tiny fungi. Thank God I never found any. I think it was the wrong time of year. So I had to satisfy my quest for getting high with wine or beer.

Sgt. Sandy Flemming had made it clear that she wouldn't be around much. She wanted to go a little farther afield than Aviano and explore what else Italy had to offer. So even though she was my supervisor, I was pretty much on my own; a young man with a set of keys, a forty-five passenger bus, and most of the day and night to kill. I'd drive airmen into Aviano in the morning and pick them up later in the afternoon. But picking them up for lunch was out of the question; this was my time. If they made too much fuss, they might not get picked up at all. I didn't care if they had transportation or not; it was my bus and I used it for my own purposes.

A sergeant with many stripes in charge of a bunch of aircraft mechanics told me I would need to take his men to some place other than Aviano once in a while to boost their morale, some place more pleasurable. I didn't care for his forceful tone and told him I wasn't in Italy for his men's pleasure. I was there to shuttle his airmen to and from their base so they could mend planes and do whatever else it was they needed to do to sustain the business of war games. That was all. Besides, I added, he wasn't in charge of me.

The irate sergeant made a call to the Bentwaters motor pool. He told one of my superiors that I had a bad attitude and wouldn't drive his base/hotel-bound men to his R&R spots when asked. My superior told him I was right, that this sergeant wasn't in charge of me, and that as long as I was carrying out my duties I was doing what I was supposed to do, but he'd have a talk with me anyway and see what he could do. I said I'd think about it and left it at that. Of course, I had no intention of doing anything more than I had already been doing. I'd shuttle the few people I liked into town and have pizza and beer, and we'd relish in the good times. Then, even under the influence of wine or beer, I'd expertly drive the long bus up or down the desolate and treacherous road that led back to the chateau. But nobody else got any special treatment.

My merely toeing the military line was just too much for the sergeant I'd upset, and he came to my room one day to lean on me so that I would take his people to a nearby beach for a well-needed rest. He was a big, intimidating man who towered over me, but I just lay on my bed staring out across my balcony at the hills and ignored him.

When he peeked into my room at the chateau, another cow was passing my field of vision. "You know, I called your motor pool in England, driver," he bellowed down at me as the cow bent down to eat some grass, "about the way you've been acting."

A solitary cloud now floated over the cow's head, and I was trying to decide if it looked more like a rabbit or dog. The big sergeant pushed open my door and stepped inside my room. "Listen, Patterson, that damn bus of yours is Air Force property, don't you get it yet? The only reason you're here is because the Air Force is paying you to drive people around."

"Around?" I said, turning from what I now dubbed the bunny cloud as it floated innocently toward Aviano Air Force Base in the valley.

"Yeah, around, dammit!"

"As in from Aviano Air Force Base to all the hotels and other places your mechanics are shacked up in?"

"No, I mean around, jackass!"

"You know, I talked to Sgt. Roberts. He's the one you talked to back at Bentwaters. He said all I had to do was to take you and your people to and from the base and the hotels you're all staying in."

"Listen, I tried to be nice—"

"—Nice?"

"I tried to be nice to you when you first got here, but I'm tired of this! I've been in the Air Force too long to take this kind of crap from a punk like you!"

He stepped a little closer, close enough that I could smell his heavy cologne over the scent of the Italian flowers on the vine that rose up the sides of the balcony. "Look, you're going to take my airmen to the beach tomorrow! They need a rest, and they've got no other way to get around! We'll be ready at 0800 hours! You got me? Be out front, or I swear, I'll come back here and show you some Mississippi knuckles up close!"

With that, the sergeant left. I heard him stomping down the stairs toward the ground floor and the jukebox as I turned back toward the window. Part of the bunny had elongated so that now it looked as though it had a leash attached to it. Then it was gone, somewhere just between north and west.

But this didn't end it. Later the same day of the sergeant's visit to my chateau room, out at a hangar where my new nemesis and some of his men worked, the big lifer threatened to take me "out back" as he put it, and "whup my ass." It was rumored that I wouldn't be showing up the following day to drive his men to the beach, and he said he was tired of my attitude and that he wasn't going to take any more.

"Are you going to take my men to the beach or not, Patterson?" the sergeant asked.

"Not in my bus."

"You wanna step out back and say that in private? You understand me, son?"

I almost gave in to his request to fight, but after someone who'd overheard the threat said, "Whoa, dude, he'll kill you," I came to my senses and walked away.

When the time finally came to transporting the sergeant and his men to Pordenone Beach, a locale where it was thought that women went topless, I was still reluctant to take them anywhere. Nonetheless, I was out in front of the chateau the next day; it was either that or suffer the consequences. A few minutes after eight, I sat waiting for the sergeant to arrive. The bus's diesel motor sent out oily fumes into the lovely Italian countryside. When the sergeant pounded on the bus's door, I angrily pulled the handle that caused this school bus-like portal to open. Oddly enough, the sergeant was smiling. He didn't even seem like the man of the day before. After giving me a friendly slap on the back, he plopped down heavily in a seat directly behind me and said it was a beautiful day for the beach.

I couldn't believe he was being so nice to me after the way he had acted. As we made our way to the first hotel on our route to pick up the rest of the eager airmen waiting to be led to those allegedly topless women, I thought of how I had been planning a drive to some other town by myself that day. I also kept thinking how I had been coerced into this other joyride, and I couldn't shake the feeling that I should somehow get back at my transport-ees.

Without giving it much conscious thought, I turned it up a notch. I showed them how well I could really handle that bus. I decided that if it they wanted a ride, I'd give them a ride they'd never forget. The streets in the Italian towns seemed even smaller than England's, and of course they were totally foreign to me. But I took them at ridiculous speeds, narrowly missing buildings and other fixed structures by inches. Looking in my rearview mirror, I could tell that the airmen were both terrified and in awe of my skills. Even the sergeant marveled at my ability to wheel that bus, but he held on for dear life. Later, when he was getting off the bus, he smiled, knowing what I had been up to, but he also sincerely thanked me for treating him and his men to the beach. That sincerity really touched me, and even through my fog-clouded way of thinking, I could tell that I'd finally done something right and had actually been a team player for once. Still, I didn't join the others on the beach that day. Instead, I went off by myself, not bothering to tell anyone when I was coming back.

One day, Sgt. Flemming showed up again and said I could take a break from driving. She would shuttle the troops for a while. But as I rode with her up the hill toward the chateau, I could tell she had seldom, if ever, driven a bus. She was too stiff and took the turns too wide. I now feared for my life and thought we wouldn't make it up that hill, that we'd go over one of the steep embankments and burn up in a ball of flame like in a James Bond movie.

We did make it though, without even hitting anything—except an old Italian farmer walking along the side of the road. Of course, I thought the bus would hit him, but I hoped it wouldn't. One of the bus's giant outside mirrors made pretty good contact with the back of the man's head, and everyone on the bus turned around to see if he was still alive. The grizzled farmer rubbed his head and yelled at us, but I have no idea what he said. The only Italian I knew was *ciao*. Sgt. Flemming looked with concern into the rearview mirror but never stopped or slowed to see if the man was all right. I just smiled and leaned back in my seat, wondering what that Italian thought of the U.S. military now. If I had to be in the military, I was glad it was the most powerful one in the world. After all, what could anyone really do to us if we got into trouble?

But Italy wasn't all beaches and taking advantage of Italians. I began to get lonely again, and sometimes at night on the veranda I would brood and repeatedly fill my hand with a bottle of the chateau's table wine. I would think of my pregnant Susan back in England who I seemed to be losing. I constantly wondered if I was the baby's father, or if it was Perry Ripley's. Susan had told me it was over between Perry and her, and she was living in my house, even though she thought she shouldn't be, but I sensed that she was still drawn to this Perry.

When I got back from Italy, I went straight home to see Susan. I found her in bed trying to get through a baby names book. She barely said hello to me, but I made it a point to plop down next to her and force her to take notice of the fact that I was back and that I wanted to talk.

"Find any names you like?" I asked half-heartedly.

"Well there are a lot, aren't there?" She was dressed in a white button-down nightie with lace. She was so pretty and her skin begged to be touched. I just wanted to reach out and hold her close, but I understood that our relationship was on a different level now. I still got the idea that Susan saw herself as a friend who merely needed refuge until she could sort things out. It was sad the way things had turned out. She used to have so much adventure in her voice and so much playful mischief in her eyes. Now she was looking through that damned book and having to make such serious decisions about everything. There was no longer the carefree Susan in my house; she was a stoic with a heavy burden to face. Looking at her propped up on her elbows with that incredibly young and naïve face, I wanted to help in any way I could. I didn't want her to face this dilemma by herself, but more than anything, I just wanted to hold her.

"I've always liked the name Sarah," I said, hoping to break the silence in that nearly darkened room.

"Yeah, I fancy that one, too. I've always liked that Fleetwood Mac song with Sarah in it. Really nice that song." When I heard that sweet Suffolk accent of hers, it was all I could do to keep myself from pushing back her thick hair and kissing her full on. But again, ours wasn't that type of relationship; to suddenly kiss a young unwed woman who was reading baby names was definitely not the right thing to do. Still, the way Susan and I had agreed on liking the name, Sarah, was a start—wasn't it? For God's sake, we were picking out the baby's name together.

"You haven't seen Perry lately, have you?" I said, before realizing it was the wrong thing to say at a time like that.

"Bloody hell, Ken." She shook her head and looked away from the book. And just like that our tender moment was gone. Still, Susan seemed more frustrated than angry. Then I could resist the urge no longer. I had to touch her. It had been quite a while since I'd even seen her. All I'd had to look at in Italy had been a tiny photo that we'd taken together at one of those booths in Woolworths. Now I was beside her. Facing her, I gently stroked her hair with the back of my hand. She moved her head away just enough to remind me where we stood. There was something in that small movement of hers that told me we might never again reach a point where such intimacies were allowed. My hand hung in midair for a moment before I finally pulled it away. Then I lay on my back and she returned to looking through her baby names book, but I couldn't stop looking at her.

Finally, I stared at the ceiling for a few minutes, hating the silence in that room and hating the darkness, before blurting out, "Susan, I'm sorry about this whole situation of yours. And I'm sorry I mentioned Perry's name. I guess I can't help thinking it's not over with the two of you, that's all."

I heard another page turn in the baby names book, and I looked at Susan again. As soon as the sound of the page was gone, the silence returned, but there was something new in the room: a few quiet teardrops on Susan's face. I looked away again, hating the fact that I couldn't hold her.

As heartwrenching as that homecoming of mine was, we got along a little better in the days that followed. Susan still made it clear that she didn't really want anything to do with me or Perry, and she still didn't know for certain who the baby's father was—even though when we counted back the months, we speculated that there was more of a chance that I was the father than Perry. I offered to marry her once again, but Susan still didn't want to marry me, and she didn't want me to push the issue. She was distraught over the prospect of raising a baby at the young age of nineteen, and marriage was the last thing on her mind. I still thought she wanted to be with Perry, even though she reiterated the fact that she didn't want to be with either of us. She said she just didn't know what to do. Nonetheless, it comforted me to know that I would end up seeing her more than Perry. At least I could pretend that I was still in first place when it came to competing for Susan's affections. I found out that Perry had a long rap sheet and a propensity for violence. Susan said Perry sometimes scared her.

This kind of Peyton Place drama had gone on long enough. I wanted to know for sure who the baby's father was. I wanted to protect Susan from Perry, and I still wanted to marry her. Things were black and white in my mind, even if they weren't in hers.

Susan's brother William and I got to be good friends, and I'd pour out my soul to him over drinks in one of the many pubs we frequented. William thought that his sister was foolish for not wanting to marry me and foolish for getting herself pregnant. He called her a silly cow and Perry a bastard. Apparently, the McAlister family had had a few run-ins with Perry after they discovered he had treated her poorly.

In William's eyes, I was an honest man with a future. He seemed to relate to my feelings of loneliness, since he longed for a Greek girl who had spurned him a short time before. William had learned Greek and he'd written long letters to his lost love. He told me how he missed Greece. Misery loves company, and it certainly loved us.

"I even learned Greek for that girl," Willim told me over drinks. We were in a little corner of Dukes comparing our sad stories. Neither of us seemed to be really listening to the other.

"I've done a lot for Susan," I said, eyeing some drunken English girl who frequented Dukes every Friday night. Her name was Rose, and she liked Americans a lot. Rose's date, a muscular American with a tattoo of an eagle on one of his arms, had been buying Rose drinks and making a big production of it. "I'm even willing to marry her. Marry her…" I paused to empty my glass of Fosters.

"I met Noola in a little village near Athens. You'd like Greece, Ken. The people are warmer there. Not like the bloody people here," William said, raising his voice as if wanting one of the few English natives in the pub to hear him. About the only person whose attention he got was the bouncer, an enormous Brit with a thick neck and a suit with sleeves too short for his arms.

"Maybe you just need another drink, William," I said, trying to calm him down.

"Yes, Ken. Maybe I do. That would be nice, ta," he said, suddenly sporting a smile and nodding appreciatively.

Considering our moods, I decided we needed something just as heavy to go along with them, so I ordered two pints of Guinness. When I got back from the bar, William wasn't smiling anymore, but he thanked me for the drinks and took a long sip of the rich, brown brew. Some of the Guinness sloshed onto the small, wooden table in front of us. There was a strong odor of history in the air as the drink mixed with the oak table, the unmistakable musky ancient smell of Europe.

"You see, Ken, they're all bloody cold here. Boring and cold. The English are just proletariats, really. It has to do with the Labor Party, you see…"

A couple of guys were playing darts, and I tried to follow the game as William spoke. I think one of the men got a bull's-eye by the way he shouted and made a victory sign with his fist, but I wasn't really sure. The game was just too far away for me to make out where the darts were landing and what was being said. William continued to talk as I pretended to understand what he was saying. His little speech must have lasted for about five minutes, but I was absolutely clueless about what he was trying to tell me. Then, all of a sudden, William seemed to be wrapping it up when I noticed a definite rise in his volume again, so I turned back to him and gave my best "I see" face.

"…bloody working-class peasants who are always talking out their arse. A bunch of bloody wankers, if you ask me," he added.

The bouncer gave us another look. I looked the other way this time, taking in the farce that was happening between Rose and the big American. He had his arm around her shoulders now, but I could tell that Rose was cringing slightly and trying to close herself up like those pill bugs I used to see as a kid.

I was starting to feel a slight buzz when William lodged into a lengthy explanation of United Kingdom's political structure, and my mind shut off. I just couldn't seem to follow along with what he said.

"Do you think Susan will leave me?" I suddenly interjected, trying to change the subject, but also really wanting to know what my girlfriend's brother thought.

William was caught off guard by the question. His face scrunched up and then relaxed before he finally nodded in a drunken stupor. "Well, I don't know, do I? She's a bloody silly girl, Ken. She's always been a little silly. Silly cow. Mind you, Ken, if she doesn't change her ways something really bad's bound to happen to that sister of mine. She wouldn't be this way if my father were around. He'd set her straight. Bloody silly girl."

I'd never met William and Susan's father. They told me he worked in the Middle East somewhere. His job had something to do with oil, and I got the impression that he hadn't been home in years. I pictured a tough man, English to the core. A real bulldog.

Noticing my anguish, William tried to comfort me. "Don't worry about it, Ken. You're a fine bloke. You've been a lot better for Susan than that bloody Perry Ripley. Something really needs to be done about him. He's bloody evil. I'd really like to get my hands on him some day. What he's done to my sister. It's not right, Ken. It's just not bloody right."

With that said, we just sat there, two pitiful young guys on the town, each brooding over a woman of a different nationality whom we'd probably never be able to lure into our worlds. But William had at least one major advantage over me during this time of lamenting: he was a clear thinker. He tended to put a negative slant on things but he usually had a better idea of what was going on around him. It took every bit of my compromised mental powers for me to focus. I still observed the world through my partially obscured thoughts. I reached conclusions more by means of impulse and instinct than by sound logic. In short, I was thinking the way I'd always thought, the way I probably always will think.

I knew William and I would probably have drinks again the following night. We'd try some other pub, as was our custom, since William disliked visiting the same pub two nights in a row. The next night would begin the same way; a few pints to relax us and then another of William's endless lectures on England and the English. The United Kingdom and anything related to it completely bored him with a predictability that left him staring into space, past pints of lager and clouds of smoke, to a place he'd much rather be. Then, when he'd made it clear what he didn't like, he would make it just as clear what he did like. But it didn't end there. Listening to William was like listening to a verbal ping-pong game since he'd eventually return to talking about what he didn't like again, and then back to what he did like. Ever since visiting Greece on holiday, William hadn't been the same. It was warmer in Greece. The people weren't so rigid; they hung out in little bars and cafés sipping ouzo and coffee and never seeming to be in a hurry. William said he preferred the Mediterranean lifestyle with its rustic poetic ambiance and its flavorful abundance. It was his dream to someday leave

England, to "chuck it all," as he said, for a different way of living. A Greek way. But I think it was that Greek woman named Noola. No matter how William put down his own people and the English way of life, I always saw him as quintessentially English, not the type to drop everything and become a wayward fishing village layabout clutching a handful of worry-beads.

In addition to talking about likes, dislikes, and Noola, my Ipswich friend talked of politics and history, and he talked about other subjects I didn't understand very much. I was at a loss to understand anything of depth that he tried to convey. It was as if I were back at school in Price's class, not knowing a thing that the teacher lectured on. Words. That's all they were. Endless, ceaseless words that never made it to the core of my mind. I wanted to know what the words meant, but I just wasn't equipped to decipher them, or at least the overall intent behind them. Still, even though I didn't understand most of what William talked about, he was my friend, and I was glad he was.

During one of William's diatribes in Dukes, he got up to go to the loo, as he called it. While waiting for William to return, I noticed Rose all alone at the bar. She was running a finger over her glass of sherry and I could tell she'd been crying. I observed a commotion across the room. This was fairly common, since young American airmen were apt to sow a few wild oats in the pub. These disturbances were quickly put down by the knuckle-to-floor gorilla-like bouncers working at Dukes. So I didn't pay too much attention to this particular fracas until the crowd cleared. Then I saw Perry Ripley smiling evilly by the restrooms, and I saw the bouncer who had been watching us earlier leading William to the pub's exit with a thick arm around his neck. It was all over in a minute or so. I took one more sip of my Guinness before heading for the door. Outside, I found William on the street spouting profanity at the pub and Perry Ripley. Then, in frustration, my friend told me he was going home. I stayed glued to that spot outside Dukes, marveling at my mild-mannered mate's actions. It was true that William always talked a good talk, but I never thought he'd actually follow up. I saw him in a different light after that night. I guess he'd finally had enough and decided to teach Perry a lesson for mistreating his sister.

A few minutes later I was face to face with the infamous Perry Ripley whom I'd never met until that moment. His scruffy face was inches from mine and he glared at me, a greasy friend by his side. Perry warned me to stay away from Susan, and I told him I'd see her if I wanted to. In my peripheral vision, I saw his friend stealthily remove a long knife from under his coat.

Still looking into Perry's eyes, I told his friend that if he pulled the knife on me, I'd "shove it up his ass." I guess I'd had enough too, or it was the Guinness talking. Whatever the reason for my gruff front, it accomplished its purpose. The knife slowly slid back under that coat, and the pair of Englishmen walked away, smiling that "you aren't anything" smile. I felt an evil force come from Perry, an undeniably demonic presence. I hoped we wouldn't meet again. I've always tried to stay very far away from evil.

As the saga with Susan lingered on, I returned to a groove of driving and smoking hashish. But my problems with Susan were still there, and she seemed more distant. The only reason she lived with me was because she still couldn't find a place of her own. Then, one night, she just didn't come home. I waited for her, fretting over what might have happened. I felt that familiar sense of loss and wanting.

It got late, and I hoped Susan would come home soon. She just couldn't be gone. The uncertainty of whether or not she would return soon took its toll. I fell into a deep bout of depression. Before the military, when my relationship with Carrie had gone awry, I had had more difficulty dealing with the devastation of a broken relationship. The CCC did little to distract me. Now, at least, I had the military to keep me busy, though the appeal of driving big rigs was wearing off. Driving became merely a job, something I did only to keep my bosses happy. Now that my pretend wife seemed to have run off, what did I have to look forward to? My attitude on base deteriorated once again. Fortunately, for a while anyway, there weren't any confrontations with higher ups, since I drove trucks almost exclusively and, for the most part, I was alone. Nonetheless, I laid the groundwork for trouble down the road.

Things seemed very dismal in those days, and more often than not I found myself struggling for a reason to do anything. I'd been in the Air Force almost four years and my infatuation with the military had worn off. I might as well have been a civilian delivering private sector freight. This dismal mood was, of course, heightened because of Susan. She'd been gone for an entire week.

And each day she was gone, I fell asleep waiting for her. A part of me felt that Susan was gone for good. Like a misty-eyed child in some Disney movie whose dear pet had wandered off, I imagined Susan out there somewhere, lost, another homeless stray traveling the cold British streets. Then the unexpected happened. It was late on a Sunday night when I heard a knock on the front door downstairs. I jolted awake, jumped out of bed, and headed for the stairs just a few feet from my upstairs bedroom. The staircase in our house was narrow and difficult to manage, and in my sleepy state I nearly fell down as I frantically descended each carpeted step. When I did finally reach the living room, the volume and intensity of the knocking had increased. In an instant, I threw the lock's deadbolt and flung open the front door to find Susan on the other side in a great state of agitation. There was a cabbie waiting impatiently nearby.

A moment after the door opened, and without even so much as a hello or explanation of why she had been gone, Susan flew into the living room, waving her hands and talking too fast for me to get any of what she was saying. Outside, the cabbie seemed almost as agitated as Susan. It was difficult to hear him over Susan, but I gathered from his insistent badgering that she hadn't paid the cab fare yet. I soon found out from Susan that she hadn't had any money when she hopped into the cab. I was so elated to have Susan back home that, initially, I didn't think much of the cab driver's pleas, but the seriousness of the situation quickly elevated when the cabbie decided to call the police. A few minutes later, a female officer showed up on the scene wearing a very proper and weird-looking hat, and carrying a very shiny black purse over her shoulder. The cop got right to the point. She told Susan to pay the cabbie or she'd have to go to jail. The cabbie simply wouldn't back down. I had a talk with Susan as the cab remained running and intermittent jabbering came over its radio. I told her that I would pay the cab fare, but then realized I didn't have any money either. Still, I didn't want Susan to go to jail, and I offered to write the cabbie a check drawn on my credit union account on base. He was hesitant to take a check that originated from an American financial institution. Not knowing what to do, I felt the fog creeping in heavily. My mind locked up. There were just too many emotions clogging up the works to allow me to sort things out clearly. Why was Susan suddenly back in my life? And how could I keep the cop and the cabbie happy? I wanted everything to go away for a while, so that I could untie the knots in my head, but I knew that wasn't an option. Suddenly, a tiny bit of reasoning surfaced though the blackness in my mind like a periscope in a dark sea. I blurted out that I'd give the cabbie whatever he wanted if he'd just go away. I told him I'd write the check for double the fare. I probably would have even tripled the amount if need be, just so that things could return to normal. Luckily, this wasn't necessary. The cabbie reluctantly agreed to my first offer, and both he and the officer left Bulstrode Road. I closed the door to the sound of two engines in the distance and went to sit beside Susan on the couch. I was happy to have her back again.

Even though Susan was now in a safe environment, having been rescued from the clutches of the law, she was still upset. Her hands gestured wildly as she vented about the night's events. Then she sat down on my Air Force issue couch, shaking her head from side to side before finally breathing a frustrated sigh and lying back against one of the couch's cushions. A second later, my jittery girlfriend undid the top button of her tight-fitting jeans to free her pregnant belly. It was reassuring. In my mind, undoing that button in front of me was a sign that Susan still felt at ease in my presence. Unbuttoning her pants might have been a little thing, and maybe it really didn't mean anything at all, given her physical state, but I latched onto it to keep hope alive. I pretended that Susan's return to my humble little home on Bulstrode Road meant that she had decided to get back together again.

I wanted to hold her and tell her how much I'd missed her, but she was too upset. I started to wonder what had happened to Susan that night. Why had she gotten in a cab with no money? Susan never took cabs. Then, before I had a chance to ask, Susan let go another heavy sigh, sat up, put her head in her hands, and told me the story. Everything had started around lunchtime when, by chance, she met Perry in town and he talked her into sharing a cab. She paused for a moment, lifted her head from her hands, and stared into space. She was trembling.

"He said he'd have the driver drop me off…here…and then he'd take the cab to his hotel." She stopped again, and I could tell that tears were beginning to well in her eyes. There was a dreaminess about her, a far-off look I'd never seen before. She was talking as if questioning her own memory. "I told the driver to take the next exit…Bulstrode Road, please…but Perry told him to keep going. I told him again, Bulstrode Road. I need to go to Bulstrode Road, please…but Perry just smiled at him and winked. 'Arthur's Arms,' he said, as if he hadn't even heard me. 'Perry?' I said. I looked right at him. 'Perry,' I said, 'I told you it's over, right? Don't you bloody remember?' He just kept looking straight ahead. 'I need to go to Bulstrode Road, please, driver,' I said, leaning toward him. But Perry just shook his head and looked at the driver and he gestured at me as if I didn't know what I really wanted. Then, right after that, Perry said, in the calmest of voices, mind you, 'Arthur's Arms, driver.' We just kept driving in the same direction. I couldn't believe it. The driver threw his hands in the air and shook his head back and forth. 'Look,' he said, 'you two sort out your problems somewhere else, right? I don't want any of your troubles in my bloody cab.' He stopped listening to anything I had to say after that. He just thought we were having a row and he didn't want to get in the middle of it. I couldn't believe it." There was another pause. "Then we were at Arthur's Arms," Susan said, looking at herself in the living room's glass coffee table, before hiding her head in her hands again and rocking back and forth.

It wasn't until the next day that I finally managed to pry more information out of Susan. She told me, in tiny robot-like whispers, what Perry had done after the cab had pulled to a stop in front of Arthur's Arms. About how her old boyfriend had paid the cabbie with a few crumpled pound notes and then forced her into his hotel, where he raped her repeatedly. It was only after Perry had finally fallen asleep from his drinking and sex binge that Susan had slipped away.

After running from Arthur's Arms, Susan said she had found the first mode of transportation she could, not even caring at all about what the consequences would be for not being able to pay for it. In what must have been a quick, frightened command, she said she told a different cabbie to take her to 17 Bulstrode Road.

Now that I was up to speed on the situation that led to Susan's abrupt arrival at my door, a mixture of intense anger and sadness filled me. Of course, I sympathized with what had happened to Susan. I wanted to kill Perry. After a brief pause, I brought my hand down on the glass coffee table in the living room and sent a crack racing through it. Then I got up and paced the floor with Susan crumpled in a ball on the couch. I just couldn't believe that Perry had raped her, and my foggy mind couldn't compute the ramifications of such an act carried out on the girl I loved. I stared down at the coffee table. In the crack in the table's glass, I saw a split image of myself. A warped image. One side of my head ascended, and the other descended. I was now permanently out of alignment. The whole world was. And nothing could set things back the way they had been. Still, I had to try. Everything would be all right now. My life would be complete. Susan was back home where she belonged. We'd act as if nothing had happened. We had to. But even as I thought this, I couldn't turn away from the split image in the glass. It was an ugly image, just as the world was an ugly world, and secretly I knew things wouldn't be all right.

After that night, Susan became moody and even more faraway than ever. She seemed to be using my house as a place to keep her safe from the outside world while she dwelled on her next step. To make things worse, Susan internalized her emotions. She didn't want to talk about what had happened, and I couldn't seem to console her. The crying had long since stopped, and she seemed immune to the pain, but she also seemed immune to being happy. I tried to cheer her up with flowers. We took trips in the country on the back of my motorcycle and trips to the sea, but it didn't matter what I did. Nothing seemed to get through to her. She was like a radio whose ability to receive incoming frequencies had been lost forever. But I hoped I was wrong. I could still be her baby's father; she had to consider this. Certainly she wouldn't want to leave me for good, at least not until the father's identity was definitively known. There still could be a plan for the two of us to follow, couldn't there?

As the days went by, this was all I thought about. The possibility of my being a father had changed my way of thinking. Even though my father wasn't the best role model, I grew up watching reruns of shows such as *Leave It to Beaver* and *The Brady Bunch*. The fathers in these shows were always responsible, predictable, perfect providers, and extremely stable. The fact that I might have to live up to this image was a wake-up call, and I tried to get my act together, gain absolute control of the fog, be stronger emotionally. I think I even dropped my normal tone of voice a few octaves. But all of this was a facade. No matter how I tried, somehow, deep down, I knew I couldn't ever live up to the stringent guidelines for fathers set forth in TV history.

Then it happened again: Susan disappeared for a while. But this time, instead of pining for her at home, I decided to go out. I needed to go out, or the confining walls of that Bulstrode house would suffocate me. I walked through a narrow alleyway between the crowded houses and onto the main drag that led into town; past my favorite fish and chips shop, over the wide canal with the ever-present sailing vessel that looked as though it belonged in some swashbuckler movie, and toward the heart of Ipswich with its shops and crowded pubs.

I happened to glance into one such pub. To my astonishment, I saw Susan and Perry seated at a table that looked out onto the street. She had an "Oh God" expression on her face. She acted as if she didn't see me, but I know she did. I don't think Perry saw me though, and I just kept on walking toward town.

I was deeply hurt. I wondered if I'd been played or if Susan just felt the need to go back to Perry. I came to the conclusion that it must have been the latter reason, but I didn't know why. At the time, I didn't know that there were women who went back to guys who abused them. I was too naive when it came to the opposite sex. To me, life was simple: if someone hurt you, you either hurt that person back or ran away from him. The only deduction I could make about why Susan had gone back to Perry was that she was the kind of girl who seemed to prefer the bad boy type. And since I knew I wasn't that type—not when it came to women anyway—I had very little chance of winning her back. In fact, even though I still loved Susan, something new was happening in me when it came to understanding her behavior and how it related to me. And it wasn't just her behavior I began to think about, but the behavior of the other women who had been a part of my life. I began to realize that the women in my life were engaged with me initially, but then their interest waned. Even though the reason for this waning interest could be easily traced back to a root cause, its recurrence in my life was extremely disheartening—to say the least. After seeing Susan in that pub with Perry, and having had ample time to reflect, I began to consider the reasons for the demise of my relationships. I began to look inward, to investigate the possibility that I might be doing something to hamper the evolution of my relationships with women. That perhaps there was some innate weakness in me, which compromised a relationship's growth. Maybe I was bad after all—not in the sense that I wanted to hurt women like Perry Ripley did—but bad when it came to communicating or empathizing effectively enough to keep a woman satisfied. This was all speculation, however, at this early stage of my development into understanding what made me tick. I had nothing concrete to go on concerning my so-called "badness."

I soon discovered that Susan left Perry and was living in a government-run home for women in her condition. I visited her, and she was kind to me. Perry visited her too. But Susan told me she'd had enough of Perry's behavior, and she still didn't want to marry either of us. She was firm in this conviction and started getting ready for the little girl who was due to enter the world soon. All Susan's attention was devoted to this upcoming event; the sheer nature of its impact on her life forced Susan's hand. Nonetheless, I sensed she respected the fact that I hung around so much, and maybe for the baby's sake she leaned toward being with me when she could. I think she wanted a male around, especially if there was a good chance that that male was her baby's father.

2 1

The Final About-Face

I KNEW I had a propensity for badness. It lay in a desire to shuck authority
and follow my own rules, though, at that point in my life, I drew the line at
committing crimes. I was merely a mouthy nonconformist who was trying to
find his way in the fog, not by design, of course, but out of necessity. And this
nonconformist attitude surfaced every chance it got now that my future path
had changed once again.

My desire to follow orders was automatic, a response to Air Force conditioning. But my enthusiasm was waning. My focus on goals and my sense of
self-importance dissipated. I was only a shell of a man, and my shell was
cracking under the pressure. I saw only the need to fulfill my military
contract and find another pursuit.

In many ways, I reverted to the way I had behaved at Ellsworth AFB. I
drew into myself again, and away from the team spirit that the military
demanded. This change in attitude became apparent to those around me.
The only difference from the way I acted at Bentwaters and the way I had
acted at past bases, however, was that I pushed things just enough to irk
superiors, but not enough to have them bring any action against me. I'd been
in the Air Force a long time, and I now knew how the game was played. For
most of my tour in England, I managed just enough decorum and control to
keep myself in check without stepping over the line. But even the most
looked after bomb will explode if it's handled wrong. And now there was a
fuse connected to the volatile elements building up inside me; the fuse had
been set in place during my ongoing troubles with Susan.

Then the bomb went boom. It exploded during one of the exercises that Bentwaters occasionally sprang on us. I was smoking more hashish at the time, trying to escape the rigidity of the military and dealing with a sketchy relationship with a young woman. The last thing I needed was a nuclear exercise, a war game designed to keep airmen on their toes. I hated the bulky gas masks and cumbersome shoes we donned on such occasions. They made me feel even more controlled by a power I had no control over.

Sgt. "Chilly" Chilson was the last person I wanted to see during nuclear exercises. I tried to stay clear of him. Everyone knew he was a "lifer" and I wasn't. I just wanted to do my three more months against my four years and leave the Air Force quietly and quickly. He was in it for twenty. He was a man who loved the military, someone who probably saw himself collecting a pension after his service, then touring the U.S. in a massive RV with all the frills.

I just wanted to be handed the keys to one of the cold, bone-jarring rigs in the yard, attach it to a trailer, and drive somewhere far so I could be with my own thoughts; the farther the better. But the military has a way of changing your plans.

So there I was in a suit I could have worn for Halloween, half-stoned and in a fog, right in Chilly's sights. I was a perfect target for him that day. Lifers don't like short-timers. They look at them as different creatures, creatures who shrug off good order and discipline and merely take the wonderful fringe benefits the military has to offer; short-timers are creatures who should be brought down and made civilians. Lifers especially dislike disgruntled airmen like me who aren't team players and have to be told again and again to trim their hair or polish their boots.

Then came the actual moment when the burning fuse that had been set on fire outside me reached the powder keg inside. I was milling about in the motor pool's yard, longing to take off that damn, stifling mask, when Chilly told me to get in a pick-up. It was just as simple as that. Why, I didn't know, and I don't remember where we ended up. I do remember that I started to get in the front seat with him and another airman, and he said "No, you get in the back," in a demeaning and uncalled for voice. I had to respond. I had to break the strict code of military conduct that so many had drilled into me. It took only two words. One expletive and one pronoun, and my life was forever altered. Enough to affect both my future and something deep inside me that I would dwell on for the next sixteen years. But that came later. At the time I said the words, I merely apologized to Chilly and told him it would never happen again. I realized the impact those words could have in the military, and I just didn't want to go down that road.

Immediately after the apology, Chilly responded with "Just don't let it happen again," and we drove on. I thought for sure that I had appeased even the well-pressed folds of his military mind, but I was wrong.

The following morning, when I showed up for another day of the same old song and dance, I was promptly summoned to the commanding officer's office. The meeting between my commanding officer and me was swift. He simply eyed a very official piece of paper and asked me if it was true that I'd said my expletive and pronoun to one Sgt. Chilson, and I said yes. What followed was just as swift. The military likes dealing with things this way. It's the quintessential well-oiled machine, and well-oiled machines need to work efficiently or they break down. I was nothing more than a bit of grime that had gotten caught in one of its many moving parts.

I could have fought the maelstrom of neatly piled paperwork that flew through the normal channels that would lead it in, and out of, in and out boxes, but I went with the storm. The stronger the negative winds blew the better. This was the chance I'd been waiting for, even if it wasn't exactly the way I wanted it to go down. I needed out of the military once and for all. I wanted to grow my hair long and wear what I liked to work. And I wanted to get away from people like Chilly. Of course, in the back of my mind somewhere, I knew that was impossible, whether in or out of the military. Still, I was on my way to being a civilian, and by the time the paperwork was processed, I *would* do my four years, even though I'd leave with an Under Honorable Conditions discharge. It wasn't a really bad discharge as discharges went, but it wasn't the best either, and as I would find out later, it would keep me from reenlisting in the Air Force or any of the other military branches.

Nonetheless, at the time I was being discharged, my attitude improved immensely, and I couldn't wait to breathe air as a civilian instead of as a government indentured servant. I'd certainly never have to wear another gas mask. Some airmen, Gonzo for example, longed for what I was about to receive, but didn't have the moxie to follow in my footsteps—not that what had happened to me on that day of the nuclear exercise was by design, unless Chilly had planned it, of course. Even if he had, my actions were just one more example of how the fog and its impulsive behavior had gotten me into trouble.

Not everyone liked the idea of my leaving the Air Force. When I told Susan, she turned cold and more detached than ever. She knew the discharge would take me back to America. Even though marriage still wasn't an option for her, I think Susan wanted me to stay around at least until her baby's paternity was determined. By this time she had been moved from the girl's home to a hospital, and I think she'd gotten used to me visiting her in its sterile, impersonal maternity wing. Susan must have also gotten used to the approving looks from nurses and other patients who were glad that this young unwed girl had someone to look after her. The hospital admittance gurus stuck Susan in a far-off corner of the ward, a dark and lonely place, with few patients nearby to witness her dilemma.

I remained close to Susan, even when she left the hospital. I tried to understand all the paraphernalia and hype that went into caring for a baby. I watched her fumble with diapers and baby bathtubs, breastfeeding and burping, and all the other oddities. Not everything seemed so frantic and strange to me when I was around the baby, however. There were times I kicked back in the eye of the hurricane. Sometimes, the scene with Susan and her baby was amusing. Like the time when Sarah, Susan's new little girl, peed a fountain of urine just like a boy would have in a tall arc toward her mum. Susan was the quintessential inexperienced mother who seemed nonplussed when it came to even the tiniest of mishaps pertaining to a new baby, let alone a fountain of urine in her face. Even so, she usually handled incidents such as this one with a combination of smiles and frustration. But when she wasn't smiling or mildly irritated, I saw her another way; the incarcerated prisoner now having to pay a debt to some unknown higher power for her irresponsibility. I'd catch her staring off into space in between Sarah's bawling and diaper changes. How did this happen to me? the look seemed to suggest.

But Susan wasn't the only one struggling with a new turn of events. I was, after all, entwined in her dilemma as well, and now I had to cope with my discharge and an uncertain future. Maybe it was lucky my ADD sidekick the fog was around, because somehow, no matter how engaging or serious, nothing seemed to soak in. I took in the events the way a photojournalist might have: a witness to the activities at hand, but not really a participant because of the camera separating subject and reporter. But the photojournalist had one significant advantage over me. The film in my mind's camera didn't record images very well; it didn't hold them there the way cellulose does. My pictures of life were coming back from Wal-Mart a little overexposed. In a nutshell, a lot of life was entering my camera, but not enough substance, not enough realism. I went through the motions the way I always had done, and somehow showed up to work on time and dreamed of my next dreams.

Soon, it was time to leave the birthplace of the Fab Four. Apparently, the military had a rule that wouldn't allow its people to be discharged in England. Given the short notice of my actual departure to the States, I sold my motorcycle to another airman for a lot less than I should have. I tied up other loose ends and vowed to come back to the U.K. as soon as I was discharged at McGuire Air Force Base, New Jersey. When I told Susan I had to leave England, she seemed more aloof than ever, as if I'd never return. It was really about to happen now; I was on my way home at last. I guess in her mind, the most likely father of her baby would end up a far-off memory who wrote occasionally and exchanged photos with his daughter. Nonetheless, even with Susan's fears, and although she had no aspirations of being my wife, I told her I'd already purchased a return airline ticket and would be back as soon as possible.

Before leaving England, I'd made friends with Judy, a nurse who owned a home on Bulstrode Road just a few houses down from my place. Her sister, Melanie, had knocked on my door one day to ask if I'd lost the kitten she was holding in her outstretched hands. I said yes, since it was a kitten I'd inherited from Susan. Melanie introduced me to her sister, and the two of us hit it off. Judy especially liked my poetry, or at least me.

This kind-hearted nurse was a lot older than I was, and she was very reserved and together. Even though she rejected the kitten, I think she likened me to a stray she needed to take care of. Or maybe she thought I was a neat artist type to have around since I was still prone to writing poetry and had almost finished my first novel. It was rough and very crude stuff, but Judy enjoyed reading what I wrote, and that helped me a lot. Whatever the reason she took me in, I'll never forget it. I desperately needed a place to stay where I didn't have to pay rent since I was low on money after my discharge, and out of work. But staying at Judy's would still be a few days away. First, I had to fly to McGuire AFB and cut the Air Force umbilical cord that had sustained me for so long.

It took me about six hours to reach McGuire in my birthday month of January back in 1984, and I now sat at a desk in a beat-up classroom with a bunch of other soon-to-be civilians listening to a man take us through discharge proceedings. The exit briefing seemed rushed and cheap, without the pomp and exuberance I'd experienced upon joining the military. Those around me were as forlorn as I was because the finality of the situation had finally settled in. Sure, many of us had yearned for this for years, but I believe we secretly never dreamed it would happen. It was as if we were attending a funeral and the speaker before us was delivering a eulogy, one obligatory Air Force goodbye, words meant for our dying military careers. I barely focused on anything the man said, dwelling instead on the coldness I felt within. Our guide to exiting the military didn't allay our grief though. He knew we were leaving him, leaving the Air Force, so why should he care too much about us?

We weren't kin to him anymore. We were leaving the Air Force family, the way some children leave a wonderful home, and most of us would never depend upon the generosity of our governmental father again.

After a few more boilerplate sentences involving the all-important significance of our DD214, an Air Force separation document, we were outcasts sent back into the undisciplined world with little more than what we had come in with: a few pieces of civilian clothing and a desire to be a part of something giant. We were confused men and women, no longer with rank or swagger.

When I returned to England, I felt very much alone and vulnerable. The good ol' U.S.A. was no longer my backer. I had to fend for my own food and lodging. I had to take care of myself. I'd lost a big brother who had been looking out for my interests the past four years. I also had to do a lot more of my own thinking. The Air Force no longer told me what to do, or how to do it. Fortunately, Judy was there to help make the transition from military life to civilian life a little easier. She'd been a nurse for many years and had seen one human disaster after another.

Judy offered a warmth and understanding that were well-needed departures from the harsh reality of being kicked out of the military. It also comforted me to know that I could hold her at night and discuss my future without any pressure to leave. Being at Judy's place was like being in some sort of peaceful purgatory. I wasn't able to go back to the life I'd known, and I wasn't certain of my future. Sometimes drifting day by day in limbo can actually expedite the planning and self-awareness process.

I kept close tabs on Susan, and thankfully neither she nor Judy felt any jealousy given the circumstances. Susan hadn't accepted me back as a boyfriend, so I was free to do what I wanted. But I told her I'd be there for her as long as possible, and if she changed her mind about getting married, I'd gladly oblige. I still thought it was the right thing to do since I believed I was the father. Judy had no aspirations to make me her husband, though we had a wonderful sexual relationship.

It didn't take long for me to realize, however, that Susan's situation didn't merit my staying in England. Things just didn't feel the same since I was booted out of the military. Before, I was kind of a novelty in England, an essential American soldier abroad whose differences could be respectfully observed for a while before I went back where I'd come from. But now I was just a longhaired leech without direction, disconnected from the great U.S. military machinery. Even though I only spent a short time in England after my discharge, I was mostly unemployed. The only job I remember taking was in an apple orchard. One of Susan's friends told me about the work, and I needed some spending money, so I picked apples all day for lager or fish and chips. The more apples I picked, the more money I made.

It seemed that the gang I hung around with in England no longer thought I should be there, even though they never told me this. I started to feel the same way. I needed a new path to follow. I needed to regroup. And England just wasn't the place to do this. At some point foreigners need to go home where they belong. I thought I could get hold of another career in the U.S. and come back to be with Susan if she wanted me.

So after two full years of European life with funny accents and my fill of plaice, I boarded a wide-body jet and headed back to California. I was a scruffy vet', with a brand new start.

I decided to take a pack of Greyhounds from New Jersey to San Francisco. The Greyhounds changed drivers and passengers about every five hundred miles. I met so many people on the bus that I can't even remember them. I got away with passing a bottle of wine around amongst a few of us at the back. I also met a girl from Israel who seemed to be escaping from something.

Jake met me at the bus station. My old friend kept eyeing my black leather jacket that zipped up on the left side. I guess he was wondering if I'd become a biker or something, but I just liked the jacket's look. People got away with tacky dress in England; it didn't seem to draw as much attention, so I fitted in there with puffed-up leather. Neither Jake nor I said much as we drove down U.S. 101, but we sized each other up to see if we could spot any significant changes. So much had changed with me; he seemed pretty much the same. Strangely, it felt as though I'd never left America.

I kept thinking about that Israeli girl I'd met on the last leg of my trip into San Francisco. She seemed very mature for her age. I got her phone number and said I'd call her so that we could go bowling sometime. It was a stupid thing to say. I never saw the girl again, just as I never saw another day in a military uniform.

2 2

Labor Pains

MY DAD WAS a hard worker. He even brought his work home with him. There were many mornings when I woke up bleary-eyed to cross the living room carpet on my way to the kitchen for a bowl of cereal, and I'd step on sharp steel shavings left there by my dad's size eleven oxfords.

Often, I'd see my father's strange machinist tools on the kitchen table: micrometers and other specialty gadgets that were used for exact measurements and precision tool and die work. Even when my father wasn't working, the fog and I would sometimes accompany him to flea markets or garage sales so that he could get great buys on all those funny-looking gadgets of his.

Most of the time, my father's tools were kept in a large wooden toolbox with an assortment of tiny pull-out drawers. Many of the things in that toolbox were worth a great deal of money, so it came as a great blow one day when it was stolen along with the family car. The theft occurred in San Francisco. The tools were in the car's trunk. The day of the theft, the Wildcat (the same car that had previously blown up) was parked at the San Francisco Zoo while Mark, my father, and I were enjoying a rare outing.

But temporary setbacks such as the loss of his tools weren't enough to deter my father's work ethic, nor did staying out all night in the bars, or the fact that he hated being a blue-collar worker. My father often told me to go to college and use my mind so I wouldn't end up wearing my body out before I was thirty. I think he always regretted the fact that he'd passed on a couple of college scholarships in his younger days before devoting his time to tool and die work. With a family to feed and clothe, he simply hadn't had the time to invest in college. So he got down into the trenches and never looked back, except during those late nights at the bar, of course. Even with my father's encouragement, only two of his five boys, Mark and I, would obtain college degrees—and I didn't get mine until my father had passed away. Still, all through my childhood, my father had high hopes for me concerning college. His other sons had let him down, but it didn't appear as though I would. As I matured and he didn't have as much influence on me, my dad saw his dream of having a college-educated son slip away. Confirmation of this came when I dropped out of high school and it was certain that I *wasn't* going to college.

But through it all, my father trudged onward in those greasy shops, which were bereft of aesthetics or proper ventilation, sacrificing more than just college scholarships the way so many parents do, just so he could provide for his family. Unemployment simply wasn't an option in our household.

Dad passed on his noble work ethic to his children. We became hard workers too. As long as we were putting some change in our pockets, we were following in our father's footsteps.

My brother Danny had a paper route. I'd often watch him prepare for the hour or so of newspaper deliveries; deliveries that took place with as much predictability and devotion as the mail, no matter the weather conditions or inconveniences. Seven days each week, morning and afternoon, a single heavy bundle was dropped off by an *Examiner* truck. Danny carried it into the house and I'd watch him quickly fold newspapers, the smell of ink on the living room floor, the snap of rubber bands filling the room as they were rolled over each folded paper. Then Danny loaded the papers into cloth bags and placed the straps over his head. Although I doubt he ever read one of his own newspapers, my brother felt the heavy weight of the day's breaking stories on his back and chest. These were the same bags that I would wear later, and I can attest to the inconvenience that the weight caused. Just bending over or riding a bike became a challenge; a challenge I couldn't wait to have myself, since I admired what Danny did. To me, the idea of being a paperboy filled me with pride. With this first job I would be an entrepreneur earning my first paychecks.

Before Danny handed down the prestigious position of paperboy, I'd sometimes go along with him to deliver his newspapers, early on Sunday mornings when the papers were thick with comics and many inserts, or late in the afternoon when the papers were thinner with just the facts, as Friday on *Dragnet* used to say.

When my brother got too old to deliver newspapers and moved on to some job that paid more, I finally inherited his route. The responsibility was immense. I discovered that I alone had to make sure newspapers made it to each driveway, porch, or path. And I had to collect money from my customers, including a few who liked the idea of reading the paper, but didn't want to pay for it.

But the self-respect I felt when I got my pay from one of the blue *Examiner* trucks that drove around our neighborhood made up for all the trouble. And I'm sure I found favor in my father's eyes. After all, I was now a working stiff, toeing the line and learning about responsibility.

Although the paper route was my first job, it certainly wouldn't be my last. At last count, I noted at least twenty-six jobs in the past forty years, not counting temporary employment with various agencies, friends, and relatives. And the reason I took on so many jobs wasn't necessarily due to that work ethic which my father instilled in me at so young an age. The reason I accumulated such an extensive employment background was mostly because I couldn't hold onto a job.

ADDers and jobs just don't mix; at least I've found this to be true in my case. I've decided that I have trouble holding onto a job because I'm not equipped with the appropriate tools required to excel in the working world. Whereas Dad's toolbox was full of the most precise instruments for his job, I lacked the two most fundamental tools for any job: interpersonal communication skills and information processing. A lack of good people skills has compromised my ability to perform satisfactorily. Employers don't have any patience with a worker who's difficult. Whether my unsatisfactory performance was caused by a failure to communicate effectively or a failure to process information effectively, the inevitable result has been the same: unemployment.

At pivotal times while working for one company or another, I've felt a tremendous amount of friction between myself and other employees. In comparison to other ADDers, I'm sure my negative family life and poor fatherly guidance certainly played a part, but I've always felt my less than adequate upbringing was secondary. There was always something else at play that I just couldn't put my finger on, and it nearly drove me crazy at times.

Because I misunderstood instructions, misinterpreted intentions, or just wasn't able to cope with fellow employees' or bosses' personalities, a familiar scenario played itself out again and again. I'd quit while I still had the chance, or I'd let something run its course until I got fired and had to carry the pieces of another burned bridge into the next job interview.

Of course, sometimes my inability to hold a job had nothing to do with people. Just not being able to do the task was enough to get an infamous "pink slip," or short goodbye. Now that I have the luxury of hindsight, I think that more often than not boredom, frustration, or even mental blocks were most responsible for my losing so many jobs.

I'm very intelligent and creative, and I have my father's strong work ethic, but the fog has compromised both. Unemployment, shoddy workmanship, and a poor attitude have been some of the side effects. Furthermore, so many jobs and so many negative dealings with employers left me with a sense of futility and kept me from reaching many of my realistic goals. I went into a job with lowered expectations. I always knew I wouldn't last long in my new position. I knew there would eventually be conflict, and I constantly anticipated negative repercussions. I also knew that I could never hold a job long enough to achieve a high place in a company. I would always be a subordinate, and I would not achieve success as I got older.

In addition, because of my unstable employment background, potential new employers who might have offered more prestigious positions declined to do so. For example, failing the police exam with the Hillsborough Police Department wasn't the only time I was turned down for the position of police officer. When I applied to other departments and passed their civil servant tests, I was ultimately turned down for the position of police officer due to my extensive employment history. According to police department officials, the fact that I'd held so many jobs showed a lack of stability and was reason enough to reject me.

Of course, the fact that I'd been fired from so many jobs didn't look good on police department applications either. At last count there have been eight jobs from which I was fired (including the military, of course) and eighteen I've walked out on. This tally doesn't include temporary jobs or the time I walked out on my brother, Richard, while working for him hauling brush. The worst part of leaving that job was the fact that I had to walk ten miles home from the job site.

There's also the interesting diversity of jobs I've held. In fact, I've had almost as many different types of jobs as number of jobs: from lowly pizza cook to legal clerk to respected park ranger. I think it's important to elaborate on my job history to show the pattern that can arise in an ADDer's working life. So let's go back to the beginning.

My first paying job after outgrowing the paper route was busboy for an Italian restaurant. Nothing significant happened while I was employed at the restaurant, and I was never threatened with being fired, but I wasn't there long enough to merit any trouble. Nonetheless, the restaurant treated its employees poorly, and the pay was low, so I didn't have a great deal of incentive to stay. I lasted about two months, shuttling dirty dishes from one place to another before throwing in the dishtowel. I just got tired of picking up after people.

About a year later, when I quit high school, I got a job with Mail Courier Service, the company that made it possible to fill my pockets with a bit of folding money and, of course, helped me get laid for the first time. But when I backed one of the MCS delivery vans into a dumpster at about thirty-five mph, the job and I had to part ways. To this day, I attribute the accident to impatience and a foggy lack of focus. Just before modifying the delivery van, my license was revoked because of all the moving violations I received. So I would have lost the job with MCS anyway. It was my first failure to toe that old working-class line. I felt inadequate, and it wouldn't be the last time.

After recovering from losing the job with MCS, I got my G.E.D. and entered college, only to quit school shortly thereafter so that I could take a job with the California Conservation Corp and pursue Carrie, my first love.

The CCC gave me another chance at being gainfully employed and, at seventeen, I was again stashing money away as I set my sights on success. The work at the CCC was hard, but during my Carrie phase, of course, I didn't care. I felt important when I wore my forest-ranger-like uniform, and I knew I was learning valuable skills for working with the parks department. But once again, a foreign element compromised my ability to keep this great job: the breakup with Carrie—well, that and the fact that I had brought a .22 rifle onto CCC grounds. Since my CCC home was way out in the boonies, I thought it would be fun to plink away at cans when I wasn't working, but firearms weren't allowed on the premises. Even so, the fact that I'd broken this CCC rule shouldn't have been enough to force me to hand in my uniform. I had a good enough record with the CCC at the time. They probably would have overlooked the gun offense, but Carrie dumped me, and I was an emotional wreck. I felt I had no choice other than to seek a new career path. Looking back on the situation, I realize that I should have been able to see past my problem with Carrie and stay focused on becoming a forest ranger.

But ADD clouds rational thought and heightens irrational behavior; impulse takes over and logical conclusions are ignored. Even though I've been able to recognize that this irrational thinking repeatedly takes over my work life—albeit after the event—I still haven't been able to keep it from causing havoc. The bottom line is that emotions are my dictators and they rule my life.

I've always envied the robot-like people who worked with me, who blocked out boredom and routine, or dismissed a boss or co-worker's harsh words just to stay on track and keep a job; or those individuals who didn't let a relationship with a significant other jeopardize job security. I can only surmise that, because of aforementioned bouts of irrational thinking, I've just never been able to see the big picture and maintain the right perspective.

It was this lack of perspective and irrational thinking that led to my enlistment in the military after the CCC and to the long road of discovery I'd have in khaki. But there was another job just prior to military service. I was a cook for Marine World Africa U.S.A.—a theme park situated in Redwood City on California's marshlands.

I spent most of the day at this new job preparing for the onslaught of hungry theme park patrons. I always felt anxious about a half an hour before they arrived, and I endeavored to lay down row upon row of hamburger patties and buns as quickly as I could. After each park show, the lines of ravenous people showed up like clockwork on the other side of the grill. And that led to the main problem with this job—pressure. Pressure and ADD just don't mix well. Because of this, it was inevitable that I'd have a run-in with my overbearing boss. One day, I was just a little too uppity with him. I actually challenged the way he ran the kitchen. He overreacted by brandishing a meat cleaver and threatening to kill me with it. About ten minutes later when things had settled down, my boss threatened me again, this time with being dismissed from the park. Had I stayed there a week longer, I'm sure I would have been handed my walking papers. Luckily my delayed Air Force enlistment came to an end, and like the cavalry that arrives just in the nick of time to rescue a lost cause, the military whisked me away from burgers and culinary hatchets for a life with screaming sergeants and even more pressure.

During my stint in the military, I took another job washing dishes at a country club, but only for a very short period. I should have known better since I realized it was a boring job. It wouldn't be until 1984 that I'd land my next job, or I should say series of jobs.

After returning from England and the soap opera that had gone on there, I looked for the first job I could find. I didn't even think about a career. I just needed money. I didn't have the luxury of thinking that the job I took would be beneath me.

Haag & Haag, a camera store in Palo Alto, California, fitted the bill. The store tried its best to train me to use its photo processing equipment so that I could develop the locals' never-ending influx of film, which I eventually turned into portraits of babies' first steps or remembrances of the family's trip to Disneyland. I hated sitting in the store day after day. The machine was noisy, and a chemical smell filled the air. I did my best to stave off the urge to walk out onto bustling University Avenue, the same avenue that turned into Palm after it crossed El Camino. It ultimately led into the heart of world-renowned Stanford University, where students worked on becoming some of the most important ants in America's enormous lucrative colonies.

The notion of Stanford's importance and its close proximity only added salt to the wounds of failure. When I had entered the military, I had thought I'd make something of myself; I'd be a success after my discharge. But at Haag & Haag I was just another worker holding a menial entry-level position, and I was no better off than I was before the military. I had traded four years of my life for an elusive notion of stature and ascension wrapped in the guise of rank and a well-meant contribution to God and country.

But now, no longer a part of any military family, I was just a film developer with a deadline, in a job designed for desperate teenagers hoping to earn enough to buy that first car so they could drink beer in some parking lot or get laid if luck was in their corner that night.

All the while, Stanford's crème de la crème were working to find a cure for cancer or test some new technology that would give America's military an edge on its competition. And I would never be a part of any of it. Even so, as insignificant as it was, I sought to keep that tiny little job of mine. Although it wasn't science or technology I had to focus on, I strained my mind to keep up with the workload and the film-developing process. In the end, it was all for naught. Somewhere in the never-ceasing instructions and explanations from my Haag & Haag supervisors, I became lost. Numbers and plus and minus signs floated before my eyes. I knew that, somehow, all these numbers and symbols had something to do with proper film development. If they weren't applied correctly, photos would end up too dark or too light, or blurred like some impressionist's masterpiece. But I just couldn't fathom the precision of what I was supposed to do. Unfortunately, every photo-processing disaster known to the camera store—and a few more I invented myself—took place when I was at the helm of the large photo-developing machine that almost filled Haag & Haag's entire store. When all was said and done, and customers came to pick up their orders, they usually weren't happy. Who would be? Who wants a photo album full of unrecognizable or blurry friends and family members to record life's journey? Some of the photos were even more poorly developed than my mind.

All too often, those who oversaw my work had to do it again just to keep customers satisfied. Obviously, because of this, I soon became an ever-present burden to the Haag & Haag mission. After all, I was pulling superiors away from their more important work. They should have let me go, but my employers gave me a lot of latitude. I think the owner decided that he'd keep me on no matter what. He assumed that I'd eventually catch on to the work I had been hired to do. He liked military veterans too much to fire me. I'm sure it was because I was a veteran that he'd hired me in the first place. But in the end it wouldn't be my boss who would kick me out of his shop; it would be me. I had to fire myself, to run away from a daily confusion that completely overwhelmed me; from an embarrassment that drove me to the point of not being able to face any more of my superiors' heavy sighs or bouts of hair pulling. I politely, and appropriately, left my little stool by the big machine at which I worked and left Haag & Haag forever. I doubted I could ever again muster the courage to take my own film in for developing, lest I would see one of those photo-processing machines again and be reminded of my fall from camera store grace.

This time I decided to seek jobs that didn't require very much thinking, but for one reason or another, even those that demanded little mental effort didn't work out either. I lasted about a day at a Round Table Pizza restaurant down the street from Haag & Haag because the place was just too frantic for me, and about the same amount of time at a gas station because I couldn't figure out how to use the cash register.

A few weeks after leaving Haag & Haag, I got a job at an oriental carpet store. I helped to flip carpets so prospective customers could look at them. On the other side of these massive and intricately woven rugs with their elaborate patterns and colors was my fellow flippee, a young man with a daily wise-guy smile and patronizing gaze. With each heavy carpet's backflip, (so the next could be viewed), I would get a barrage of silent disrespect from my younger co-worker, Kevin. And when customers weren't in the store, my carpet-flipping comrade would comment on how I had screwed up my life, and how I was the sorriest individual he'd ever met. I learned from the owner's son that this young man was a recovering cocaine addict, and I think his drug usage contributed to that flippant tongue of his.

I really hit rock bottom taking that carpet store job, and I often yearned to be like those together types who came in to buy the expensive imports that probably covered floors in mansions in nearby Atherton or Los Altos. Sleek watches and cars to match indicated the carpet customers' successes in life. These expensive material possessions also indicated prestigious degrees and professions. And there I was with my mindless, insignificant robotic movements, clad in my thrift shop clothing and turning over carpets to suit a discerning yuppie's whim or decorator's color scheme. I barely made enough money to buy half of one of the non-slip mats to be placed beneath the carpets.

Somehow, I managed to look past the stares of my tormentor as I mind-lessly flipped carpets. I got used to Kevin's behavior, and even though I didn't enjoy the way he delivered his assessment, he was right about what type of person I was and what I had done with my life.

I soon lost myself in the store's piped-in classical music, in the brilliant movements of masters long dead, and I made sure I knew when the carpet store owner wanted me to help a customer. A few snaps or minute head movements were the signals for my co-worker and me to move.

When that unmistakable nod was finally given for a carpet to be rolled up and thrown into an awaiting delivery van, the carpet store owner smiled and fawned over a customer like some sort of grateful Bedouin in a seedy marketplace where camels spat and women looked furtively through well-placed veils. When I had to help carry the carpet to a customer's car, the bent-backed owner and his wife always lingered by the door, nearly salivat-ing, as one of the five-thousand-dollar ornate objects left its brethren.

The job wasn't all insults and finger snaps though. I did have an affinity with someone in the store, Terry, a wannabe novelist seamstress who mended carpets in a dark corner. Since this woman seemed to have more writing experience than I did, I listened to her advice on polishing the novel I'd been working on since the military about a man who wanted to be a rock star. Terry's encouragement meant a lot to me, and it gave me the hope I needed during this dark time in my life. The idea that someday I might be able to publish something I'd written spurred me onward. It was the only thing that my foggy mind had to hang onto; a great feat to overcome all my shortcom-ings. After that, the carpets seemed to get lighter, and I treated my tormentor with the same wise-ass comments and patronizing smiles he sent across the piles to me. In fact, I think I even one-upped him. I might be a nobody now, my looks seemed to say, but you just wait. Someday, I'll be a household name, and you'll still be snorting cocaine and flipping carpets. I couldn't feel any more elated—that is until I allowed the seamstress to read an excerpt from the novel. Terry's succinct comments about the lengthy piece of fiction I'd given her summed up my writing abilities so that even the comatose would understand. In short, the work lacked what it took to make it to bookstores, and I needed to acquire basic grammatical and punctuation skills. Her recommendations: read more and take an English 101 class.

After that advice, the carpets got heavier again, and I lost hold of my dream of becoming a famous writer. The man on the other side of the carpet helping me flip again represented everything I hated in the clear minded; at least in those who ridiculed and sought to cause others to feel abnormal and lacking. Kevin once again knew he had the upper hand. He knew I'd taken a blow to my already fragile self-confidence, and he would take advantage of this new turn of events. I could almost hear my nemesis across those large plush rectangles saying, "What made you think you could be a writer? Just flip. Flip, boy, flip. Welcome back to the land of flakes and fools."

Another series of wise-guy smiles and patronizing looks had returned with unsurpassed commitment. His smugness said it all: he'd won again. And with every flip of those heavy carpets, I got one step closer to crossing the line, to literally bridging the gap between us.

"Come on, man," my adversary had begun that day before we clashed. "It's simple. You just flip when I flip. We flip together, get it?"

The customer we'd been showing carpets to earlier had us flip carpets almost all the way to the bottom of the stack so she could get a good look at each one. Now we had the laborious job of flipping the carpets back over so they would lie atop one another as they had before the picky woman had walked into the store. It was the same thing over and over: walk back to a flipped up carpet, grab an end while Kevin grabbed another end, and pull the carpet back down to a flat position.

"So I heard about your book." There was that smile and look of his again. *Walk. Grab. Pull. And Flip.* That's all I kept telling myself so I could avoid Kevin's words.

Kevin shot a look at the store's owner, who smiled back before pretending to look back at some paperwork. "A rock star, huh?" Kevin added.

I only looked at him and walked back to grab another carpet.

"Like a Van Halen type maybe, right?"

Walk…grab…

"You know, a little..." He did an overly dramatic air guitar rift before grabbing his end of the carpet.

I gave him another stare. Then he gave up strumming, chuckled, and grabbed his end of the carpet. We pulled it back down. I tried to take in the intricate Arabian designs of the carpet, its velvety sheen, the vibrant reds, blues, and yellows. Anything to keep my eyes away from another one of his demeaning looks. But just as with the number of carpets we had to pull back down, there seemed to be no end to the looks Kevin cast my way.

"My little brother likes to write stories, too. You know, he plays at it like you. Once upon a time and all that crap."

Walk...grab...pull...flip...walk...

"Maybe you two could get together some time."

Then, thankfully, we pulled the last carpet back into place, and I lingered near the front of the store and away from Kevin. I stared out at University Avenue. A steady flow of cars went by, west toward Stanford University and east toward Highway 101. They represented all the possibilities that lay beyond my little enclosed world with Kevin. He came over by me and leaned against a pile of carpets, staring out of the store just the way I was, but I could also tell that he intermittently looked at me. There was a plan in his head; he was trying to get a rise out of me, and it was working.

Kevin turned toward the pile to smooth out a few tiny wrinkles, but the carpet didn't really need smoothing. "You want me to set up some time you and my brother could meet?" He shot another look at me and then smiled and shot a look at the back of the store; probably at the owner again, but I couldn't be certain since I was still trying so hard to ignore Kevin.

"Of course, you'd have to wait for Timmy to get home from school. He rides one of those big yellow school buses. You know, with the flashing red lights that make you have to stop what you're doing in life. I hate those. I just want to zoom by them. But everything gets put on hold, right. Just like everything gets put on hold in life, huh? You think you're going along at a good pace, and then wham," he said, striking the carpet with the palm of his hand, "you're stuck right where you are."

A woman stopped outside for a moment, put her face to the storefront window and cupped her hands around her eyes so she could see in better. It seemed as though she looked right at Kevin and me, but I knew it must have been at the carpets behind us. I turned to see the owner get up, a hungry look in his eyes, but the woman turned to go, and the owner sat back down.

"Yeah, stuck, man," Kevin reiterated, turning to face University Avenue again.

"But how can you ever feel stuck, Kevin?" I said, leaning back by him.

"What's that?" he chuckled. He turned to face me and then shot another look in the owner's direction.

"Well, I mean how can anything slow you down with all that coke always shoved up your nose?"

Kevin's smile faded and he straightened up. He started to walk by me, but even though there was plenty of room to do so, he bumped into my shoulder. I pushed him away. Then, swiftly, Kevin had me in a headlock.

Immediately, I thought of all those little martial arts tricks about striking someone's genitals or simultaneously striking a person's back and stomach with both fists. There was any number of things I could do: proven movements that would get someone to release you instantaneously. But as much as I hated Kevin, I just couldn't bring myself to seriously hurt him. I was angry about the damned headlock but I became angrier at my reluctance to inflict damage. After all, he deserved to be hurt. We stayed like that for only a few seconds longer before the owner came over and detached us. In a fury, I pushed Kevin back again, and he rushed for me again, but the owner stopped him. I didn't move until the owner did so. By then everything had taken its toll: the monotonous carpet flipping; Kevin's taunts; the harsh appraisal of my manuscript; the fact that I'd taken a job that I felt was beneath me; and too many other things to even name at that moment. I turned toward the back of the store, all the while yelling at Kevin never to show his face to me again. But he wasn't angry in the least. He couldn't even give me that. Kevin knew he'd won again, made me lose it. The patronizing smiles were back. Even the owner joined in, but tried not to show it. I glanced at Terry as I stormed passed her, and just like that, I flung open the back door to an uncertain future.

For the next hour or so, I walked aimlessly around Palo Alto, still thinking about why I'd gotten into that headlock and how I could have gotten out of it. I imagined my fingers gouging out Kevin's eyes or clutching his genitals and pulling, the way I'd pulled hard on those heavy carpets. But I also thought that I should have been able to just strong-arm my way free without using any of the harsh tactics I'd been taught. And then my anger turned to self-pity. I kept running the headlock scene over and over again in my head. In the scene, I saw how I had suffered the humiliation of the store's few onlookers until the owner eventually forced my attacker to release me.

All the while, I imagined the seamstress steadily sewing those tattered carpets at her little table in a little cove filled with dust and dim lighting. Her head probably only momentarily lifted to view the commotion in the prettier part of the store.

I never returned to that carpet store. I even tried to avoid seeing it when I had to drive down University Avenue. Later, my self-pity turned to anger again. In fact, I was more than angry; I was livid. Still, when I had time to dwell on what had actually taken place, I began to see things in a different light. I saw that I had blamed the way I had been treated on someone else, but I now knew I was the only one to blame. Yes, the man I worked with was a jerk. He should have been a little more compassionate, but it wasn't necessarily his behavior that was the impediment between a peaceful work environment and me. It was my inability to ignore his attacks and keep my job. This lack of self-control was the fog's doing again, its nature of blocking out reason and negotiation, like the child who can't work out a problem on the playground. It's easy to see this now, but I was in a state of confusion at the carpet store, unable to think clearly and, as usual, subject to the uncontrollable impulsiveness that leaves me with only one way of dealing with confrontation: confrontation.

But it didn't matter that I was able to analyze the situation after my dramatic carpet store exit; I had burned another bridge and I needed to move on. I've always found that one of the best things to do after setting flames to the past is to return to something familiar. So I went back to an old friend: driving. Since I usually drove alone, I was less likely to get into trouble.

I got a delivery job at Baker Graphics, a printer/copy shop around the corner from the carpet store. I was hired to pick up blueprints for architectural firms needing copies. The job at Baker Graphics went fairly smoothly, but there were occasions when I was at odds with the people around me. A burly printer from New York threatened to kick my ass after I told him I'd never live in New York. Another driver who rode with me during a short training period was driven crazy by my unwavering refusal to exceed speed limits. And there was the time when I rammed the rear end of a car waiting to merge onto a busy on-ramp with the tiny station wagon I used for deliveries.

But even with occasional minor problems like these, I managed to do what was expected of me. Most of the trouble I got into took place when I'd hang around Baker Graphics during the daily lag time between assignments. As with those idle times in the Air Force, these periods were filled with busy work: emptying trash, sweeping, or cleaning vehicles. When these things were done, I'd just stand in front of my boss's glass office and gawk at her, hoping for a delivery so I could get on the road again. My boss at Baker Graphics was a lovely woman with long black hair. I dreamed of being intimate with her. I guess the only reason my dream didn't come true was because that black-haired beauty was married—well, that and the fact that she probably wasn't interested in me.

There was another woman at Baker Graphics I befriended. Camille was a Hispanic free spirit who worked in customer service. She was constantly on the run at Baker Graphics, and I don't even remember how I got her attention. But it didn't take long for us to begin hanging out together after work. My Hispanic honey's true love was art, and one night I got a glimpse of the galaxy she'd painted on the bedroom ceiling of her apartment, replete with glow-in-the-dark stars and planets. Camille introduced me to San Francisco's Erotic Exotic Ball, a hedonistic event, which deepened my obsession with sex.

But my new friend's companionship wasn't enough to keep me satisfied for long at Baker Graphics. Eventually, I yearned for more than making deliveries and being laughed at behind my back by the skilled co-workers and professionals with whom I interacted.

After reevaluating my possibilities, I decided to go back to driving tractor-trailers. The advantages were twofold: more money and more respect. Although I still knew how to drive semis, a slew of television commercials for a truck driving school sold me on the idea that I needed to hone my skills for civilian big rig use. In hindsight, I'm sure I could have gotten by without the added lessons. However, there was one thing I needed that wasn't in dispute: a Class One license. I got by in the military without one, but as a civilian I needed one of these driver's license endorsements, and truck driving school was one easy way of getting the use of a rig for a day's drive to the Department of Motor Vehicles for a driving test.

So I said goodbye to Baker Graphics and hello to Superior Training, a truck driving school in Rialto, CA. In six weeks, the time it took to complete my training at Superior, I had my Class One license, and I was back up in Northern California looking for another job.

But I soon discovered that most companies I applied to did not care that I had a pretty little certificate from a truck driving school and that I had driven rigs in the military. They wanted me to have current experience driving trucks in the civilian world. I almost gave up trying to get a job in this field when, out of the blue, I was offered one by a very small company owned by a couple of tough Irish brothers.

So began my new career in a dirty lot next to Candlestick Park where Willie Mays and the San Francisco Giants used to play. Working for Scannell Brothers Drayage was not what I expected from all those pretty Superior Training commercials inserted in between "Gomer Pyle, U.S.M.C." segments. In the commercials, truckers drove fancy, state-of-the art rigs for major companies that paid drivers major salaries. In reality, I accepted a job working for an obscure company where I drove old trucks that pulled rusty trailers. They were kept in a yard with barely enough room to maneuver. The yard was unpaved and grew thick with mud when it rained. In addition to the lousy trucks and working conditions, I had to deal with deteriorating wooden docks and mechanically unsound pallet jacks, which were ill equipped to handle freight.

The crude working conditions were better suited to some third world country. I delivered freight that workers reluctantly forklifted into dreary warehouses until such time that it was summoned forth to be moved again. Although I was ecstatic to be a truck driver again, the incredible workload and the depressing surroundings took their toll. Maybe if I had been earning the money I merited given my skills and credentials, I could have overlooked my predicament and held on longer at Scannell Brothers, but that's a big maybe.

Each morning at five-thirty, I'd sit in that cold San Francisco lot in my brown Audi 100 a good half hour prior to beginning work, listening to a U2 cassette, dreading the first step into that mud and into one of those jarring rigs. I'd wait there like that, clad in green overalls and seated in my German car, Bono's working-class vocals blaring out over the steam of my coffee, until the absolute last second before leaving my pampered and insulated world. Finally, on one particularly nondescript day, I made the decision to take this separation between my world and Scannel Brothers one step further and I left the rough-hewn trucking outpost for good.

Even though I was happy to be leaving, I wondered why I couldn't be happy where I was, even if that place was an industrial wasteland completely void of soul and aesthetics. I think the lack of aesthetics was key to my leaving. For some reason, I've always drifted toward environments where there are lots of trees, or where there is at least an ocean within view. Nature is another kind of stimulus I've clung to in my life. My dad used to take me to his shops so much I got burned out on those industrial complexes with all their metal and grime. I needed more natural surroundings, the smells and colors of trees. I toyed with many ideas, as I folded my truck driving overalls and placed them into the farthest recess of my duplex's closet. Whatever the reason, I'd get myself far away from San Francisco's working-class environment, but I didn't know what I should do next.

Ideas are wonderful, and they've helped me to gain perspective in my life. But I didn't have the luxury of dwelling on the next long-term venture after Scannell Brothers. I needed money. So I took another delivery job, this time delivering flowers for Lum Toy Florist in Atherton. The job was simple: deliver flowers. Flowers were prettier than freight and, incredibly, even though the workload was lighter, the job paid as much as the one I'd held with Scannell Brothers. The surroundings were better too, mostly wealthy homes surrounded by well-trimmed yards, many in the California foothills.

People were usually happy to receive flowers. These happy customers were a breath of fresh air after dealing with workers who seemed indifferent to, or bothered by, loads of freight. Another benefit to delivering flowers was that it didn't require as much effort as delivering freight. Flowers were relatively light and didn't require elaborate tie-down procedures or weight distribution considerations. The delivery schedule could get hectic when the holidays came along, but during these times I held to a system I'd painstakingly plan out before embarking on deliveries with many stops. Delivery plans like these became almost military-like in their conception in order to maximize efficiency and decrease flower wilting. Before getting into one of Lum Toy's vans, I'd study large maps in the small floral war room. As with any delivery plan, a number of factors had to be taken into consideration. Traffic. Construction. Speed limits. Pre-set delivery times. Even weather. I loved the challenge. After all, order and methodology were some of my favorite pastimes. Remnants of all those elaborate games I used to play as a child with all those inanimate objects. An ADDer's heaven.

I didn't seem to have any problems I can recall with my position at Lum Toy. In fact, I developed a friendship with a floral arranger named Connie who invited me over her house a few times, someone I also later visited at a bar where she worked when Lum Toy went out of business. The store's closure took us both by surprise. I showed up for work on a Saturday only to find a San Mateo County sheriff's notice and padlock on one of the florist shop's large sliding doors. I found out later that one of the owners of Lum Toy, a really nice guy, had apparently been involved in some sort of theft of the store's assets, and the police had to force the business to cease all operations immediately and take possession of its property. I remember thinking how odd it was for such a thriving business to close its doors to the public so suddenly. And then I moved on.

I believe this was the start of my infatuation with law enforcement, and I yearned to be a police officer someday. I watched all those cop shows on TV wondering if I could be part of such a demanding profession. All the action appealed to me. Car chases. Foot chases. Drug busts. The whole lot. I began studying for civil servant tests and doing some research about what it took to make it as a police officer. In 1989, I tested for an entry-level police officer position with the California Highway Patrol. The organization turned me down because of my background.

But before the CHP rejection, and shortly after losing my job with Lum Toy, I got a job with San Mateo Security Service. It somewhat fulfilled my desire to be a cop. I was handed a pair of handcuffs, a pretty police look-alike uniform, and a shiny silver badge. But unlike a cadet who's just graduated from the police academy with loads of special training, I received absolutely no training whatsoever from San Mateo Security Service. Nonetheless, I was sent out to protect life and property—or at least to pretend to. Instead of all that cop show action I longed for, I spent the day or night watching for suspicious behavior requiring police notification, should there be a need for notification. Of course, there never was.

Most nights, I nearly fell asleep from boredom, but there were a few exciting assignments. One such assignment occurred when I was sent to keep an eye on a picket line near the San Francisco International Airport to make sure scabs didn't cause any trouble; not that I would have known what to do if they had. And there was a New Year's Eve party at a bar bursting with boisterous airline mechanics; I made sure that I stayed glued to an extremely large security guard co-worker on that one. Then there was the time they sent me to a McDonald's in a busy mall where I made sure loitering teenagers didn't bother customers. I did see action on that assignment. One of the teenage boys threw ice at someone, and I had a talk with him. That ended the ice incident. But I'm sure the teenager snickered behind my back, the way people on "Mayberry RFD" scoffed about Barney Fife.

Ultimately, I had to hand in my badge at San Mateo Security Service. The overall monotony was just too much for me, and the idea that I really wasn't trained to be a security guard always stuck with me. What if something truly hairy goes down? I remember thinking. I won't be able to handle

it. The bottom line is that without the preparation and backing of a city or
state, the rent-a-cop thing just doesn't work.

But I still needed to pay off that expensive Superior Training loan I'd
rung up, so after terminating my employment with San Mateo Security, I
rushed out to find another job. Basically, I closed my eyes and thrust a finger
at the want ads where it landed on a job listing for restaurant help. I found
out it was an ad for a pizza restaurant owned by two guys who had left the
mainstream and tried to make a go of it on their own. One of the owners,
Shawn, had spent the past twenty-five years working for one of the Round
Table Pizza franchises in California. The man was a jolly, likeable fellow
with keen business sense, and he never seemed to get flustered, even during
the busy lunch hour.

On the surface, the other owner, Mark, was an amiable man too, who
kissed up to his customers, but he patronized his employees and governed
them with an iron fist. He was a spiteful recovering alcoholic who didn't like
me, and if it hadn't been for Shawn I wouldn't have lasted a month. As it was,
I managed to stay on about a year, working as hard as anyone ever could. I
performed every duty required in the small restaurant. There were usually
three of us, max, working at any given time. And each of us was required to
prepare any pizza, salad, or pasta dish on the menu, along with other selec-
tions, from scratch. We were also required to man the bar, wash dishes, make
pizza dough, sweep, mop, and do a myriad of other tasks.

There was a fringe benefit to working at Mark's Brick Fournous Pizza
Restaurant: one free meal a day. This was important, since I was now living in
my large Pontiac Catalina. Thanks to an agreement with a mechanic friend
of mine, I parked on a gas station lot about fifteen miles from work. He also
let me use his shower. It wasn't that I couldn't afford a room. I just couldn't
pay rent and pay off my truck driving school loan at the same time. I decided
to forgo paying rent with the hope of getting rid of that nagging debt.

It wasn't too bad living in the car at first. There was ample room for
sleeping in its back seat, and I liked listening to some loudmouth radio DJ
when I got off work around eleven-thirty p.m. Before taking in the DJ's
show, I'd play chess with Shawn, or I'd visit one of the nearby bars where I'd
long for some drunken woman to wander into range. Of course, this only
happened twice the whole time I frequented the bars. Whether I scored or
not, I'd always be back at Mark's the next morning making pizzas.

Working at the restaurant was sometimes tedious, but at least I stayed
busy. Everything was fairly straightforward and within my powers of com-

prehension. There were occasional times when I had trouble using the restaurant's cash register and I'd catch flak from Mark, but nothing else really threw me. I think I made a better Greek salad than anyone else who worked there. In fact, some customers took me aside and requested in a whisper that I be the one to prepare the salad that night. It had to do with the way spices, red wine vinegar and Pompean olive oil were combined. To this day, my hands recall the proper shakes of spices and liquids to add to this epicurean delight, and now, some sixteen years later, I often prepare the salad just the way I did then.

I saw a lot of employees come and go while working at the restaurant, but my position seemed secure. The owners hired a couple of really good managers to oversee things occasionally so they didn't have to be there all the time. I wondered why they didn't make me a manager, but it didn't really bother me too much. At least I seemed invaluable to my employers, and the fact that I held the top score on an arcade game in the back of the restaurant was a testament to the fact that I invested a lot more than just work time at the restaurant.

Still, things heated up between Mark and me. He talked about me to other employees when he thought I didn't know it, and I could see him snickering from the other side of the one-room restaurant in a wall-length mirror, eyeing me suspiciously, wondering what mistakes he could catch me in to further his cause toward my dismissal.

It wasn't long before Mark convinced Shawn that I was bad with customers and that I should be let go. I suppose I was a little short with the drunken softball players who broke the day's tranquility every so often when they suddenly filled the restaurant with their vociferous conversations. Oscar the Grouch from Sesame Street would have been proud of their messes. I could have been a little more cordial with customers, but the fog had retreated into another place that was calm and orderly, and most of the people who frequented Mark's disturbed that peaceful place.

Just because I didn't smile enough when serving drinks or ferrying pizza didn't mean I should have been fired, but that's what happened. I felt that Shawn really liked me and didn't want to see me go, but his hands were tied. So now I was both unemployed and homeless. To make matters worse, I became very sick one day after eating at a restaurant near my parked car. I'm not sure what caused the sickness, but it landed me in the emergency room where I was pumped with fluids and told I had too much oxygen in my blood.

I ended up moving into my mother's duplex, a place I'd spend most of my pre-marriage years because of money problems. In fact, I'd only rented two other rooms prior to becoming homeless and prior to moving in with my mother, both of which I was unable to keep because of a lack of funds. One of the rooms I rented was in a house in Belmont, and I especially regretted losing that room since I'd developed a friendship with a roommate who used to go to the movies with me a lot as long as his epilepsy stayed under control.

It was embarrassing to live with my mother, so I usually neglected to tell people about my living arrangements. She had always been a strong little woman with only her children's interests at heart. I liked looking at a photo of her taken with my dad sometime in the forties. The picture showed a beautiful black-haired woman wearing gloves and a black veil that flowed from a tiny hat. I could tell by the way my mother smiled in the photo that she must have been a fun person to be around. But sharing time with her when she was much older, I knew her only as a pushy, exacting woman who constantly told me I needed to go to church and live life another way. I know she always meant well, but my mother's interest in my life was exceedingly invasive and taxing. I had reached another low in my life. A man in his mid-twenties shouldn't have been living with his mother, and he should have had a career. But obviously things just weren't working out, and I had few options. Since I needed an eventual way out of my mother's depressing post-divorce brown duplex, I enrolled in the county's Regional Occupational Program (R.O.P.) for free training to become a park aide.

The county course taught the rudimentary skills one needed to work in a park; things such as basic tool knowledge and plant identification. It was all very mundane stuff, but it was fun being outdoors surrounded by trees and other people who had the same goals as I did. We were all pretty much simpletons, rejects from one place or another. Most students were younger than I was, dropouts from high schools and dazed pot smokers trying to get their lives on track, so I fitted right in. I've often felt that I fit in with society's losers and wannabees. There's much less pressure around this ilk of people, as long as they aren't the criminal or badass types.

My R.O.P. teacher was a very knowledgeable blonde woman who I immediately fell for and went out of my way to please. If she needed a volunteer or additional help moving some brush or chainsawing a log, I was her foggy man. Amazingly, given her incredible patience and knack for teaching, I was able to learn just about anything, even things that would have normally been beyond my scope, such as surveying.

All in all, I liked what I was doing on the park aide course, and I attacked tasks with a fervor that I hadn't felt in a long time. I was a new person with the dream of someday becoming a forest ranger. I thought I was off to a good start in realizing this dream while working along with the rest of the class one day to repair one of the county park's maintenance sheds. The head ranger of the park was looking for seasonal park aides, and the way I busted my butt to put on the roof convinced him to hire me. I felt fortunate to be picked from the rest of the group. Landing a job as a park aide was very competitive, and not many R.O.P. students were as lucky as I was. My teacher was happy for me, but she told me that I seemed too eager to please those who were in charge and that I should relax a little.

But I didn't pay much attention to this advice as I embarked on a new path with my new job at Huddart Park. I kept right on working as hard as I had been doing with R.O.P. and no task was beyond me now that I wore a park uniform with a California bear on it and packed a heavy radio like those the rangers carried. Working in the forest reminded me of my stint with the CCC. The smell of California bay laurels triggered memories of being with Carrie, and some of the work was similar to that done with the CCC. Things such as trail building, running chainsaws, and periodic park maintenance. But the majority of work I did at the park did differ from what I'd done with the CCC, since emptying garbage cans and barbecue grills and cleaning restrooms took up most of my day. Because of this, I soon began to feel like a glorified janitor, and it was difficult to justify staying in a position that pretended to be more than it was.

There were select occasions, however, when I felt I was performing more than janitorial work. One time, for example, when the public came to witness the building of a handicapped-accessible trail, I was the center of attention kneeling there in the redwood duff as I drove in a steel stake meant to hold a guide wire for the visually impaired. That is until I was distracted so much by one person's questions about what I was doing that I missed the stake with my five-pound hammer and struck one of my fingers instead. Later, at a nearby hospital, I received seven stitches for the throbbing gash. The attention paid to me earlier didn't carry as much weight as the hammer, and I kicked myself for once again not staying focused.

Another time, I had to respond to a rare park emergency, and that made me feel I was worthy of more than just making sure that restrooms had enough toilet paper and that barbecuers would find a clean pit when they came to raise hell. As with most emergencies, this one was unexpected. One afternoon, my co-worker Rick overheard an urgent call on the radio and we had to speed off to offer assistance. Apparently, a young boy had fallen off a log into a creek and landed on some exposed rocks. The rush to get to the boy was something beyond anything else I'd experienced since working at Huddart. It was the closest I'd ever come to being like those police officers I still admired so much.

When we reached our destination on the forest road near the accident, a boy of about eleven or twelve flagged us down. We jumped out of the truck, leaving both doors open, and ran over to the breathless boy.

"He's...he's in there," the boy panted and pointed at a trail which led up into a thick growth of bushes, ferns, and redwoods. Without hesitation, Rick and I followed the boy up the trail. It was tough going, with jagged granite outcroppings and thick roots that had all but overtaken the path. Rick was just as eager as I was, but I could tell that he wasn't up to the challenge the hill presented. He kept stopping to catch his breath and lean against a tree. Once he stumbled on some loose gravel. I thought he was going to fall down into a crevasse that ran beside the trail, but then he caught hold of a branch and pulled himself back up. Things didn't get any better for him. About halfway up the narrow trail, Rick stopped and bent over. He spit out phlegm and we both knew he wasn't going to be able to continue.

"I can't...make...it," he said between spits. He slowly stood back up and handed me our only handheld radio and first aid kit. "I'll go back and wait for the paramedics," he panted. "You go on ahead." He turned around and descended the trail we'd just climbed, and I turned to face the boy who had been leading us.

"Come on," the boy said. "He's not much farther." After about another two miles, the trail wound down into a lush valley. I heard the creek before I saw it. It had the lovely trickling sound I'd heard so many times before when hiking in these same hills. There was a pleasant smell of bay laurel in the air, and the poison oak I hated so much was brilliant red. Every now and then, I glimpsed the sun through a space where the trees didn't absolutely block out the rich blue sky. The sun's rays illuminated the ferns. It was such a perfect day and such a magical forest that I could almost imagine a band of tiny fairies coming to guide us to their secret city. If I hadn't known there was an injured boy ahead of us, I might have thought this was just another nature hike.

Then, all of a sudden, I saw a doe and her fawn bolt about fifteen feet from us, and I heard someone yell out in pain just beyond an immense boulder. When I rounded the boulder, I was met with a sight in stark contrast to the tranquil forest setting. A boy lay about twenty feet below a redwood that had fallen across two boulders. It was a tempting bridge. A pristine creek ran between the boulders. Its indifferent waters flowed past the boy as he cried out to his friend who was now beside him.

"Hang on, Pete. I brought help."

At first, I took in the scene as if it were all in my imagination. Surely, I was at home dreaming up some television-like action drama before the day's monotony of emptying out all the park's beerbottle-and-chicken-bone-filled trash cans. But of course that was just silly. And there were no tiny fairies either, just an injured boy lying face up with blood covering his face. And I was the only one who could help him.

I knelt down in the creek's icy water, drenching my thick, brown park-aide pants. I tried to locate the source of the blood that flowed over my outstretched hands. I carefully parted the boy's hair until I found a deep wound a good four or five inches in length. The boy had cracked his skull wide open. Blood was gushing everywhere and I wasn't sure what to do. I had secretly hoped I wouldn't be the first person to reach the boy, and now my fears had become a reality. I may as well have been back in my diabetic brother's room waiting for my mother to save the day. But there would be no rescue that day, not yet anyway. We were too far from any other help.

Pete's friend looked at me, unsure that I knew what to do, but I continued to eye Pete's wound. There I was in that important uniform without a clue. I felt the sliminess of the blood on my hands and quickly washed them in the creek. It wasn't that the blood bothered me, I just wanted something to do. Pete had a dizzy look in his eyes as he reached out to grab hold of my shirtsleeve.

"I can't feel..." Pete began. "Can you...call...my mother will be," he said. Then his eyes slowly closed and his hand on my sleeve grew weak. Finally, the hand slipped down to rest somewhere between my leg and the cold water.

"Pete?" his friend called out. But Pete's eyes had closed.

I thought back to my Red Cross class down on Veteran's Boulevard near the Salvation Army store. I had learned basic first aid techniques. It was all a jumble in my mind but I had to do something. Somehow I had to take control of the situation. Then I remembered something from my training. Direct pressure. That was it. I needed to stop the boy's bleeding. That should have been obvious. I frantically undid the first aid kit's two metal latches and fished around until I found what I needed. I tore open a large package with a cross on it. Seconds later, I pressed the gauze to Pete's head.

"Everything's going to be all right," I said, but I didn't really know that. I only knew that that's what people always said on TV.

"Shouldn't we move him?" Pete's friend had tears in his eyes. "I mean, at least get him out of the water and…"

"No, just leave him where he is. He'll be fine where he is. We might hurt him more if we move him." I'd heard that on TV, too. "Everything's going to be all right. You stay here with him while I go for more help."

Pete's friend gave a feeble nod and I got up out of the creek.

"What's your name?"

The boy looked up and said, "Kenny."

I couldn't hold back a smile at the sound of my childhood name. "Keep pressing this against his head. I'll be right back. Don't worry. Everything's okay now." I stood up and looked at the boy holding the bloody gauze against his friend's head. "You did fine today, Kenny," I said, before turning to go.

I headed back to the trail and hiked to the main road where I found a couple of newly arrived paramedics. Without further delay, I led the paramedics to my patient and Kenny.

We carried Pete out over the rough terrain using a Stokes litter, but we had to stop every so often to turn the odd-looking stretcher on its side so the boy could throw up. When Pete was loaded in an ambulance, I saw Kenny sitting next to him. He looked at me as if he wanted to say "thank you," but then the doors closed and the ambulance sped down the main road with its siren blaring and its lights flashing. Rick was over by our truck still talking to the paramedics, and I saw him laugh about something when he saw me notice him. But I didn't care. After all, I had saved the day this time. I decided to walk back to the maintenance yard, so I headed downhill after the ambulance without even saying goodbye to my out of shape park-aide buddy.

A few days later, the head of the parks department sent me a letter of recognition which both thanked and commended my efforts that day, and that made me feel even more proud of what I had done. Even so, the excitement of the emergency call quickly wore off, and I knew my days with Huddart were nearing their end. I became more withdrawn and impatient with the whole routine. Most of the other workers thought that I was too serious and didn't hang around me much. Once, while we were sitting around a long table eating lunch, one of the other guys joked about my being thin and how women wanted a man of substance so they could put their arms around him. After that, I became even more unsociable. That comment has always stuck with me. During the same lunch, a ranger asked me why one of my sideburns was longer than the other, and the way he put the question made me feel inadequate.

Later that afternoon, I tried to fit in by joining in some extracurricular ATV activity with the guys (even though the head ranger had told us not to race around on those four-wheel workhorses), but when I tipped my vehicle over, my so-called buddies laughed their heads off in a way that further told me I'd never really be accepted by anybody I worked with there.

When it began to get dark that night, some of the same group of jokers sprayed each other with hoses in the maintenance yard. They didn't include me at first, and then I became the only one they wanted to douse. But I made sure I wouldn't be a victim of this humiliation, so I jumped a fence to get away from the hoses' reach and ran into a dark wood. I walked blindly for miles not really knowing where I was until finally, by sheer instinct, I found the maintenance yard again. The others weren't anywhere in sight by then, so I snuck up to my car and sped off, never to return to Huddart Park.

It's a shame the fog made me so sensitive to my plight at Huddart; the park aide position really could have led into something worthwhile. I guess the main reason I wasn't able to hold my job with Huddart was due to my thin skin. Years of criticism and being the target of every mental bully I'd come into contact with had left me a shell-shocked wreck incapable of interacting with others. And it didn't seem to matter how hard I tried to do what was expected of me. Huddart was a perfect example of how the fog would come in to snuff out promising beginnings, so that sooner or later I'd end up in the same boat. And being in the same boat meant falling back on the same mainstays. After deviating from my new path with the seasonal park position, I returned to the tried and true. A new job with Hamilton Press literally placed me back into the driver's seat of another delivery van. Hamilton Press competed with Baker Graphics for the privilege of copying local companies' precious blueprints and other assorted documents.

Ironically, many of the companies I frequented with my new employer doubled as Baker Graphics customers. My sharp, smiling new boss was a male version of my old boss at Baker Graphics. He even had the same hair color. Of course, my new boss wasn't as pretty, but I couldn't have asked for a better, more positive, and supportive individual after the disaster with Huddart. I think the man's name was Bill, and Hamilton Press was just a stepping stone for what he really had in mind. I wouldn't be surprised if Bill is a successful executive today. God knows he put enough hours in on the golf course while at Hamilton Press to rival the most impressive self-made men of our times. While I was at this new company, things quickly became rote, and I soon forgot about trails and trees. In a matter of months, though, I aspired for more.

This time, I stayed a little closer to home in my career ambitions, deciding that driving was my expertise and I'd at least use this to my advantage. I got wind of a program Sears was offering that trained people to become driving instructors. I eagerly accepted the challenge, choosing to say goodbye to yet again another dead-end job.

A few of us took a ride through the streets of Hayward where a well-groomed man oversaw a whirlwind course meant to prepare even the most unprepared for all those nervous teens and adults biting at the bit to get behind the wheel. At the time, the task of becoming a driving instructor seemed daunting enough with its thick manual of rules and etiquette, but at least the format was clear-cut. A step-by-step method described in my student text outlined a very comprehensive way of training someone to drive a car. Notice the word "method." I later learned that "order" and "control" were a part of this so-called method, since they were essential tools for a driving instructor's success. My childhood buddies reared their heads once more in my life. And I soon used my God-given powers of manipulation to move students through their paces just like all those coins and strange-looking objects I used to play with. But this wasn't the only perk the job had to offer. Teaching people how to drive meant that nobody criticized or berated me. Things were done on my terms once I was in the instructor's seat. And even though I wasn't some type of Hitler bent on dominating his subjects, I did have a mission in mind every time I got into a car with a student.

It had only taken me a matter of weeks to convince my Sears teacher to grant me a passing grade and the status of instructor. Having attained this level of proficiency, I saw to it that a new batch of needy individuals not only got a chance to explore the open road under my direct supervision, but also got the opportunity to experience California gridlock with all its smog and aggravation.

My new job as driving instructor sent me throughout the Bay area in a loaned brown Toyota to any number of sites and situations. Sometimes I would end up at high schools to take a group of smiling speedsters out for a spin, and other times I'd pick up an aging adult who had never gotten a driver's license for one reason or another. There were special cases too. Once, in San Francisco, I had to give a few lessons to a man who was too scared to get behind the wheel. He started the first lesson with a death grip around the Toyota's steering wheel. By the last lesson, after my calming effect he was absolutely relaxed and able to traverse the most nerve-wracking streets of the city by the Bay without a care.

Another time, I had to certify that an elderly man, who had had his license revoked by the city, could get back on the road. The man was barely able to move, let alone operate a motor vehicle, but other than driving way too slowly— which I'm sure had caused his license to be revoked in the first place—he showed me that he wasn't a real hazard to other motorists. So I monitored his driving one day and helped him get his license reinstated. Perhaps I shouldn't have done it, but I just didn't have the heart to turn him down. The man's wife had recently died, and he was lonely. Since he could hardly walk, his only way to get around was by car. Besides, he told me that the only place he really went anymore was the local supermarket. So what was the harm? People had often said that I was incompetent, and I couldn't do certain things. Now they were saying it about this nice old man. Well, here was my chance to stand up for the rights of the incompetent.

I was a really good driving instructor. I think it was because, unlike other instructors, I got to know my students long before we ever moved away from the curb. I even had fun with some of the teens. One thought he was Mario Andretti and didn't need California's mandatory six hours with an instructor.

I knew the only way I could keep this guy interested in continuing with the six hours was by resorting to drastic tactics. So I removed my magnetic Sears sign on the car's side and took him up a mountain I used to speed down when I was a teen. When we reached the mountain's top, I told Mario to show me what he could do, and the car bolted off like a rocket ship. After zooming around some hairpin turns, I told him I still wasn't impressed, so he took the turns even faster. We barely stayed on the road, and I could see the fear in his eyes, but I wasn't afraid. As always, I enjoyed the motion and wanted more. When I started to mock his abilities, he pushed the envelope even more, until he finally got too nervous and slowed down. At the bottom of the long and winding road, I asked my young student if he'd gotten racing out of his system for a while. He said yes, so I put the Sears sign on again, even as the smell of burning rubber still filled my nostrils, and we pulled out slowly, once again going through all the official driver-training motions.

Virtually every one of my students got his or her license the first time out with a DMV tester because I took it upon myself to learn every aspect of the test and test route and all the pitfalls that could do a student in. I imparted this wisdom to my students, and they performed wonderfully. Other instructors' students often had to try more than once to get their licenses.

Everything concerning the job was rolling along smoothly, until one day when I was sent out to evaluate a student in a lower income area of South

San Francisco. From the get-go, supervisors at Sears had told us about the different packages that instructors could offer students and, as with my other customers, I tried to sell this new student as many lessons as I could. But after seeing where this kid lived, I decided that his parents would hardly be able to afford a car, let alone a bunch of driving lessons.

So I suggested the basic plan to the student's mother, much to the chagrin of the soulless salespeople back at Sears. They thought I wasn't trying hard enough to sell more. But it wasn't the first time this happened, and I got fed up with their greed. In fact, I was so disgusted with these parasites that I told them I'd be turning in their car for the last time when I got back to Hayward; a dumb move, since I didn't have any way to get back across the San Francisco Bay to Redwood City. I should have told them to pick up the car at my mother's place. Fortunately, one of my brothers was able to drive me home.

About a week later, I took a new job with Stanford Driving School, which was located a lot closer to home and had a far less money-hungry staff. Even the fire engine red cars were a more welcome sight than all those browns and silvers that Sears had to offer. The format was similar to that of Sears however, albeit in a much more personable environment.

I settled right into teaching at Stanford, soon filling my schedule more than most of the other instructors. The reason for this was that I had a lot of teens to teach. They seemed to get along with my easygoing manner and my approach to helping them get those coveted licenses. It didn't take long for word to spread in their close-knit circles—I should be the one requested when mom or dad finally made the call to pay for them to attend driver's ed.

Having all these teens to teach wasn't without its pitfalls, however. Many were playful young girls experimenting with their blossoming bodies, and obviously I had to discourage the moves they put on me at times. In addition to fighting the whims of these young sirens, I had to fight the urge to move on again. The job just wasn't paying enough, and I didn't feel as important in that all-powerful instructor's seat as I thought I would. But even before I had the chance to set my sights on another career venture, I was told to leave Stanford.

It seems that the DMV had revoked my instructor's permit because that government-run organization claimed I had incorrectly filled out the paperwork to acquire it. I was accused of not being absolutely honest when answering a question to do with my criminal background. The question had asked if I'd ever been convicted of a felony, and of course I answered no, since I hadn't. Nonetheless, the DMV said I'd withheld information, since I'd been convicted of a misdemeanor. There was no question on the Driving Instructor's Application asking if I'd been convicted of a misdemeanor. I was prepared to appeal the decision to revoke my instructor's permit when I abruptly changed my mind, deciding it was fate moving me away from being a driving instructor. My boss was sorry to see me go. After all, I was probably earning him more money than anyone else. In fact, just prior to leaving the driving school, new students were being turned away because I didn't have any room left for them in my busy days.

Still, the momentum of change pushed me into another uncertain future, and I handed in my car keys. Back at my mother's duplex, I put my thrift store briefcase back in a closet and immediately set out to find another job.

I've often pondered the possibility that I could have somehow filled out the DMV Driving Instructor's Application incorrectly. I wouldn't have lied about anything in my past, but I have been known to fill out forms incorrectly just because I didn't fully understand a question or simply because I neglected to give information when asked. Once, after submitting a card that was meant to secure me a place on the waiting list for the next San Francisco police officer application process, I neglected to check a gender box and was unable to move on to the next phase. The fact of the matter is that sometimes I just hurry through paperwork when I should take my time. Sometimes I just get bored with all the questions.

Because of the monotonous nature of most forms, I think the fog is often overcome with an urgency to hand the things in whether they're complete or not. The occasional inaccurate filling out of employment applications hasn't been the only problem for me when it comes to paperwork. Credit questionnaires, school documents—you name it—I've probably penciled in wrong information or failed to include information on just about every type of white-collar form. I can't stand paperwork.

On the other hand, many times my creative and honest answers have helped me with an employment application. Once these impersonal pieces of paper got me past the initial protocol and into a prospective new employer's office for an in-person chat, my charm and heartfelt enthusiasm often got me hired.

North American Van Lines saw that I had tractor-trailer experience. The moving company hired me to drive its trucks, but first I had to learn how to load them, since arranging a houseload of items or an office full of furniture and other assorted things into a trailer was somewhat different from moving standard freight. At North American, I spent my days with gruff moving men, many of whom were ex-cons or meaty guys just needing to make a buck. The atmosphere was one of tattoos, tough talk, and which bar to drink in after the day's work was through. I had difficulty adjusting to an environment like that. It seemed so limiting and predictable. But I tried to fit in, moving one blanketed thing after another into long box vans and securing the lot for transportation to some new city or state. Later in life, I'd see the hilarious movie *Moving* with Richard Prior, and my thoughts would drift back to the smell of musty blankets and men who didn't say much.

While I was working for North American, I found nothing to laugh about, and in fact, I ended up getting into an altercation with another lumper before I ever had the chance to drive one of the company's trucks. As with the fight I'd had with my co-worker at the carpet store, the fiasco with this moving company person ended disastrously, and I left North American Van Lines without even saying goodbye. I often chose to leave abruptly; it seemed easier. Mostly, I think I was avoiding the looks I imagined getting from superiors who I'd let down. I often felt guilty having to leave an employer that had trusted me to get the job done. When I quit, I also felt that I had failed again in my life, and I was depressed enough with this thought without having to deal with questions or disapproving looks from bosses.

A few days after leaving North American, I delivered flowers for yet another florist. Redwood Florist shared a building with a funeral parlor and the business's paychecks were about as lifeless as the bodies that never ceased to visit next door. A few months later, I got another trucking job with a large firm called TNT Bestway. I pulled box trailers for TNT, hauling any number of things. The truck often got loaded with tires that I delivered to Kmart, or box upon box of foreign-marked cartons that were usually delivered to some nondescript company off the beaten path, where heavy-smoking, non-English-speaking people hurriedly took their well-traveled loot through dreary backdoors. Many times, I'd deliver big-screen TVs to private residents. I had to manhandle the enormous televisions from the truck without the aid of a liftgate or buddy to assist me. The burden was made worse by the fact that, more often than not, the TVs were loaded in the nose of the long box trailers I pulled. This meant that I'd have to inch the oversized boob tubes to the end of the trailers, then use every fiber in my tiny body to slide them carefully to the ground. Only then could I use a handtruck to deposit the televisions on a sidewalk or porch, much to the dismay of the customers who wanted me to wheel the TVs directly into their houses. When I told the red-faced consumers I wasn't allowed to bring items inside houses or apartments, they often got irate. Some customers would swear at me and call my supervisor to complain. Thankfully, my supervisor always backed me up by saying that I was doing what was expected of me since TNT didn't want to risk damage to customers' property.

The job with TNT was extremely taxing, and I'd barely make it to my scheduled deliveries on time. My dispatcher called me throughout the day to ask where I was or why I hadn't delivered something yet. He constantly put pressure on me to get things done, and I tried as fast as I could to appease him. I'd speed my truck through the worst parts of San Jose, frantically making an effort to drop off some seemingly insignificant trinket at its appointed destination.

Sometimes, I'd see my old friend, Jake, wheeling his own truck, calmly taking his office furniture deliveries to the next radiant building in Silicon Valley. The computer industry was in full bloom. The buzz of computers and power lunches was taking place all around us. Santa Clara County's elite, cutting-edge technological businesses, with their elaborate fountains, well-maintained grounds, and flashy cars, were in strange contrast to the nearby ghetto-like districts with run-down houses, graffiti-painted walls, and dirty streets. But I didn't have much time to dwell on these contrasting worlds. I focused my time on getting those damn deliveries done so I could go home and heat up some high-cholesterol dinner and then lay my exhausted body down in front of that blue-collar television god which filled my meagre duplex room with all the stimulating and pretty things I liked.

Each morning I'd wake up early and each night go to bed late, me behind my brown door and my mother behind hers. And each night I'd wonder where my life was taking me. Sometimes I'd go out cruising with Jake in his truck and relive all those teenage experiences of ours. He'd put on more weight since our teenage days, and he'd even started losing some of his hair, but he still had the same sense of humor and desire for mischief.

"Remember when..." we'd usually start off, before going into a reconstruction of some silly past escapade that only the two of us knew about. Or we would drive around with fast food in hand looking at all the pretty Bay area women who seemed to lead such interesting lives. We never went into clubs, though, since Jake didn't like that scene. Instead, we'd just leer from afar, each of us lost in his own lascivious fantasies. We rarely had women of our own. We just didn't know how to get them or, more importantly, hold on to them. This was contrary to my being able to date women in England, of course. Women were different in America. I got the sense that most American women were more concerned about how much money I made, or what type of job I had. Since neither my bank account nor job reflected the kinds of things they were looking for, I didn't qualify as a potential boyfriend.

Nonetheless, Jake and I made do without being lucky enough to lure many women into our worlds. But we never stopped talking about how much we liked looking at women and how we wished we could have girl-friends of our own. To help deal with this lack of female company in our lives, we'd go on long drives. On our "cruises" we'd listen to all our favorite loud bands like Led Zeppelin, The Who, or The Doors and inevitably comment on the decline of good rock and roll. Rarely did our activities deviate from this repetitive format, which culminated in going back to Jake's place to watch TV or pornos, so that we could salivate over more beautiful women. The fog has always felt right at home with Jake, no challenges, no confrontations, no stress.

The nights with Jake always seemed to end too soon, and before I knew it I'd be back at work the next day, where the uncomfortable nit-picky world would take on the fog full force in the form of a screaming TNT dispatcher, an unhappy customer, or an angry driver who I might have accidentally cut off in traffic on one of the Bay area's crowded roads.

Sometimes, while driving out there, I'd get lost in some unfamiliar terri-tory and my foggy mind would seize up on me. When this happened, I'd drive around in a daze, not caring if I ever found a delivery address or not. Then there was the occasional mishap with that big truck I used to wheel around. Once I drove into a trailer park to make a delivery and the box trailer got stuck on a low-hanging overhead wire. I wasn't even aware of what was happening until a man flew out of his trailer home yelling at me, and I finally spotted the wire hung up on the truck. The telephone pole was being pulled to the ground. When I called my dispatcher, I thought I'd be fired for sure, but I got another chance. I'm sure everybody back at the dispatch office had a good laugh after hearing about what happened. The accident was due to pure lack of judgment, something that has gotten me in more trouble than I've needed in life.

Even with the accident, it looked as though I'd be keeping my new job at TNT for a long while until, after returning from a day's work, the old ADD curse—or maybe just a case of bad luck—kicked in. The incident started out very innocently, and I didn't think anything of it. I was talking to a dis-patcher who was behind a counter that separated drivers from dispatch office personnel. At some point during our talk and juvenile banter, I pulled out the tiny pocket knife that I kept on my belt for those times when I might need to cut straps or shrink wrap. I don't even remember what I said, but before I knew it I was waving the knife in the dispatcher's direction, never even remotely intending to use it. Still, that was all it took for me to be called into the headman's office for a chat. It seems the dispatcher I'd been playing with had reported the incident, and now I was on the defense to keep my job. Even though I emphatically told my boss that I'd just been playing, I got the axe. As with a few other times in my employment history, I think the higher ups were looking for any excuse to fire me. I'd just become too much of a liability working for TNT.

The termination caught me completely off guard. I couldn't believe I'd been fired again. The familiar pattern of getting a job and losing it had repeated itself once more. I began to wonder if I'd ever be able to keep a job, any job. If other ADDers are anything like me, their most commonly used word must be "why?" Unfortunately, when it comes to some things—especially employment—it really doesn't matter why. The only thing a person can ask himself is "when can I get another job?" In my case, the answer came in a few weeks. And if you've been paying attention and recognize the pattern, I'm sure you can guess what type of job it was: that's right—delivery driver. But at least this time, I'd be a delivery driver with a large company, not that this would fetch me more money, however.

Wong Sum is probably the biggest florist in the San Francisco Bay area. Although I got the same salary I earned driving for other florists, at least I worked for a well-known company. Instead of the usual solitary delivery driver, Wong Sum had four or five, and most of the time we were out there rolling around. A tall, good-looking jock named Mark Bess coordinated the whole affair and most of the time he made sure deliveries got to their destinations on time. In addition to delivering flowers, I delivered large fichus trees, small plants, and other decorative items to top-of-the-mark hotels, usually in San Francisco. I used the company's largest vehicle, a one-and-a-half ton truck. None of the other drivers had truck-driving experience. Most were too young to know about wheeling around anything larger than a van, so I got the honor of using the big truck, even though it was smaller than most of the trucks I'd driven in the Air Force.

When I'd set out with the truck, time-consuming decorating affairs took me away from deliveries for most of the day, and I welcomed the change. I liked it better when floral arrangers didn't tag along. They tended to be backseat drivers, even though the truck didn't have a back seat, of course. Once the nagging got so bad that one of these shotgun-riding arrangers complained about my driving in the slow lane to Wong Sum's president as soon as we got back from a job decorating the Fairmont Hotel in San Francisco. I didn't get in trouble, but I wasn't happy with the flak. Things started out jovially enough at Wong Sum, and I got along fairly well with my co-workers, but in the end leaving this company would be the second most horrific and stressful parting I was to have with an employer, second only to leaving the United States Air Force. This time, the problem would have nothing to do with my insubordination.

I couldn't have asked for a better filler job. I was even on the company's softball team. But my ADD soon got in the way of a good thing when I developed an obsession with Julia, the tall blonde girl I pursued until I almost landed in jail. I cringe to think that I acted that way and that I was so obsessed. I know the idea of holding onto such an out-of-whack idea like this might seem ridiculous and outrageous to most, but to an ADDer, pursuing a misguided principle or unhealthy obsession is justified because often he doesn't know any better. By the time reason has shown me the error of my ways, the obsession has run its course. Incredibly, when this epiphany finally arrives, memories of the obsession are merely vague recollections of something that happened which just got out of control. I hardly give Julia a second thought these days. I haven't seen or heard from her since the early nineties, and I doubt I'll ever see her again. When I do think of her now, none of the incredibly obsessive and outlandish pursuits I held onto concerning her even enter my mind. Unfortunately, I still live with obsessive spurts. It comes with the territory when you have ADD. The only thing I can do when an obsession comes along is to hope it won't devastate my life.

At the time of the Julia saga and shortly after getting the axe, all I could think about was how unfair it was for her to do what she did. For a long while, I couldn't trust anyone. The ordeal, especially on the heels of my disastrous affair with Susan, severed my trust in humanity. Now I understand, of course, how I affected Julia's life. While it's still tough for me to come fully to grips with why she decided to stop being my friend, that sad reality didn't give me the right to force her to be my friend. Unfortunately, issues become larger than life for me—especially when I think someone has wronged me in some way. I find it difficult to let go of my need to make the situation right. Sometimes the difference between right and wrong gets muddled for an ADDer. The fact was that Julia hadn't wronged me; she simply wanted to live a life without me in it. And, of course, she had every right to do so.

After Wong Sum, I tried to move on with my life but it was difficult to keep from dwelling on what had happened. I finally got another truck-driving job that kept me busy. This helped to take my mind off the past. It was common for me to work ten- or eleven-hour days at my new job. Still, I wasn't ready to let go of my obsession with Julia. The new company I worked for, AF Xpress, was a small trucking outfit run by tough Italians who often told war stories of the times they'd driven trucks themselves. One of the Italians, now a dispatcher, told me he carried a gun because people were still looking for him.

I hauled strange loads for AF; things such as car seat foam, which I got from a company in Livermore; or load upon load of some fine powder which was extracted from the bay. Everything and everyone in the powder's company got covered with the white substance, whatever it was, and every time I pulled a load from the place, I became whiter too. I mostly hauled containers that I picked up from huge shipping ports in Oakland, or from train yards like Southern Pacific. Pulling containers was easier than my prior experiences of driving trucks when I had to load my own trailers. With this new job, most of the containers were pre-loaded, and I just took them from one location to another. Even though I didn't have to load trailers anymore, I'd never been busier shuttling loads from one place to another, and the biggest challenge was to stay awake.

Delivering flowers seemed worlds away from my new job duties. But transitions like this were commonplace when one moved around so much in the working world. It was back to the rut of smelling diesel, and coupling and uncoupling trailers to shaky rigs; roach coaches parked by the sides of dusty roads; rock and roll and pallets; shrinkwrap and shippers. The whole gamut of a truck driver's experience, though I wouldn't be reliving the experience long.

This job, like so many others, would have a tragic end. It happened after a long day of driving. I backed a trailer into a familiar dock where I was to pick up a load of Budweiser. In my haste to get the beer and drop it off so I could go home, I forgot about a short pole that couldn't be seen on the truck's blind side. Memory of the pole was triggered by the sickening sound of crumpling fiberglass, and as soon as I heard the noise, I knew I'd just lost another job. I called my boss and told him what had happened. He confirmed my earlier premonition, and once again, I found myself unemployed this was the straw that broke the camel's back in my topsy-turvy working life. I decided to take a break before rushing out to look for another job. Still, there were those ever-present bills and needs that would keep me from a lengthy and well-desired rest. I wanted some sort of break before getting into the working trenches again. I set my sights on the idea of collecting unemployment insurance, one of the few times I did so. I thought, other people collect money from the government, so why shouldn't I? But I didn't like collecting money from the state because it meant having to apply to jobs each week, even if they were jobs I didn't want. In addition to this manda-tory unpleasantness, I had to fill out and mail in paperwork that I didn't want to deal with.

To make matters worse, AF Xpress contested my receiving unemploy-ment insurance since the company didn't think it was obligated to pay for my dismissal. My position was that if the company hadn't pushed me the way it had and gotten me to a state of absolute exhaustion, I wouldn't have struck that pole with the truck. And besides, I hadn't struck the pole on purpose. I would have remained working for AF if it would have allowed me, but it wouldn't. In the company's mind, one accident was more than enough to terminate an employee. I attended a State of California unemployment hearing to determine whether or not I should be awarded unemployment insurance. The hearing was also attended by an AF representative in cowboy boots whom I'd seen hanging around the company's dispatch office a few times. Three silent, poker-faced government judges sat across from the two of us at a long table. The AF guy made a good case, and within a few minutes of the hearing's start, I thought I wouldn't be getting those meager little unemployment checks. But a week later I was notified by mail that I had won.

I've only had to stand up for my rights three other times before impartial bodies. Two cases took place in small claims courts where I complained about people who had sold me cars that had not lived up to my expectations. I won each case. The third time was when I tried to upgrade my Air Force dis-charge, so that I could enlist in the Navy. I know fighting to join the military again might seem like a crazy idea, but remember I lack the judgment that others take for granted. Anyway, I only got a few votes in my favor from those on the military hearing's panel, so I guess the ADD gods determined my fate that day.

I would rather have stayed away from the hearings and the court cases, but I couldn't. I had to stand up for my rights. I think ADDers are probably easy targets for those who take advantage of people. Because of our poor judgment, we often aren't as savvy as others when it comes to ascertaining whether or not a deal is sound or a punishment is worthy of being enforced, so we rely on other, more litigious venues to decide for us. I'm sure most ADDers stand up for their rights the way I do. Because we constantly make mistakes, we are constantly trying to defend ourselves.

Quickly tiring of unemployment checks and daytime TV, I went back to work with another florist. All I have to say is thank God people like flowers. Los Altos Florist was located in downtown Los Altos, just below Apple Computer founder Steve Wazniac's house. I spent the afternoon in the computer genius's house one time when I was in a play with his wife, who had invited the cast over for a rehearsal. Even though I didn't know who Steve was at the time, I knew he had to be important since I saw a photo of him shaking hands with the then President, George Bush Sr., in the living room. After the rehearsal, Steve's wife took us on a tour of the Wazniac estate, where she showed us her herd of llamas running freely in a lush, green meadow set in the middle of a forest of oaks and redwoods.

My new boss at Los Altos Florist was kind of snobby, with heavy make-up and gaudy jewelry. I had to play the part of the well-mannered servant who had to show complete obedience when in the presence of the company's wealthy customers. Even though I loved Los Altos's surroundings, I hated the prevailing attitude of the place. I've always had this love-hate relationship with wealthy communities, but I keep coming back to them because they're cleaner, more orderly, and often more eccentric. I think I gravitate to these areas of the country because a lot of artists and freethinkers tend to congregate in them, and I'm very drawn to art and abstract thought, no matter what the medium or idea.

Nothing of note happened at Los Altos Florist until I started flirting with one of the floral arrangers, a young, thin woman who didn't like the attention at all. It wasn't as though I was obsessed with the woman in the way I had been with Julia. I think I unconsciously chose to mess around with her because I was bored and needed an outlet. The flirting was really superficial. Still, it was enough in the eyes of Los Altos Florist's owner to pull me aside one day and stiffly, but politely, say that my kind of behavior didn't fit in with the shop's atmosphere. I gladly handed in my van keys and left the peaceful little hamlet in the hills for my mother's disgusting brown duplex, more daytime TV, and many more walks on the beach.

Now I was at another crossroads in my life, and I decided to make a drastic change in my career direction. For years I'd heard about the importance of computers. I thought I should get on board and learn how to operate one, but I just couldn't compel myself to do so until one day somebody told me it would help with writing books. Up until then, I had labored over antiquated typewriters to put words to paper. I had struggled with ribbons and whiteout, unable to move around pieces of text. When I finally got over my hatred of all those plastic electronic boxes with those tie-wearing nerds running them, I was amazed at what I could do.

The Regional Occupational Program came to my rescue again and broke me into the computer world with its lengthy Automated Office Occupations course, designed to get dinosaurs like me up to speed with the rest of the world. The course not only taught me how to use a computer, but an adding machine too, and it acclimated me to the office environment since it was designed to prepare students for an entry-level office position. As well as using computers and adding machines, we took turns manning a single phone in the large, open-bay classroom to get hands-on receptionist experience. The phone was set up to take incoming calls for those interested in gaining information about the Automated Office Occupations class.

In addition to showing us the common tools of the office environment, our very knowledgeable teacher versed us in proper office etiquette, so that by the time we had graduated from the course we were well-rounded candidates prepared for any assignment. I caught on well to the WordPerfect programs. In fact, I couldn't get through the word processing program quickly enough, and I rapidly surpassed others who didn't seem to be in a hurry and happily dragged their feet when it came to learning. Sometimes I would get stuck on the more advanced elements of WordPerfect though, and I'd hit a brick wall. It was then that my teacher's patience and positive attitude were most helpful, and even these stumbling blocks were eventually conquered. But I'd be hard pressed to recall any of that advanced computer stuff now.

Even so, I was at the top of my game back then, and I was the first to put up my hand when the teacher announced a job opening to the class. I was so eager to get started in this new world.

I applied for a couple of temp jobs and was hired for both of them. Although they were only temporary gigs for an engineering firm and a law firm, the experiences and references I built up for later jobs were worthwhile. In fact, later in my office working life, many temp agencies sent me out on assignments too numerous to recall here. I soon had a plethora of computer programs and other tools in a bag of goodies that was quite useful to employers, especially to one company in particular.

Just before I graduated from the R.O.P. course, a job opening was announced in class for a position in a large patent/trademark law firm. The job was a permanent, full-time position and would pay well. I applied and was offered the position. The office was on the fifth floor of a large building down the street from none other than Stanford University.

Working for Cooley Godward Castro Huddleson & Tatum was a gravy train. My cubicle was in a quiet, air-conditioned area with soft lighting, and I basically governed my own actions. My duties included maintaining the file room for a boss who worked on the fourth floor. My new boss was a nice woman (a Navy brat whose father was now a retired police officer). Peggy was an outgoing woman who was in control, but who really didn't want to be bothered. As long as I did what I was supposed to do and made sure that I only dressed down from my suit and tie on Fridays, she was happy.

I'd usually get done with my duties by mid-morning and then go back to my cubicle to wait for lawyers to call. These were busy men and women with paperwork scattered across their desks. They constantly pored over detail after detail, making certain that patents and trademarks couldn't be contested. At least that was my understanding of what they did. When I retrieved the files they wanted, I would usually drop them in an in-box and take any files or loose documents from an outgoing box back to the file room. It was extremely simple and uninteresting work. Consequently, given my low tolerance for boredom, it didn't take long for me to go stir-crazy from the routine, and I'd yearn for each day to end so that I could run to my waiting car and soon to be blaring radio to make up for all that placid silence and monotony during the workday.

Back at work, a ritual soon developed. At first, I'd repeatedly take the elevator to the floor below to ask my boss if there was anything else for me to do. Ninety-nine percent of the time she'd say no, and I'd go back upstairs to wait for lawyers to call, or I'd make the rounds again looking for outgoing files (even though I knew there probably wouldn't be any) just so I could take a walk. Then, I'd meander back to my cubicle and start the ritual all over again about an hour later. Unfortunately, after a while, this meager ritual wasn't enough to keep me sane, so I developed other distractions to save me from the boredom.

Sometimes, I'd bother a science-savvy woman who sat in a cubicle behind me, just so I could break the monotony. The scientist was really nice, but she was usually too busy making sure patents and trademarks were scientifically accurate to have much time to spend with me. I also made friends with a guy in the mailroom on the fourth floor who used to bring me my mail. He entertained me with his easy-going manner and sympathized with my boredom, but he was usually too busy to stay long, too.

I took long lunches. Sometimes two hours or more, worrying that when I came back I'd be disciplined for my flagrant misuse of law firm time and money. But most of the time, nobody even knew I had been gone. All that free time on my hands at Cooley didn't help to keep me out of mischief. It was in the file room, when I was alone and completely secreted from visitors, that I left a few musical messages on my old Wong Sum pal's family answering machine. A trickle of my obsession with Julia still remained, and if it hadn't been for the boredom I was experiencing with my new job, I probably wouldn't even have bothered with the calls. Fortunately, the few silly pop songs I left for Julia that reflected the way part of me still felt, didn't get me in any trouble.

To help me keep a proper perspective on things at Cooley, I put some artwork in my crowded file room so that I could at least dwell on something that I thought mattered in the world: Monet, Waterhouse, Bouguereau, and some guy from the Romanticism period who had a yen for redheads. The paintings reminded me that there were more than ties and brown file folders out there.

When I finally ran out of options to fill the day, I'd sit at my computer—the one I didn't even need since I never used it for any job-related duties—and write. I wrote a few plays. I even submitted them to theaters later on but I didn't get any bites. After I was replaced at Cooley, I learned the new file clerk read those plays (even though I thought I had deleted them). He thought they were good. The praise left me feeling a mixture of accomplishment and embarrassment. But this review of my work and the feelings associated with it would come later. At the time I was writing the plays, I still had to deal with Cooley and the immense boredom I continued to experience on a daily basis.

The tedium at Cooley became so unbearable that I considered extreme measures. I was desperate for adventure. I read an English guy's account of his five years in the French Foreign Legion so I sent away for some literature about this hardcore military organization. After getting a quick reply from a

Legion outpost in France, my hopes went up. I now had a plan to get away from the mundane world of files, no matter where it might take me.

I had wanted to return overseas since leaving England in 1984. If I served five years in the Legion, I could attain French citizenship. This was definitely a plus because I knew it only took about two hours to get to England by ferry; a lot shorter trip than the time it took to travel from California to England.

I worshipped my French Foreign Legion two-page flyer with the picture of a traditional legionnaire on its cover—even though, other than the legionnaire's picture, the flyer was as austere as I'd heard the Legion was. Still, as blunt and no-nonsense as the flyer was, it gave me the information I needed; the nuts and bolts of what to expect after signing up. The cut-off age was forty. The first place a new legionnaire might be sent was Morocco, or it could be Algiers. But most importantly, the flyer told me I was qualified to join this elite group. And the idea of joining the Legion more than intrigued me, it completely exhilarated me. Romantic images of remote places popped into view. I also thought that living the rough and ready life of a legionnaire might inspire me to write more meaningful novels. Who knew what I would find out there amongst the camels and hidden faces of Arabian women? I thought I might have a promising future again as a part of another military organization. It might even make up for my failure with the Air Force. So, being the flighty, impulsive person I was, I put in my two-week notice at Cooley and bought a ticket for England.

My plan was to spend a little while in England and visit with friends, and also check out any possibilities I might have there. If nothing panned out in the U.K. by the time my money ran out, I'd move on to France and the French Foreign Legion. It was during my last two weeks with Cooley that I met my future wife, Pamela.

I had lunch one day at a Round Table Pizza Restaurant, which was only a stone's throw from Cooley on California Street. The restaurant was packed with other office people trying to gulp down a quick slice or salad, while a jukebox in the back played songs that could barely be heard over the lunch-time din. I was fortunate to find a place to sit, and when my number was called I left my tiny table to get a ham and pineapple individual pizza. When I got back to my table, a young blonde woman was seated at it. I plopped down in a seat opposite the woman, not really caring that she had stolen my table, and I started to eat, all the while staring at the thief—or at least at the book that hid her face. A few moments passed before I broke the silence between us and asked the intruder about her book. The woman seemed put off by my trespass into her privacy, and it looked as though she wondered why I was at her table. Nonetheless, trying to start up a conversation, I continued interrupting her literary trance until she finally had to talk with me. It was obvious I wasn't going to let her read her book. I often feel the urge to talk to strangers, and I usually don't consider the fact that other people might not want to talk to me.

I found out from my lengthy interrogation that Pamela also worked nearby. She was a transplant from Houston, Texas, who had recently graduated from Berkeley. Now she worked as the manager of a company that sold vending machines. When lunch was over, I walked my table thief back to her building, which was only a little shorter than the one I worked in. I asked for her phone number. Throughout the rest of the day I thought about the fair-haired Texan I'd shared a table with, and I finally got up the nerve to call Pamela from Cooley with the intention of setting up a date. I was surprised when she accepted. I looked forward to the date and couldn't wait for the week at Cooley to end.

On Sunday we went to Stow Lake in San Francisco's Golden Gate Park. I rowed Pamela around the lake and we ate lunch in the November sunshine of a beautiful Bay area day. Then I pulled the boat into a little island cove and we got out to look at a waterfall. I kissed her and knew that we were involved in something that had potential.

The following week we started talking on the phone. Pamela probably thought I was a little weird, but I also thought she liked me. Back on California Street, we had lunch at a Chinese food restaurant that had a fish tank in it. I liked walking my new girlfriend back to her office. Even though the building I worked in was more impressive than Pamela's, her job paid more and the position she held with her company was much more important than mine. I sensed that Pamela was a lot smarter than I was and that she had a very promising future. Because of this, I didn't know why she wanted to be with me. I decided that she must be lonely like me and, contrary to what she told me later, that she wasn't really pursuing me, but was being pursued by me. Whatever the reason for our whirlwind relationship, I told her that I couldn't stick around since I'd already purchased a ticket for England, and I was probably going to join the French Foreign Legion. I added that now something new had entered the equation, I'd have to see how things went overseas and maybe come back if I had a change of plans concerning the Legion.

When my last two weeks with Cooley ended, I had a little time to kill before flying off to England. I moved into Pamela's tiny room that she rented in a house in Menlo Park and spent the day doing things for her. She let me use her car since I'd sold mine, along with virtually everything else I owned. One day I cleaned the Toyota inside and out. I also watched Pamela's small TV, and I played with one of her roommate's cats—anything to keep my mind off an uncertain future and the possibility that soon I would be making the biggest mistake of my life. Mostly, I just goofed off, treasuring what might be the last few days I'd have in America for quite some time. Just prior to leaving for England, I visited the graveyard on Arastradero Road in Palo Alto where two of my brothers lay side by side. My brother Stephen had committed suicide. My brother Danny had died after plowing his Volkswagen head-on into a van on California's coast highway after he'd had too much to drink. But it really didn't matter how they died when all is said and done, they were both just as dead.

When the time finally came for me to leave the U.S., Pamela and I had a touching moment together, but I couldn't look back, not now. I'd only known this girl for a month. I'd made my plans to join the Legion long before meeting her, and it just didn't make sense to get too involved. Still, I couldn't help but remember how much fun we'd had during those few days before I had to go. I had gotten to know a lot about my new girlfriend. I knew that she was smart. Just the fact that she'd gone to Berkeley told me that. People regarded this university with the utmost respect. In fact, Pamela had told me herself—not in a bragging way, of course, given her humble nature—that her boss at the vending machine company where she worked was so impressed with Berkeley that he only hired Berkeley graduates.

Pamela was also the kindest woman I'd ever met, and that was important to me since kindness was the number one thing I looked for in a girlfriend. She was the type of girl who might take in stray cats or help little old ladies cross the street. Of course, I'd never seen her do either of these things, but I knew she was that kind of girl. In fact, the more I thought about it, the more I liked Pamela. I guess there's just no other way to describe the way I saw her, except to say that she was a woman with a girl scout's soul. She was loyal to a fault, somebody I definitely felt I could rely on. And her eyes were a beautiful sky blue with aspirations of goodness and grandeur at their core. I felt I could share a future with her. And then one day—just as it happens so often when you find a good thing—I was gone.

When I got to England, my friend William found a room for me to rent in Rochester, where he now lived. Even though I'd left Pamela behind and thought about her often, I was glad to be embarking on my new adventure. After all, this is what I'd longed for while being cooped up in that tiny Cooley office that was so far away from me now. Unfortunately, I didn't seem to be having much of an adventure—even though I liked being back in England. I didn't even do very much until the evening. And then it was basically an attempt for William and me to take up where we'd left off all those years ago. Mostly, we'd just go out pubbing so that we could air our feelings about the world. Just as in the old days when I was dating his sister, William mostly talked about Greece or how he detested the way things were set up in England. And just as in the old days, I'd tune out most of what he said since either I didn't understand or I'd get lost in my own thoughts. After we were well soused and had had our fill of William's favorite kebabs or let some greasy fish and chips slide down our gullets, we'd go back to our quiet, dark English dwellings.

William rented half of a house on a hill, and he said I could stay there if I wanted to save some money. But William's place was too messy for me, too disorganized, and I needed somewhere that was neat and tidy. I needed the fewest distractions possible while I thought about what to do next in my life. When I left William's house, I'd take the long walk back to my primitive little room on the ground floor of another house closer to downtown. I had to walk over an archaic-looking bridge that spanned a deep black inlet that wound its way through Rochester. In the distance, the town's cathedral looked down at me with medieval superiority. One day, I took a cold walk up the historic building's staircase and bought a wooden placemat that I'd later use as artwork tacked upon a barren wall.

Rochester was as lonely as it was beautiful, and I felt a connection to the cobblestone streets as I walked their uneven surfaces, an American trespasser in limbo. I was lonely and stuck in a timeless fog, just as the city was stuck in a sort of timelessness that had never quite moved into the twentieth century. Part of me would have enjoyed staying in that limbo for another few months but, unfortunately, as usual the luxury of loitering comes to an end when pockets are left with nothing but lint. Since I wasn't lucky enough to find some sort of paying venture in England, I had to start thinking about my options. It was just about the time when the yearly Rochester Dickens Festival nears its end, and I had to make a decision about my future. Like

Dickens, who had spent a short time in Rochester to finish one classic or another before moving on, I too had to find new digs.

I strongly considered following my plan to go to France, but the more I thought about it, the more it seemed ridiculous. The boredom of Cooley had long since worn off, and I started to see things in a new light. Still, it seemed I had one of two paths to follow. On the one hand, there was an adventure with the Legion no writer could turn down; on the other, there was a kind woman who could give me security and a settled life in California. In considering my first choice, I had to take into account the likelihood of failure. What if the Legion didn't take me into its ranks? I'd be a penniless, unemployed American in a non-English-speaking country with few alternatives. Even if the French Foreign Legion did allow me to join its arduous and never-look-back life, there was no certainty that I'd end up staying with the military organization. I guess, ultimately, I took the well-traveled coward's path—the sure thing. But what if I hadn't? That's a question I've asked repeatedly over the past ten years.

So now that I'd made the decision to return to the States, I called Pamela from one of those pretty red phone booths that are so commonplace in England; the intriguing ones I used to see in Peter Sellers movies. The phone booth I used was located across the street from a fish and chip shop where bored Middle Easterners waited patiently for that next customer with a fast food craving. It was also a phone booth up the road from Dickens' old hamlet, that had a plaque in front of it for all those who passed. Lovers of his work could feel they'd brushed up against a landmark that had once held his genius. In the end, it was just a phone booth. But once I entered it and made that call telling Pamela I'd like to come home to live with her, the adventure would be over.

I made the call quickly, not wanting Dickens' ghost to pull me away, as it yelled, "Live! Dammit! Take a risk for once in your life! You're a writer! You're not meant to settle down!" But nothing supernatural stopped me that day. So I said goodbye to Rochester Cathedral and William on the hill; to Dickens's hamlet; to the man who rented a room above me in that confining house near town; and to his striped kitten that liked to wander the narrow carpeted stairs; to England; and most of all, to the undiscovered and dodgy life that might have been. The fog and I went home. It would be the third time we'd left England in the past ten years, and the third time we'd lost touch with the wanderer's dream

23

School Daze

BACK IN PAMELA'S room in Menlo Park, I was alone with her housemate's cat and my own mediocrity. In a few weeks I found us a better room in a house in Redwood City's Emerald Hills. We moved into a former carpenter's pine-paneled converted basement that looked like a boat, and I quickly hung up my Rochester Cathedral placemat.

Pamela and I ran aground in Emerald Hills, just as Noah's ark supposedly came to rest on Mt. Ararat after the flood. Below the house was a vast suburb that led to the shores of the San Francisco Bay, the Pacific Ocean, and somewhere on the other side of the world, England.

Now, like Pamela's former roommate and the bloke in England with the striped kitten, we had a cat of our own. He watched me play a Sonic the Hedgehog video game every day when he wasn't looking out the window for the gopher who'd taken up residence in our front yard. I'd become hooked on the silly game and nothing else seemed to matter. The game belonged to Pamela, and it was the first time I got a taste of this new type of juvenile diversion. I hadn't played video games since the old black and white versions shown to me in the seventies, and I was amazed at how far technology and fun had come since then.

Sonic quickly became another of my many wasted pursuits. I feverishly tried to get an animated creature through level after level of pleasurable lands and villains attacking. There seemed to be nothing else to do while exploring my options. There was enough food in our college-size refrigerator and enough heat to keep out the cold. I was unemployed, but I knew another plan would germinate somewhere in my mind if I just gave the fog enough time to burn off.

After a few dead-end jobs that did nothing more than get me out of the house, I decided to go back to school. Like driving and florist shops, school was an old friend of mine. When in doubt about what to do next, sometimes I'd seek out a class on some subject somewhere. At least school would be more productive than video games. I thought school was always a safe, fun place too; a place to goof off without worrying too much about consequences. I had a long history of attending different schools. Being a student frees one from normal responsibilities, and even though I've often been out of work while attending school, I've never felt any guilt associated with studying for a better future.

In addition to the two R.O.P. courses I'd taken that had prepared me for work with Huddart Park and Cooley Godward Castro Huddleson & Tatum, I'd also embarked on a carpentry course with the county training center. But after just one class, I dropped the program. I've always struggled with numbers, and they were too integral to carpentry.

I'd also taken a bank teller's course with another county-based outfit similar to R.O.P., a trade school dubbed Organizations Industrial Centers West. I passed the course, but thought better of trying to get a job with a bank since I knew I didn't really belong in a place handling people's money, with my aptitude for figuring things out. So I shoved the bank teller training certificate in a briefcase with my other training diplomas and my G.E.D., and temporarily went back to work. But I'd soon return to another school. I guess I was just hooked on the idea of getting one more useless diploma, although this time I decided to focus on something other than driving trucks or pounding nails.

While stationed in the military overseas, I'd racked up a few college credits by taking some classes with a branch of the University of Maryland. I thought I might be able to get a college degree someday. I wasn't sure what I'd do with one, but others had told me that college degrees helped people earn more money and get better jobs. Besides, I had to get one. Pamela already had a two college diploma lead on me.

So I told my new steady I was going back to college. She agreed that it seemed more productive than video games and watching the cat watching the gopher. I enrolled in a junior college named Cañada College since it was nearby and would help me to get into a higher college later on. Although a lot older and more jaded by life by the time I started college again, I was nonetheless right back where I'd been a few years before. It was the same campus where I'd set my sights on getting a degree until I met Carrie and tossed my college books in a trash can so that I could embark on an adventure of romantic destiny and, ultimately, military servitude.

This time, the students in class with me at Cañada were just slightly older than I'd been the first time I'd entered the school's tidy grounds. They were eighteen to twenty-two years old. They had little real-world experience but were eager to get some. They were all smiles and playfulness, and I was a seasoned older man set on nothing else but rapidly getting an A.A. (Associate in Arts degree) in Journalism. Some of the classes did help me with my writing—especially when it came to structure. Of the non-writing classes, I did best in subjects such as Oceanography, California History, and my favorite, the one that delved into the early Native American experience.

Even though I wasn't sure how elective classes would help me become a better writer, I'm sure they made me a more rounded person. From a purely practical standpoint, I knew elective classes would help me with my future goals since I needed them to help obtain my A.A. degree. I found classes like these interesting, but I knew they'd have no value out there in the working world. I could probably have learned the same things from reading books on my own without the aid of a teacher. Math was the toughest subject to get through, and I don't think I would have done so without Pamela and all those late nights spent poring over equations and logical conclusions. By the end of our stressful study sessions, my emotionally battered girlfriend was usually in tears, and I was full of anger and frustration.

But the hard work paid off, and not just in mathematics. Somehow, I managed to pass each of my subjects and earn that treasured degree. I was ecstatic. This was a benchmark achievement, something I never thought myself capable of. It was one of the proudest moments of my life. The fact that I could earn a college degree gave me new hope. Still, one degree wasn't enough. I wanted to take my college education one step further, so I enrolled in San Francisco State with the intention of earning a B.A. in journalism. Pamela had gone to a big school, so why couldn't I? All it took was a few student loans and credit cards.

San Francisco State seemed a lot more prestigious to me than Cañada. It had dormitories—like the ones I'd seen at Stanford all those years I circled the Palo Alto campus in my delivery vans or Jake's Bronco late at night. I wasn't privileged or wealthy enough to live in one of the SFSU apartment-like dwellings. Nonetheless I'd become worthy enough to sit in the same classes as those who did. Just walking the college grounds made me feel important. People lay out on lawns talking about weighty subjects. Protestors often carried signs around or handed out pamphlets. It seemed as though I was in one of the intellectual hubs of America, fog or not, and nobody seemed to care whether or not my thoughts were disjointed, just as long as I continued to be part of the giant scholastic think tank.

It was about this time that my Berkeley degree-holding girlfriend also decided to quit working and go back to school. But instead of a modest state-run school like mine on the fringes of a large metropolitan city like San Francisco, Pamela chose none other than Stanford University. After all, the school had accepted her, and she couldn't pass up the opportunity. So now both of us were unemployed students living on loans and credit cards, filling our days with reading and writing, speculation and speaking out.

Pamela's attending Stanford hit a little too close to home for me. It wasn't fair. She wasn't even from California, and she was getting an M.B.A. just a short walk away from such former employers of mine as Haag & Haag and the oriental carpet store. I was still jealous of anyone who got to attend Stanford, and I told her so. She said it wasn't a big deal, but that only made it worse.

Even though I wasn't going to an Ivy League school, I was still proud, and I attacked my subjects with a fervor that I hadn't experienced in years. I got so good at doing what was required of me that I ended up on the Dean's List most of the time I was at SFSU. The first time the words "Dean's List" showed up on a report card with my grades on it, I had to ask Pamela what they meant. She told me that they meant I was doing well, and that made me smile a lot more. I changed my major from Journalism to Creative Writing because I was a lot more interested in writing fiction than nonfiction. Just as at Cañada College, I felt many classes at San Francisco State weren't essential to becoming a better writer, but they helped me understand more about my world.

As a prerequisite for obtaining a B.A. in Creative Writing, I had to take a lot of literature classes, and literature classes meant lots of reading. I hadn't done much reading prior to these classes. I found books tedious and difficult. My concentration would wander, and I'd often lose track of characters or events. I still do. Many times I read passages repeatedly until information sinks in. Like in the rest of my life, I'm lucky if I retain anything. Many of my memories seem fuzzy, and I can't trust myself to remember names and dates accurately. But that's the way it's always been for me. I tend to recall the gist of an experience, and not the exacting details that most are fortunate enough to call forth. Sometimes, however, I remember little details that even surprise me to this day. For example, I still know the phone number of my childhood home on Eighth Avenue—even though neither my family nor I have lived in this home for over twenty years.

I came to the conclusion that reading novels didn't necessarily help me with the process of writing the way teachers thought it would help. I think the teachers' theory was that if students read certain literature, they would subconsciously absorb what they thought was proven good writing, and this would make for a better writer. I thought that more writing would help us become better writers. But I still had to go along with the program if I wanted to graduate. Even so, I barely kept up with my reading assignments because I just didn't care for most of the books I was forced to read. I'd often just scan them to get the gist of what they were about. Even when I was fortunate enough to finish a book, I usually didn't understand a lot of what I'd read. I developed a bad rep with some teachers when I told them I thought some of the classics they had me read were difficult to get through and not really worthy of my time. But I filled papers with information I plucked from books and commented on it so teachers would keep giving me good grades.

Still, I felt I wasn't getting as much from college as I would have liked. Mainly, I wanted to learn more about editing and polishing my writing. I came to believe the overall college experience focused on theories about writing and the craft of writing, but lacked conviction when it came to the more commonplace nuts and bolts of writing. I didn't feel I was learning what I needed to learn to help me become an accomplished writer. I got so frustrated with my instruction that I began to lose the initial momentum I had had when I entered SFSU. I started to throw together papers filled with a lot of double-talk and fluff. I waited until the last minute to hand them in.

Thankfully, attending SFSU wasn't all for naught, though. We read a few authors whose work I really enjoyed, and I doubt I would have been introduced to them had I not attended the college. Author Paul Auster was one of my favorite forced reads. I eventually read everything he wrote, even though I didn't have to. I considered him a genius with an original voice. I also liked Jerzy Kozinski who wrote *Being There*, which was later made into a Peter Sellers movie. Joyce Carey's *The Horse's Mouth* was worthwhile, as was Tim O'Brien's *The Things They Carried*, about Vietnam. In spite of my misgivings, college gave me a love of reading I hadn't had before. After college, I seemed to need to read, whereas before college I only did it when I had to.

Good books made me laugh and wonder why they were so good; bad books made me wonder how they could have gotten published in the first place. I became quick to notice all the boilerplate formulas in books that were so predictable and without salient literary value. Even though I couldn't stomach the supermarket stand novels, I had a hard time with books like *Catch 22* and *Moon Palace* that both intrigued and confused me. Still, I wanted to write like the Joseph Hellers and Paul Austers of the world. I wanted to leave my mark. Unfortunately, even though many people told me I had a lot of talent, the same people would criticize some of the confusing and jumbled prose that I tried to pass their way. Teachers would say that my work was often too predictable—the very thing I loathed in all those cookie-cutter murder stories. Teachers also said my work was often too linear, and that drove me crazy. I strained my foggy mind to come up with fresh and, hopefully, more abstract stories. Of course, it wasn't until years later that I developed my own voice and some of my work began to get recognition.

It wasn't until December 1998, upon receiving my first award for a short story, that I was able to understand how some of the literary works I had been forced to read might have actually seeped into my writings. The most worthwhile knowledge gets planted in my mind through subconscious saturation. When I consciously try to soak up anything taught to me, I often struggle to receive and process certain information. There were many times that I simply couldn't follow a teacher's lecture. It wasn't because I'd stop making attempts to understand what was being said, but ultimately I'd just get frustrated since I had trouble concentrating. Then I'd tune out most of what was being said. I'd sit there and daydream about what the people were like in the room with me, where they might live, or what kinds of jobs they might have. Or I'd wonder what I'd have for my next meal, or what kind of story I wanted to write next. All the while, in the background, it was as if a teacher was speaking with the wah-wah kind of voice the Peanuts characters used to hear in the Charlie Brown cartoons. I did learn to make up for the loss of information in the classroom.

Many epiphanies came when I labored over a textbook or piece of literature away from class. Somehow, when I was on my own, I was able to focus on enough of what I read to write about it. So even though I got frustrated in the classroom and had difficulty retaining the information I needed, there was still a good reason why I maintained my Dean's List standing. Most of my grades reflected my independent study efforts. I had learned to live with the drawbacks of ADD and, indeed, overcome them sufficiently to become a

better writer. I was even able to begin to enjoy some of the college experience.

In addition to taking pleasure in some of the books assigned me at SFSU,
I also relished some of the elective classes. They were avant-garde. There was
a class on comedy where people got up on stage and did stand-up acts for
grades, or they wrote humorous plays. I learned to love theater almost as
much as I loved writing, and there was a performing arts class that allowed
me to stretch my acting muscles.

There were also a few SFSU writing classes I enjoyed, and I'd labor over
short stories, novels, poetry, and even plays for my teachers. But as much as I
enjoyed many of the things I did at SFSU, ironically, I often felt lonely and
unfulfilled. I couldn't seem to make any friends at school, and I usually spent
my limited time on campus by myself, mulling over some archaic piece of
fiction as I sat in a common area drinking coffee or secluding myself in some
musty corner of SFSU's gigantic main library. The drab coloring of the
school and San Francisco's frequently overcast skies combined to fill me with
a feeling of gloom. Consequently, much of the work I turned in to teachers
was riddled with pensive passages or at least had a melancholy feel to it. This
prevailing melancholy got to at least one teacher when, during a one on one,
he said that I might consider not being so negative. Unfortunately, I took the
comment as an insult from someone who just didn't enjoy my style of
writing. But being defensive is just another symptom I've had to live with as
an ADDer. It's always been extremely hard for me to take criticism.

Either way, regardless of how I felt about teachers who were criticizing
my work, and regardless of what I was getting from the college experience,
there was no getting around the fact that after my first semester the initial
excitement of attending college had worn off. I continued to go through the
motions, trying to turn in assignments on time so that I could just move on
with my life. I only wanted everything to run smoothly so I could get
another little piece of paper to tack up on the wall and be even with Pamela.
But things didn't always run smoothly. As I did in the working world, I inevitably found myself involved in confrontations with others—mainly
teachers, who I often thought were talking down to me. In a utopian literature class, I got so outraged by a student teacher's comments that I loudly
voiced my objections and walked out of the classroom before class had
ended. I did the same in a class on Edgar Allan Poe. But at least I wasn't alone
in thinking the teacher of this class treated his students poorly. He was an
old, crotchety, bent-backed professor with one giant eyebrow. He growled at

students when they said anything he didn't agree with. The guy always had a disgruntled look and outlook on things. He looked like he belonged in an insane asylum, alone in some room going over conspiracies in the world that had no validity to them. Not only did his eyebrow have the singular objective of running amok over his eyes like some long forgotten lawn that had overtaken two lost sprinkler heads, but so did his mind. It was constantly working itself into a frenzy over all the things which could be read between the lines of Poe's writing.

This teacher was a true Jekyll and Hyde in the flesh, only he always remained the monster who couldn't turn back into the level-headed gentleman. I'm sure Poe would have been proud of him. The professor wore on me like a shoe that didn't fit right, and I usually matched his screwed-up facial expressions when he shot down anything I had to say on Poe's work. I dreaded coming to that class, and I'd linger in the hall as long as possible before entering the classroom. It was the worst kind of ADDer's nightmare.

Things got so bad that ultimately I paid a visit to the head of the Creative Writing Department and registered a complaint. It turned out that I hadn't been the only one to protest. I was told the former class had also lodged a unanimous complaint. The students were all studying for their Master's degree and had planned a one-day boycott of class in protest at the way they were being treated. Only the teacher had shown up on the day of the walkout. But this hadn't affected the professor's job security. That was the problem: the teacher had tenure, and he was immune to being fired unless he did something so outlandishly evil that even his status would no longer help him. Each day he glared at his students and threw out tidbits of wisdom about Poe and his work.

The teacher constantly espoused his theory about Poe being a necrophiliac, and he said this obsession with dead people was made clear in at least one of the writer's stories. I didn't necessarily see this as being the case, but I didn't care one way or the other. In fact, I had grown so disinterested with the class that I didn't even participate in its round-table discussions. Instead, I inserted a magazine inside my open notebook and read from it, completely oblivious to what was going on in class. Unfortunately, Mr. Bentback circled the room one day as he preached on Poe and saw the open magazine. Without missing a beat of his lecture, he told me to put the magazine away. I paused for a moment, maintaining eye contact with my professor as he reached the other side of the room before slamming the magazine shut.

The professor's single eyebrow rose slightly, but he went on with his lecture. Suddenly I decided that I'd had enough that day and went to the door, slamming it behind me hard enough to send reverberations throughout the room. My mind then shut down, and I wandered SFSU's sunny grounds until I reached the cafeteria where I sat, taking in the people near me. I did come back to the remaining Poe classes, even though I wondered why I did so, since I was sure I'd get a failing mark. I didn't. In fact I was later amazed to find out that I'd received a B in the class.

As my college days continued on a course destined for a B.A. in Creative Writing, I tried to earn a few extra dollars taking a night job with an editing firm. I worked in a room with a few other editors in a South San Francisco high rise. I was hired to make sure the legal text conformed to a particular format for publication. A couple of very bright teenagers sat at computers on either side of me doing the same work. They were best friends, and it seemed way ahead of other teenagers, and probably some adults, when it came to editing. They were certainly better at editing than I was. I felt bored and out of place between them and not too sure about what I was doing, but I stayed as long I could just to earn some well-needed funds. During a break, while the teenagers racked their brains over a newspaper's crossword puzzle, I called Pamela from a darkened office and told her I didn't want to stay another night staring at one of those impersonal computers. As I vented on the phone, I could see Candlestick Park in the distance, and I thought of its openness, of the fun all those baseball fans and players were having. In the end, I didn't return to Barcly Law Publishing. I took advantage of the regained chunk of time to concentrate on my studies.

2 4

All the World's a Stage

IN THE LATE eighties I went through a stage where I felt I needed a hobby—something to invest my time in that didn't revolve around careers or earning money. I'd been out of the Air Force about four years, and I was still bouncing around from one job to the next. I needed something that would allow me just to express myself, something that would accept me. I got wind of a series of acting classes being offered at a local junior college, so I enrolled in one. Acting seemed like a good choice for someone who had always been so interested in TV and movies.

The beginning actors' class at Foothill College was a perfect start for someone like me who'd never had any acting experience. The teacher began with a basic explanation of stage terminology; what things like downstage and the fourth wall meant. Then we actually got ready to act. There were warm-up exercises designed to make the actors less rigid, and improvizational exercises which helped actors think on their feet. Finally, there were scenes we had to perform from plays I'd never heard of.

I fell in love with Janus, my teacher, from the start. It wasn't romantic love; it was admiration of her techniques and open method of teaching. My teacher had been in a few movies and had a strong background in the theater. She was a beautiful brunette with a laid-back personality who believed in exploration when it came to acting. I often thought she would have fitted right into a place like LA, where eclectic actors hung out and dreamed of making it big. She also believed in having her students empty their minds before class. In one exercise intended to help us achieve this goal, we lay in a darkened room with our arms by our sides while Janus spoke softly of a beautiful garden and the waterfall in it. She wanted us to fully relax and only see the things she was describing, but I couldn't relax. I can never relax when somebody tells me to relax. And as far as focusing on the garden and water-fall, I failed. Instead, I thought of things like what I would eat later, or how my job was going—anything but things such as the flowers and plants she was describing, or the waterfall's gently falling water.

I liked everything about the theater at Foothill College, from the large velvet curtains that framed the stage to the single bulb that was always left burning when nobody was there. And I liked acting too. It brought out a lot of different emotions in me—even though these emotions got so intense that they were sometimes difficult to deal with. But even then I relished the chance to act. It was finally a way to express myself without getting into trouble or feeling awkward. I could play the fool or the villain, and no one cared as long as I got my lines right.

The fact that I enjoyed acting wasn't the only reason I excelled in it. I was good at it. Playing a character seemed easy for me, and it surprised me when I saw that it was so difficult for others. I was amazed that I could actually commit something to memory—word for word—because of my past trouble with so many other subjects. On the Hillsborough Police Officer test, for example, I had much more difficulty remembering a few details in a one-page story or criminal penal code than I did in recalling line after line of Shakespearean dialogue. But how could this be?

I did some thinking and figured it out. For one thing, on a test there was intense pressure to come up with answers while people were watching me and time was short. ADDers don't usually do well under pressure. But there was another reason I had more trouble taking a test than I might have had remembering the lines in a play. Memorizing lines in a play is rote memory work. I say them to myself repeatedly until I can retain them for a play's short run. The Hillsborough Police Officer test required more than just rote memorization; it required memorizing information and then applying it to a problem that needed solving. I had to actually figure things out under pressure—the same way a police officer might.

Also, I liked acting. There were more rewards if I could get a few lines under my belt and get on stage, than if I could get a pass score on a test. Having fun is key to doing something well. If I'm doing something I like, my focus is more concentrated. And if my focus is more concentrated, I do better. I've heard this is a truism across the board when it comes to ADDers. However challenging it can be, even acting becomes rote once the character is mastered and you act him out enough times. In addition to the privilege of performing before an audience, I got to play in a well-organized atmosphere, an atmosphere that suited my love for order.

But all this understanding of why I was able to memorize lines and act, and why I liked acting, would come later on. In the beginning, I just kept plugging away at something new that I felt I had a knack for. After taking my first acting class, I took another, and then another. In fact, I kept taking acting classes until I finally got up the nerve to audition for Shakespeare's *A Midsummer-Night's Dream* in Palo Alto. It was being put on at an upscale all-girls school. I landed the part of Demetrius, one of the play's four lovers, and I set about trying to make my way through the Elizabethan language. As soon as I got used to words such as "thou" and "doth," memorizing lines was a piece of cake. I even began to like the way Demetrius talked. In fact, I liked the way every character talked, and the way they moved. It was just like seeing a TV show acted out. And then I got my first chance to act before an audience.

Each night before the performance, I would be incredibly nervous until my first line was delivered, and then the pressure lifted and I felt as though I were talking to a few friends. When I got to a part in the play where I had to call out in anger and wield a futuristic plastic sword—a nouveau prop that accompanied spaceman-like garb created by an avant-garde costume designer—I always felt a little dizzy, and there was a slight pain in my side. For a minute, I was lost on stage, as if some ancient ghost had taken over my body, but then the pain and dizziness would pass, and I'd get right back into the flow of things. After the play, I got a rush from all the applause and a few of the younger girls in the play who fawned over me. I couldn't believe the feeling I got from all the attention.

When the play's run was over, I felt as though a lasting relationship had ended. If I was in the neighborhood where the theater was located, I'd look at it and remember all the wonderful times I'd spent inside. Even though I missed acting in the play, I also realized that I felt a kind of relief to be done with it; not to have to worry about recalling all those lines or missing my cues. In a way, it almost made sense that the play had been so shortlived—everything else in my life had been. But there was a difference between the play not lasting and the other things in my life not lasting. There were no guilty feelings and no enduring bad associations when *A Midsummer-Night's Dream* came to an end.

I think there was one more reason I liked the play. It was the mere idea of someone casting me, as if I'd been welcomed into some private fraternity or exclusive club. I knew I needed more of this kind of acceptance and more of the elation I felt on stage, so I auditioned for my next play at Lucie Stern Theater in Palo Alto. It was a community theater not far from the girls' school, a large and well-known theater with a steady flow of plays. The play I auditioned for was *Inquest,* which dealt with the true story of Julius and Ethel Rosenberg—two civilians convicted of espionage in the U.S. I studied hard for the role of Julius, and thought I'd be a shoe-in, but somebody else got the part. I guess the director decided that I just didn't have enough experience to tackle such a meaty role. Nonetheless, I was cast in a series of supporting roles, which included electric chair technician and reporter, but my favorite role was that of an FBI agent who got to grill Julius shortly after he was arrested. I leaned heavily on Julius to make him spill the beans about stealing government documents. Because I was jealous of the actor who played the part of Julius, it became altogether too easy to deliver my gruff G-Man lines—except for one night, that is.

Opposite the interrogation scene on the large Lucie Stern stage, was a simultaneous scene with Ethel Rosenberg talking on a weighty payphone about her husband's arrest. During one performance, a few moments into her phone call, the entire phone fell onto the stage with a mighty crash. Fortunately, every actor stayed in character even with the distraction, but for a moment my mind completely lost its focus. The noise of the crash and the payphone lying at Ethel's feet took precedence over the part I was playing. Then, my mind wandered to the actress who played Ethel, her dark hair and small frame bending over the phone as she desperately tried to stay in character. I caught a glimpse of her form-fitting fifties gray suit, her gloves, the tiny hat with black veil that partially obscured her face. I noticed the glare of the stage lights, and I was aware of someone in the audience in the front row, a plastic glass filled with white wine dangling from his fingers. All of these observations only took a few moments, but I had broken the fourth wall—a cardinal sin in the theater—and I was afraid I wouldn't be able to return to the play. My ADD mind was literally running amok and I strained to narrow my focus again, to grill Julius. I looked into the worried actor's eyes; he saw the confusion in mine. Somehow, I knew he sensed what was happening, but he also knew there was little he could do about it. Then the jealousy I felt over this actor getting the part I had longed for locked me back into the role of FBI agent. Almost as if I'd never broken my concentration, I uttered a line about how Julius should relax. I was the cool, patient interrogator offering Julius a cigarette or stick of gum as he sweated before me in the hot seat.

After that night, the play's run went without a hitch. I felt sorry for the Rosenbergs. Since I had always been under a spotlight because of ADD, I could empathize with these people. In fact, it became a trend for me to empathize with characters who were always under intense scrutiny. And if these characters were ever chastised in any way for what they did, I felt as though I were being chastised too.

During *Inquest* I got used to putting on stage make-up for the first time—even though I tried to behave as if I'd done it before. Behaving like this was nothing new. Because of my inability to pick up on things throughout my life, I'd made a point of pretending that I knew what I was doing. I often tried to fake my way through things just so no one would make fun of me. Deep down, as in those other situations when I faked it, I wanted to walk over to someone and ask how I was supposed to paint my face. But I couldn't bring myself to do it. I just watched the other actors putting on their make-up and did what they did.

There was something else I didn't know about while acting in *Inquest*. It was the meaning of the word "strike" on the play's rehearsal and performance schedule. I thought the word meant that the actors and other people connected to the play would have to carry signs in protest of something. Little did I know that when used in the theater the word strike only means that actors help dismantle the set. Nonetheless, because I misunderstood what the term meant, I thought it better not to get involved in the strike and its political implications. All during the play, I wondered when the strike would take place, but I dared not ask lest I appear too eager to participate, or unknowledgeable about something else I should have known about. After someone told me what strike meant in theater terminology, I felt unaware as ever about what took place around me.

But it didn't take long for me to learn the theater ropes, and I knew I now had a hobby that could last well into my old age. It also didn't take me long to audition for my next play, which was also being cast at Lucie Stern Theater. *God's Country* was a play based upon another true story about a racist Aryan organization—dubbed The Order—that had been disbanded by the government. It was an incredibly dramatic piece. A lot of hatred was spewed out on stage along with a great many hard-hitting images. This time, I was cast in even more supporting roles than the last play, including prosecuting attorney, coroner's pathologist, racist paramilitary leader, racist priest, convicted racist prisoner, and armed robber. At first I had a tough time keeping all the characters straight in my mind, and an even tougher time dealing with the frenzied costume changes. But after a while, I got used to this strenuous task. The theater had my costumes neatly arranged backstage, and there were ever-watchful stagehands who made sure the right costume got onto the right actor at the right time. Again, as with memorizing lines, changing costumes became a rote memory activity. As soon as a certain line was uttered, I knew it was my turn to change into the next costume.

The only other difficulty I had with the play was something that might seem trivial to people without ADD. While playing the part of the racist priest, I had to wear a KKK-like robe and hood. When I was dressed that way, I found it difficult to see through the tiny eye-holes in the hood. The stage lights were always off when we went on stage so that the torches we priests carried would be all the more brilliant. I never could understand how KKK members could tolerate those annoying hoods; mine drove me crazy. When wearing the hood, I often felt disoriented and would stumble over steps or bump into doorjambs. I once read that, even without cumbersome headgear, people with ADD often bump into things. I've never liked wearing anything on my head. Even when I wore a cap while playing baseball or watching the San Francisco Giants at Candlestick, I wished I could flick it off. I was told by the educational kinesiologist that it wasn't uncommon for people with ADD to be bothered by things like this. Apparently, ADDers are more sensitive to items of clothing touching their bodies.

After *God's Country*, I didn't get involved in another play for some time. The thing with Julia caused me not to want to play anything or be around people much. I had trouble dealing with the intense emotions I felt while on stage. Also, I felt slightly uncomfortable being cast in roles such as attorney or coroner's pathologist, when the only jobs I could really land involved menial labor or rote duties designed for people without college degrees. It was difficult going back to delivering flowers after playing the lead counsel in a court of law.

However I guess I was bitten by the acting bug; I had to go back to the theater eventually. I craved the attention. Out there on stage, at least for a moment, I was key to something happening in the world. I was a success in setting something in motion. With delivering flowers, there was only the feeling that I was serving somebody else's needs and not my own. That's the way I usually felt. My prior endeavors seldom led to any sense of accomplishment during *God's Country*; my past failures were amplified by not being able to convince Julia that she should come back into my life. This made being a success on stage a must. The bottom line was that in the play I felt important, and I felt that I had created something uniquely my own, and people knew it. I saw no other way to find this kind of importance and creativity. I was not only bitten by the acting bug, but its bite injected a kind of healing cocktail into my wounded psyche.

By the time I got parts in a couple of stage-adapted versions of the old *Twilight Zone* shows, I'd been with Pamela for a while. I was ready to forget about the past and move on with my life. This time, the theater was at my alma mater, Cañada College. Being at the college again was like hanging around an old friend. The theater at Cañada was small, but I got to act out the bizarre scenes which had appeared in a TV show that I absolutely adored. In one half of the play, I played the part of Sailor in the *Twilight Zone* episode called "The Hitchhiker." It was a kick being decked out in an authentic, all-white sailor's uniform. It made me feel as though I had won back my government's approval and been reinstated into the military once more. Soon the realization that I'd forever burned that bridge set in again, and I fell into a stupor. Then, the thought of putting on that Navy uniform left an empty feeling in the pit of my stomach, but the show must go on. Every night, I swung my duffel bag over my shoulder (the same one I'd actually used in the Air Force) and played my part.

During the second half of the night's performances, I played the part of Phillip Hall, from the episode called "Perchance to Dream." Phillip was a man plagued by a recurring dream that seemed altogether too real to him. I couldn't help noticing the tie-in to my own life, the way one similar disaster after another had played itself out. There was a young temptress in Phillip's dream who toyed with the fact that he had a weak heart. She seemed intent on pushing her victim over the edge, so to speak, and worked her best magic when she lured Phillip onto a giant roller coaster. As with the earlier plays, now I was not only empathizing with a character, but I felt I was living surreptitiously through him. The temptress was analogous to all the attacks and shortcomings in my life, and she'd come for me, not Phillip. Even though I still felt the exhilaration of getting the attention I needed on stage, I also felt an odd sensation of doom. I loathed the temptress's seductive attempts to slowly push me each night.

At the end of the dream, Phillip and I were so overcome with terror and excitement that we dove through an office building's window. By the time the play was over, I actually thought I might have a heart attack given the intensity of the things I felt just before crashing through the window. I started to wonder if this experience was more destructive than cathartic. For the first time since I'd started acting, I also began to wonder if it was something I truly wanted to do. The play tested more than my emotional state; it tested my ability to endure night after night as an actor with a big part.

It was also the first time I wasn't happy with a director, and I often felt he was doing things contrary to the way I wanted them done. I felt as though I needed less control and more freedom to flex my new thespian muscles. During one particular rehearsal of "Perchance to Dream," I tried to develop the heart attack scene so it would come across more realistically.

"You need to show signs of torment a little earlier, Ken," the director said. "It might be better if we see more terror and agony on your face during the roller coaster ride."

I thought I had the facial expressions down pat. "Signs of torment?" "Terror and agony?" My whole life was torment and agony. What did this director know about torment and agony? I thought. All I wanted was a coke in Cañada's cafeteria on the other side of the parking lot.

"Let's get back up on the roller coaster," the director said.

Let's take a fiver, I thought, loosening my tie.

The temptress and I got up on the stage version of a roller coaster, and we both held onto the wooden bar in front of us. The young actress beside me delivered the lines that were supposed to set me on a course of no return. I told her, in Phillip's terrorized voice, that I couldn't take any more. Just as things were reaching a fevered pitch, the director cut in.

"Okay, hold on. Ken, maybe you could close your eyes here or even move away from her a little. We need to get the sense that you have to get off this damned roller coaster or you're going to die. I don't think we're getting that. Do you feel as though you're going to die?"

I had the sense that if I didn't get out of that theater I would die. What did he want from me? I was showing terror. I was afraid. I was afraid that if he said one more word, I'd jump down from that coaster and take it upon myself to take a fiver. I wanted to sit somewhere by myself and stare into space. To watch people or simply not hear about how I wasn't playing my part right. What did this director want from me?

"Ken, do you know what I mean?" We locked eyes for a moment before he said, "Okay, let's take five minutes."

Now I could get off the roller coaster and find level ground again. I'd go somewhere and have control of my life for a few minutes. I'd get that time I needed to reflect on how the director's instructions just didn't fit in to my way of thinking. Then I'd go back and do the roller coaster scene the way I'd always done it because that's the only way it made sense to me.

Of course, all this rebelliousness just came with the territory. After all, it was the first time I'd got to play the lead, and I think my ADD head may have gotten a few sizes bigger. In fact, after the *Twilight Zone* appearances I felt I had a firm grasp of acting and could play almost any part thrown at me. It didn't really matter what a director said. I decided to shuck the old acting adage: "There are no small parts, only small players," and only accept leading roles from then on. Small parts were just too boring now. Even if bigger roles took a toll on me, I needed more stimulation. I just couldn't walk out on stage and say one or two lines and walk off any more. I wanted almost constant interaction with the other actors, or at least a few long monologues. That's the only way I could see making the theater experience worthwhile.

It was around this time that I registered with a talent agency in San Francisco and tried to break into TV or the movies. I submitted a batch of head shots that were kept on file with the agency, and whenever they felt I had the type of look one of their clients wanted, my face was sent out. I got a few nibbles. Once I was called in for an ice cream commercial, and I had to lick an imaginary ice cream cone in front of the camera. Another time, I was called out for a print ad for Sears. I didn't get cast for either assignment. In fact, in the end I only got cast as an extra in a handful of things. I was a cop in an episode of *Nash Bridges*.

I thought that being on a TV set would be exciting until I realized that extras had to sit around most of the day until the next scene was ready to be shot, and shot again, and again. It was definitely not exciting. I was told not to talk to the principals, in this case Don Johnson and Cheech Marin—but I talked to Cheech anyway. In addition to things not being very exciting on the set of this filming, I felt that as extras we were considered part of the backdrop. We weren't allowed to have any lines on camera unless we'd joined one of the actor's unions—which I wasn't ready to do.

I got the feeling the other extras like me were just killing time and hoping to catch a glimpse of someone famous. The crew addressed us as "atmosphere" when it was our time to do our thing. Before then, we mostly just sat in an area called holding and talked about what other movies we'd been in, or what other actors we'd seen or actually gotten a chance to talk to. Big names like Schwarzenegger and Brosnan were thrown around along with things like: "He's really cool," or "He works out every day." Being an extra and hearing about those important lives made me feel all the more small. After all, my life hadn't turned out the way I planned. I hadn't become the rock star I'd always wanted to be, I was just atmosphere; and it appeared that all I would ever be was atmosphere.

Still, being on a movie set was the closest I thought I'd ever get to the big time, so I agreed to be an extra in another *Nash Bridges* episode. This scene was again shot in San Francisco. Wearing a police officer's uniform made me pause. It was ironic that someone now wanted me to wear this uniform in the very city where I'd applied to be a cop. But that's just the way it was, and all I could do was get back into my street clothes and head home with the sad notion that there was playtime and there was reality.

There would be a few more roles as an extra: a priest in a movie called *Toby's Story*—that I never saw; a meat packer in a Robin Williams movie called *Patch Adams*. I strained to see Mr. Williams over a roomful of other meat packers but never did. Much later when I got an agent in Austin, Texas, I got a part as a protester in a movie called *The Life of David Gale*. I was glad to be in this movie because I had had such high regard for Kevin Spacey, the star, ever since seeing *K-Pax*. I had told Pamela for weeks about how I wanted to be like Kevin Spacey—so together, so focused. I wanted to wear a face like his that bespoke of no worries or troubles in life. I saw Kevin three times during the shoot: once at about five a.m. when he was still unshaven and walking a small terrier; a second time as he brushed against me on his way to lunch in a room that had been converted to a chow hall for the cast and crew; and a third time on Austin's state capitol grounds while I sat on the lawn waiting between takes for my next call to action. I'm sure Kevin had no idea what I was thinking as he sat there about ten or fifteen feet away on his folding chair. I wanted to know what made him tick, what he thought, why he was so unapproachable, so different than me. On the surface he seemed similar to me—dark hair, rounded face. We were possibly even the same age, but there was obviously a difference. He had a chair to sit on, a large umbrella, and a man at his beck and call with cell phone in hand. He was high; I was low. He was famous; I was not. He obviously had something inside that I couldn't see, some hidden clear-minded secret for success, something that perhaps he didn't even know about himself. But it was there. So I watched him carefully, unobtrusively, trying to guess what that something was. My eyes followed Kevin to a nearby trash can where he deposited a handful of orange peels, and then they followed him back to his director's chair and to the very thick book he read. I watched him take the cell phone from the man at his side and tried in vain to hear what few words he spoke in between chuckles. But there was nothing I could see that told me why I was different from Kevin Spacey. No tangible thing. Once, I thought I saw him look directly at me, lock eyes with me, but I decided that he was probably engaged in some profound thought prompted by that thick book.

Sitting there on the lawn, I came up with an idea to write a short story about Kevin Spacey and me. In the story, I whisk Kevin away to my world for a while because he's in need of a break from all his hard work. I introduce him to my wife and ask him if he'd do some acting with me. Then we become good friends. It was a crazy idea for a story, but I just wanted that kind of connection. I needed more to go on, so that I could figure out what made someone like Kevin tick.

Then, as quickly as it took for him to finish his orange, my study of Kevin Spacey and thoughts of the short story were over. He was called back to work, to his further success, and I was back to my foggy thoughts there on the grounds where President George W. Bush had walked.

Now that I had an agent in Austin, I got sent out for some other things in addition to the Kevin Spacey film. There were a handful of TV commercials and another movie called *Secondhand Lions*, but even though I again felt excited about being around a few big-shot actors, I needed to get back to the stage. I knew I would get more attention there, and I'd feel more a part of things. I landed a role in a nearby Texas theater called the Polo Barn. Just as its name suggested, the theater had once been used to house horses and paraphernalia associated with the game of polo. The theater was in a cute, but incredibly small, red barn with just enough room for a stage upstairs and a place downstairs for actors to change or theater-goers to get refreshments. Usually, the two women who ran things at the theater would put on non-mainstream plays that the theater downtown wouldn't; plays with offensive words or lifestyles that a more conventional audience might not approve of. But occasionally the theater needed to draw a bigger crowd and bring in more money, so it would offer middle-of-the-road stuff. I got a part in one such offering, a very funny play called *The Foreigner*. I played a British non-commissioned officer with a heavy cockney accent who took his friend to a favorite retreat of his. Since the NCO's friend was incredibly shy, he told the other guests at the retreat that he was a foreigner. That's when all the fun began. I got to wear a helmet and goggles in the play and even to use a homemade plunger to blow up some white supremacists' van. It was a challenge working on the small stage, however, and I had to measure my movements carefully. But there's something to be said about an intimate theater. Once during the play, another actor accidentally dropped a small prop off the stage and to my amazement it was handed back to him. There was also a person in the audience who decided to use a corner of the stage as his own footstool. Despite the small size of the theater, I gave a larger-than-life performance. I spared no expense when it came to realism. I went to extra lengths to find a real British uniform, complete with ribbons, stripes, and a beret with a British military insignia pinned to it. I shaved my mustache to look like a young David Niven, and I went to a nearby college to study its cockney accent tape. By the time I hit the stage I was British. In fact, I was so British that a few audience members actually asked where I hailed from in Britain.

Not everything was hunky-dory during the play, however. My head started to swell again. I felt I couldn't do any wrong, and that I had mastered the part of Froggy, the character I played in *The Foreigner*. I didn't need any help from the director—or anyone else for that matter. This created palpable friction during rehearsals. Whenever someone tried to give me advice, I'd find a way to push it out of the limelight or act as though I'd taken note of it when actually I hadn't. After a while, some ugly tension built up between me and some of the other cast members. It got to the point where I ignored everybody until it was my turn to get on stage and act. I'd show up just in time for a performance so I could minimize my interaction with people and just do what I was really there to do. When the play was over, I tried to get out the back door as soon as possible so that I didn't have to hang around and sip wine with the audience who so eagerly awaited us downstairs. This hostility finally reached a climax. Now I had a problem. I wanted to act, but I didn't want anyone disagreeing with my take on things. Unfortunately, direction went along with acting. I didn't mind some direction, but directors—and even actors—always seemed to cross the line in my mind. Often, it seemed as though others wanted to control what I said or how I said it, or they wanted to control how I moved on stage, or where I moved. As a result, acting wasn't as much fun, and after each new play I would tell Pamela that I'd never act in another. Nonetheless, I'd always end up on stage again.

I finally realized I needed to take a break from acting after Neil Simon's play *Plaza Suite*. I played Sam, a character who came with more lines than I'd ever had to memorize. I spent every extra moment trying to remember what to say and when I was supposed to say it. And there was more "blocking" than I'd ever had too. Blocking is an acting term that means an actor's movements on stage. It caused me a little trouble. Saying lines was one thing; saying them as you did certain things was quite another. Adding emotions to the mix meant that I had to multitask. I've always been better doing one thing at a time. Sometimes my brain would just shut down if I had too many things to do. In *Plaza Suite* it came close to doing that a few times. If I wasn't using an electric razor on stage, I was moving to the bathroom to take some aspirin. If I wasn't doing either of these things, I might be talking on the phone or going over documents that I kept in a briefcase. The director had me constantly moving on stage. It went along with Sam's frustrated mood. Sam was trying to keep his annoying wife happy while at the same time trying desperately to get away from her so he could pursue an affair with his secretary. The play's pace was frenetic and sometimes I'd forget a line or two. Thankfully, the lines I forgot didn't affect the thrust or outcome of the play. But I was still tense on stage. There had again been a lot of tension created during rehearsals, a lot more than with *The Foreigner*. But I guess the thing that bothered me most was when one of the women who ran the theater had to fill in as director and she said I wasn't playing the character of Sam right.

From the very beginning, Beth thought that my character leaned too much on his cynicism for laughs, that my Sam was too one dimensional. With Beth, I was always under a microscope. If she thought I was doing something wrong, she'd tell me. I recall one time when she filled in for the director, who had a day off, questioning the way I said a single line.

"What's the matter?" I said as Sam.

"It's 'What's wrong?'" Beth pointed out, stopping me from going on with my lines. It hadn't been the first time she corrected me. She was right, and I knew it. I had the line wrong. I kept trying to get the line right, but in the end, if I inadvertently substituted "What's wrong?" for "What's the matter?" I didn't see a big problem.

"'What's the matter?' 'What's wrong?' what's the difference?" I asked.

"People didn't start saying 'What's the matter?' until the seventies. This play takes place in 1969," Beth said.

Then I felt the need to respond. I knew I shouldn't have, but I did anyway. "So you're saying that you know without a doubt that nobody said 'What's the matter?' until 1970?"

"'What's the matter' wasn't said until the seventies, that's right."

"You're sure about that? In every conversation, in every situation, in the entire year of 1969, no one said 'What's the matter?'"

"Why don't we just get on with rehearsal, Ken?"

"But how can you be so sure?"

"Listen, the line is 'What's wrong?' Do you have a problem with that?"

"No, but I just want to get this straight. How can you be so sure that no one said 'What's the matter?'"

"Because I lived back then, okay? Is that good enough for you?"

"I lived back then too," I said, even though I knew she had been much older than me in '69. "The fact is that you couldn't have been everywhere all the time in 1969."

"I was enough places. Let's move on, okay?"

"I see, and no one anywhere, said 'What's the matter?'"

Beth looked down at a copy of *Plaza Suite* in front of her and involuntarily tapped out a rhythm with a pencil before answering. "That's right. No one said 'What's the matter?' "

"And poof, 1970 hits, and someone says it for the first time."

Now Beth put her hands through her hair, looked up at the ceiling, and blew out a long sigh. I'd seen the look before when I pushed an issue, a look of complete frustration bordering on someone who's about to lose it. "What's the matter Beth?" I asked as innocently as I could before storming off stage. I knew Beth didn't want me there, and it was a struggle just to go to the theater each night. Beth also told the actress who played my wife in the play that she wasn't playing her role correctly either. The two of us would have long talks about the abuse we were getting. I even began to doubt myself and the choices I made, but I continued to show up for each performance.

Plaza Suite would be my last show though. Later, I learned that after a couple more shows the Polo Barn called it quits too. Now the theater and I were taking a well-needed break from all that playing around. Once again, ADD had severed my ties with something that showed potential in my life. It was the combination of my inability to deal with people and my insistence on standing my ground when I should have just been going with the flow. These tendencies had again shut down the show for me. Acting just wasn't fun any more. Acting had become a solitary pursuit. Of course I was aware that other people were on stage with me, but to use the TV and movie term I'd gotten used to, these people were only atmosphere. In my foggy way of looking at things, they were a necessary annoyance, there on stage so that I could do what I wanted to do.

But this kind of attitude doesn't cut it in show biz. Ultimately, my intolerance and inability to keep dealing with other actors forced me off the stage. Even so, maybe I'll return to the stage someday, but I haven't been able to get in the mood for a play since *Plaza Suite*. In fact, the only shows I participate in now are those I see from a distance. If all the world is a stage, than I'm just making sure I do my acting away from the theater.

Something Old, Something New,
Something Borrowed, ADD too

BACK IN OUR college days, Pamela was busy studying too. Thick books and folders filled with business jargon littered our small room on Lakeview Way in Redwood City's Emerald Hills. The information in the books and folders was completely foreign and uninteresting to me. So were the smiles and charged attitudes of Pamela's fellow students whom I sometimes met. The plain and simple truth was that my girlfriend and I were on different roads. One road hopefully would lead to the publication of my fiction someday, and the other meandered toward the probability of Pamela securing a lucrative future working in a corporate office somewhere.

Even though our careers seemed destined not to follow the same path, it seemed certain that our relationship would. After about a year of living together, we thought it time to take the next logical step in our union. We decided to get married. I still saw a goodness in Pamela that overshadowed that in any of the other women with whom I'd been involved. I thought we complemented each other well, and since we had lived in a one-room flat before getting married there was no hiding who we were.

It was in that tiny room in the California foothills that we learned everything there was to know about each other: about how we both wanted children; how we wanted to get a dog someday and live in the country; about how we both loved nature and God. In one of the best summers we ever spent together, we bought a canoe and strapped it to the top of our old 1973 pick-up and headed up north to Mt. Lassen. During the trip we found every dirt road and every alpine lake we could. In the morning we rowed under towering peaks before the sun rose. In the evening, we huddled close together in the truck's rusty camper shell and played gin rummy or Scrabble. On the way back to our studio apartment, we played Johnny Cash and sang along with him until we hit Sacramento and the steamy delta. By then, I had grown a beard and Pamela said I looked like a mountain man. She took pictures of me with things like beef jerky and licorice ropes dangling from my mouth.

We were always like a couple of kids, a little on the naïve side, either one of us trying to top the other's pie-in-the-sky dreams. When we ran out of money we'd just run up the credit cards and buy another toy to stuff in our already overstuffed knotty pine basement home where animals like raccoons and possums would sometimes come in an open window at night.

If we weren't at work or in class, Pamela and I played games or watched movies and talked about what was bad or good in them afterward. Pamela helped me with things like math and grammar, or other left-brain subjects that had always stumped me. In turn, I told her how to write stories or I just sang to her with my guitar on my lap. She got me hooked on country music, and I tried to get her hooked on the Rolling Stones.

As with most couples, there were times when we got on each other's nerves, but mostly we were just comfortable together. We realized that even though we would never like all of the same things, we were, nonetheless, more compatible than we were incompatible. I admired Pamela's ability to excel in just about everything she set her mind to, and I also admired her understanding when I fell short of succeeding in the things I set my mind to. I also knew that Pamela could put up with my turbulent outbursts, my moodiness, my defensiveness, my failure to bring much money into our home, and even my inability to understand everything that was thrown at me. And I knew that I could put up with the fact that she didn't like tomatoes, avocados, bell peppers, asparagus, artichokes, and chess.

Even though I told Pamela that my love for her would never be the highly charged romantic variety most women wanted, she still yearned to be my wife. I made sure, however, to tell her about my past, and I mean everything about my past. She needed to know with whom she was getting involved. God knows there were times during that first year before getting married when I would blow my top and not listen to anybody's opinion but mine, so I think she had an inkling of how volatile living with me could be.

Still, even after the full disclosure of my past life, Pamela was determined that I should be her husband, so we threw a few bags in a car and headed to Lake Tahoe, Nevada.

It was shortly after our arrival at this beautiful mountain retreat and gambling town that we enlisted the services of a woman who ran one of the fly-by-night marriage establishments a few miles past the casinos. She joined us in holy matrimony while standing behind a makeshift pulpit where she manipulated the volume of a prepackaged musical accompaniment to her words. As she delivered her prepared message with a meaningful smile, I could see the woman cleric automatically moving the levers on a console. In addition to the piped-in music, there were a few plastic flowers and plants for atmosphere in the diminutive wedding chapel. The pastor—or whatever her ordained moniker was—also read a moving Native American piece of prose which spoke of marriage as a serious commitment that united its constituents forever.

I wore a tight-fitting white suit jacket and slacks, and Pamela wore a tight-fitting, short dress with white stockings. There were three witnesses. One was my brother Mark, who drove a cab back then in Reno. To reach the chapel, Mark had to leave Reno's flatness and drive his cab into the mountains and thin air of Lake Tahoe. When he arrived at the chapel and saw me with Pamela, he grinned and shook his head as if he doubted marriage was such a good idea. But I didn't take this to heart. As the result of our parents' divorce, and later Mark's own, he felt less than hopeful about any couple's chances of staying together. But even with his doubts, my brother seemed happy for me. The other two witnesses were Pamela's Berkeley college roommate, who also attended Stanford, and the stunning young woman's husband, a suave man whose charm could be seen a mile away.

Shortly before the ceremony, the wedding ring, which I had purchased in a spiritual shop in San Francisco's famed Haight Ashbury, broke. It was only a thin break, and both Pamela and I agreed that we should still use it as the symbol of our upcoming union—at least until we could get a replacement. Even though we were still in good spirits before the wedding, the fog and I secretly hoped the broken ring wasn't a bad omen of things to come. When Pamela and I were pronounced man and wife, she and her girlfriend cried. After the short ceremony, all but my brother and the clergywoman went to a place in the mountains for a photo op, and then to Harrah's casino to play blackjack.

In a few days, my bride and I were back in our basement dwelling, busily studying business and literature. We tried our best to live the married life, and at least I now didn't feel so alone and in need of sex. Life was fairly mundane, although it continued to have its bouts of arguing and occasional unhappiness. We watched a lot of TV, visited with the couple who had witnessed the wedding, and sometimes flew back to Houston, Texas, to see Pamela's family. I had a difficult time when we visited Pamela's family. Her father, Bob, was an engineer who had a big house in a nice part of this large Texas metropolis. I felt embarrassed to say what I did, and there was never any talk about my past. Pamela's dad was everything I wasn't: even-tempered, extremely stable, intelligent, and a go-getter. I'd seen his type in all those professional buildings I used to deliver to. The ones with the big desks and all the family photos. He was like one of the lawyers at Cooley I'd once bowed down to. And I think he knew it, and probably still does. He had to live with the fact that his daughter had married a working-class man, and not a privately educated, high-earning, positive-thinking man like himself. I was an hourly wage earner who frequently said the wrong things and who was often disgruntled with life, but I would share the rest of his daughter's.

When we stayed under Bob's roof, I felt I didn't belong, that I hadn't earned the privilege to spend even ten minutes in such a lavish home during the most ordinary times—let alone the Christmas holidays. But Christmas is when I visited the Thomas family home. And not only did I get treated to southern hospitality on the home front, but fancy dinners out too—dinners that Bob would usually pay for unless I insisted on using one of our overcharged credit cards. And there were Christmas presents. Presents such as the nice shirts Pamela's mother would buy for me from some pricey store, shirts I felt I didn't deserve to wear. And there were financial gifts as well. Checks meant to make Pamela's and my life a little better. I didn't deserve any of it.

As the years went by, it became clear that I wouldn't advance to some acceptable form of work after college. Since I was still only capable of landing low-paying jobs, I secretly resented the Thomas gifts even more. I felt further embarrassed by the fact that I knew Pamela's eventual degree would most likely earn her a six-figure salary, making her the family's real breadwinner.

Pamela becoming a high-earning professional was a given. Her father was a professional. So were her sister, her brother, and her uncles. There were airline pilots in Pamela's family, accountants, engineers, business execs, and doctors at every turn. In my family, unless you went way back, there were mostly menial blue-collar workers who sweated for every buck. And unlike the smiling, well-balanced individuals in the Thomas family, the people in my family included heavy drinkers, malcontents, mental patients, and one foggy-minded misfit who still didn't understand most of what was being thrown at him—or why.

From the very start of my dealings with the Thomas family, it became clear that what I did in life would just be sort of ignored. I was Pamela's husband and that was that. During one of our first trips to Houston, we took a drive to a nearby restaurant and I got a sense of the future of our interactions with Pamela's parents.

"That's where my dad works," Pamela said, nudging me as her father drove us by a large office building like the ones in California's Silicon Valley. Pamela's mother said something about what we should have for dinner, and her father glanced at his daughter in the rearview mirror.

"Are you ready for Stanford?" he said, turning his attention back to the road in front of him.

"I guess so."

I expected Bob to ask about my future, but he didn't. "Well, you'll do okay at Stanford. You've always done okay," Bob said, glancing in the rearview mirror again. I waited eagerly for Pamela's father to ask me about my future, but he just drove on in silence. And he was still silent at the dinner table. When it came time for Pamela and me to fly back to California, Bob shook my hand and turned around to head back home. In fact in all the years I've known him, I don't think he ever asked about my desire to become a published writer, or about any of my desires whatsoever.

However, even though neither Bob nor his wife Carolyn ever took an interest in my life, they never put me down for marrying their daughter. All the Thomases seemed so together and successful, so how could I find fault with any of them? But I did, and sometimes with a passion. The plain and simple truth was that I was jealous of such a seemingly good family, and I was also irritated with them. Surreptitiously, or sometimes overtly, they seemed to put down my ideas. They would condescendingly correct me on occasions to numerous too recall when, because of the fog, I'd inadvertently make a mistake in regurgitating some fact or incorrect information. The patronizing smiles or flicking eye movements of Pamela's family members were enough to send me into an internal rage even as I sat amongst them in supposed calm. I've often revealed this resentment when alone with my wife, bringing about occasional discontent in our marriage. But my new wife understood all too well my disenchanted view of people and the world around me, so she didn't pay too much attention to the way I felt.

When Pamela did take notice, she tried to allay my fears that her family didn't like me and that my observations of their reactions to me were just overreactions or fantasy on my part.

"Why doesn't your father ever allow us to pay for dinner?" I said one night after another visit to Houston.

"I don't know," Pamela answered. "That's just the way it is when I come home. I never get to pay for anything."

"Is it because I don't bring in any money? We're buying dinner in California. He must know we have some money. He won't even let me reach for the check. And he never asks me about what I do with my time. None of your family does."

"They don't ask about what anyone does."

"That's not true. Your father always wants to know how you're doing in school. I'm going to school now. Why doesn't he want to know how I'm doing in school?"

I considered the things I might have to tell Pamela's father. How I could tell him about the teacher with one eyebrow. How I could say "Have you ever read *Moon Palace*?" I might even have been able to let him read one of my stories. But then I realized that I really didn't want to say anything to Bob, because I knew he'd only smile that "Oh" smile of his that told me that what I had to say was nice, but it wasn't really necessary. We all know about what you do, the "Oh" smile would add. And even though I knew he wouldn't really have cared about what was happening in my life, I wanted him to ask me about it anyway.

"I don't know why my dad doesn't want to know about your school. Why don't you ask him? Do you ever ask about his life?"

"No, because I already know about his life. He's an engineer. And even though I don't really know what engineers do, I know they make a lot of money, and that's all that counts, right? Just the way everybody in your family makes a lot of money. Just the way you'll make a lot of money. I just wish everybody in your family would value what I do and what I say sometimes. Instead they all try to avoid me with a smile and a look back and forth between one another when I do have something to say."

"We like to smile Ken, that's all. That's all there is to it, okay?"

I considered this point, but still the uneasiness stayed with me. And I knew that even if I had overreacted to some of the things that occurred with Pamela's family, or addressed the way they avoided me, I wouldn't have been able to do anything about it. Once again it would have been one of those examples of realizing the error of my ways when I ruined everyone's evening with an accusatory tone—whether it was justified or not. And what if I was wrong about them? I had been wrong about people before.

There were definitely times when I wished I could have kept my mouth shut; times when a less obsessive person might have chosen to let things slide. The salt shaker incident was one such time that shouldn't ever have been brought to the dinner table.

It was Christmas dinner, 2001. We had just sat down for a feast that included turkey and homemade giblet gravy. Mr. and Mrs. Robert Thomas's dining-room table was decked out in linen, and there was pecan pie waiting for us in the kitchen. Pamela's brother had flown in to Houston from San Francisco, and her sister had come from San Antonio, easily a good two-hour drive. And of course Pamela and I had driven from Georgetown, Texas, which was even farther away from Houston. To add to the long drive's tedium, we had our four-year-old daughter Kristina in tow. Now seated at the dinner table with us, Kristina sat to my left on two thick phone books, so she could reach the fixings. She was beaming and couldn't wait to dig in.

In the beginning, when events like these had been new to me, I couldn't believe my eyes. But ironically enough, since Pamela and I had flown back to her parents' home for get-togethers like this before, what I now saw was almost second nature. Everybody at one table. No yelling, no swearing. A family actually seated in a lovely dining room, like the ones I saw in those feel-good family movies as a kid that had always seemed so fake to me. A scene like this one still generated feelings that led me to believe I had somehow been cheated out of a few good holiday extras as a kid. How I had always wanted a scene like that in my home on Eighth Avenue. I would have given away a trunk full of toys just to have a single Christmas dinner like that one. Smiles on everyone's faces, a sober father like Pamela's who had just said grace and was about to carve up the turkey. And all that jovial talk around the table of Christmases past, or how nice a new Christmas sweater might look on someone. It was a Norman Rockwell moment, but I'm sure Mr. Rockwell would have never painted in a person with ADD. Because if he had, the painting might have taken on a twist.

"Is something wrong?" Pamela's brother said, across the table from me. I hadn't eaten a thing on my pristine china dinner plate. For some reason I couldn't yet. I was too drawn to the salt and pepper shakers. I'd been staring at them for a good long time and I still wasn't sure why. But I must have been wearing a nonplussed look for Keith to suddenly ask his question. He seldom butted in to people's business unless he felt there was a good reason. Keith's an incredibly smart man who chooses his words carefully. He's also a man with a memory I'd kill for.

"I'm not sure," I answered.

Keith shoved another piece of turkey into his mouth, but he was still eyeing me. I could feel the stare more than see it, and I knew that he'd probably already shot another few sly looks at his father. But the rest of the Thomases didn't pay much attention to what was happening between Keith and me—not at that moment at least.

Then I reached out and grabbed for one of the shakers. They weren't see-through, so I balked. The one with the single hole, I thought, or the shaker with multiple holes? I wanted salt, but it suddenly occurred to me that I wasn't sure which shaker would have salt in it. I had to choose one of them, so I chose the shaker with one hole and flicked it twice over my turkey before realizing that pepper, not salt, was coming out.

I paused again and looked at the shaker. Then I put it down and stared at both shakers again. Keith took note of what surely must have been a look of consternation on my face this time. "It's pepper," I said, trying to flash a smile at Pamela's brother. I knew Pamela had now glanced over at me, and so did everyone else except my daughter. The Thomases are a family that doesn't miss much.

"Yeah?" Keith said, shooting a look at his father and then back at me.

"I don't know," I said, now reaching for the shaker with salt and sprinkling some on my turkey. "I guess I just thought it would be salt, that's all."

Pamela looked at me again. I could tell she knew something was brewing in my foggy mind, but she had no idea what.

"The pepper shaker has fewer holes," Keith said, as if to help me out. He confirmed this with a look at his father again. Bob looked at me and smiled. I smiled back and then shook my head.

"Didn't you want pepper?" Keith had to ask.

"No, I didn't. It's just that, well, I don't know. I guess I expected the shaker with the single hole to have salt in it."

"No, the pepper shaker always has fewer holes. It always has fewer holes. That's how you can tell the difference between it and the salt shaker"

"I don't think—" I began.

"So you don't pour out too much pepper," Keith cut in. "But people want to pour out more salt, so there are always more holes in salt shakers," he added.

"But I thought salt would be in this shaker."

"The pepper shaker always has fewer holes," Keith reiterated.

"Always...no, I think I've used salt shakers with two holes...even one hole. Yes, I've definitely used a salt shaker with one hole before."

"No," Keith laughed as he quickly shot a look around the table to help confirm his reply. "Pepper shakers always have fewer holes."

"No—" I began again.

"Ken, it's not a big deal," Pamela cut in.

"It is a big deal—with me it is. Everyone always thinks he's right around here, but I'm not laughing the way he is. I'm just being serious. I'm just stating the facts. Salt shakers have fewer holes than pepper shakers, and I've used ones with one hole before."

The sound of silverware on china sliced through a short pause before Keith spoke up again. "No, we can't give in this time, I'm sorry. It's just the way things are. With salt and pepper shakers I mean. Like Pamela said, it's not that big a deal," he said, flashing looks around the table.

All of the Thomases smiled back—except Pamela, of course. She just looked down at her plate forlornly.

"You can smile at everyone all you want, goddamit! But it won't change things!" I yelled and shot out of my seat before quickly going upstairs to the guest bedroom.

And that was where I stayed for the rest of our visit with the Thomases. Later, still fuming, I told Pamela about that I didn't want anything to do with Keith or her family. She just said again that she thought it wasn't a big deal, and that only made me angrier. I snuck out when everyone was asleep and walked past all the happy store-bought snowmen and reindeer, all the Santas and strings of multicolored lights, turning street corners without even knowing where I was or where I was going in that foreign Texas neighborhood. When I finally tired of walking, I somehow found my way back to the Thomas home and snuck back into bed. Now I felt bad for ruining Christmas dinner, but I also felt that I had to take a stand with the Thomases for once.

I stayed awake all that night, finally succumbing to sleep in the wee hours of the morning. When I awoke I remembered what had happened the previous night, and I began to put on my stone face again. Pamela and Kristina came rushing upstairs playing some kind of game. Pamela said there might still be some breakfast left if I wanted it, but I said that I didn't, and I just wanted to go home. I stayed in the guestroom until it was time to leave, and then I stormed downstairs and shoved our bags into our Isuzu and sped away without saying goodbye to a single Thomas who was staying behind.

Shortly after returning to Georgetown, Kristina and I accompanied Pamela on a business trip to California. While in my old stomping grounds, I visited Jake and told him about what had happened at Christmas dinner. I laid out the whole shaker scene. I asked him how many holes he thought were in a salt shaker and he said there was usually more than one. I shook my head and said, "Oh man. Are you sure?" and somehow, deep down, I knew he was right.

Later, I checked our salt and pepper shakers at home, but this didn't help because both shakers had the same amount of holes. I also checked the salt and pepper shakers at Denny's and noticed that the pepper shaker had fewer holes. Again, I felt guilty, and stupid. What must the Thomases think of me now? I thought. Why do I always have to act this way? Why did I think salt shakers had fewer holes? I don't get it.

About a month later I took a much-needed vacation. I went back to England to see my friend William. I always needed to visit Europe again every once in a while. William drove me to Felixstowe at my request. It was one of the towns I had lived in about thirteen years earlier; the same town where Shelly had slapped me on the butt on the boardwalk when I was a skinny airmen living by the sea with Dennis Clannihan; and the same town where I had written "Fuck England" in larger-than-life letters on a black-board at a party with a bunch of Brits standing around me.

That was all history now, and as Roger and I sped by the North Sea listening to some unknown classical composer's masterpiece, I looked for that mischievous young girl I used to know. Of course I knew I'd never see her—and even if I did, I wouldn't recognize her. I had William try to find the old house I used to live in, but I couldn't be sure exactly where it was. I recalled the American flag Dennis and I had hung along our house's upstairs balcony and wondered where that rowdy big brother of mine lived now. Shortly after being discharged from the Air Force, Dennis had sent me a photo of himself with both hands giving me the middle finger. Dennis was always such a joker.

William pulled into a little restaurant by a marina, and we went inside for fish and chips and ale just the way we used to. I reached for a bottle of vinegar so that I could drown my fish in this condiment the way the English did. William and I were in good spirits, already a little tipsy. I automatically reached for the salt shaker, without even recalling the Thomas Christmas dinner a month earlier. But this time, instead of reaching for a shaker with lots of holes, I reached for a shaker with one hole. I shook the shaker over my fish and a beautiful shower of white granules floated down toward my plate.

"It's salt," I said.

"Yes, well, what the bloody hell did you think it would be?" William replied.

"Salt. Look. Salt, goddamit." It was then I realized that for some reason, at the Thomas Christmas dinner, my cross-wired brain had remembered some insignificant detail from years before. There were salt shakers somewhere with one hole in them, but of course Keith wouldn't have known that. He'd never been to England. So as far as he knew, there weren't any salt shakers with one hole. Still, I relished the fact that I had been right about something in my life. For once I had known about something without even knowing I knew it. The next day I told William that we needed to go into Chatham, where he still lived. I told my old English friend that I needed to buy a salt shaker and I needed the shaker to actually have the word salt on it. I said that I needed to send the shaker to my brother in law with a short note, a sort of "See? I told you so!" But I never did send the shaker. Instead, I called Keith when I got back to America. I told him I was sorry for the way I had acted at Christmas dinner. I was surprised to discover that Keith didn't even know what I was talking about.

There have been other run-ins with the Thomases—silly, unfortunate ADD misunderstandings. Sometimes I still harbor anger over things they've said to me. Sometimes I misread the looks or smiles directed my way, but we still manage to get through the holidays together, and I don't think they notice as much when I put my foot in my mouth. Thankfully, my feelings toward Pamela's family, and all the other stuff she's had to endure, haven't affected our relationship to the point of some tragic marital outcome. Not yet, anyway.

Just as I predicted, Pamela got a high-paying job after graduating from Stanford with an M.B.A. A plastics company in San Jose, California, hired her, and even though we had now incurred an incredible expense from our student loans, we began to live a life filled with all the luxuries a good job can bring. One of the first things we did was to move from our basement room to the upper portion of the house we'd been living in, which had previously been occupied by an attorney and his wife. After four years of living in a space not much bigger than a large hotel room, we were suddenly introduced to two bedrooms, a living room, and a kitchen with a stove. And now, we could even see the San Francisco Bay from a roomy redwood deck.

Just as the song from the old Jeffersons sitcom used to say, we were "moving on up." And it wasn't just our living accommodations that improved; it was our whole lifestyle. Pamela's new company was good to us in many ways. Of course, the obvious increase in cash flow helped us to breathe easier, but it also gave us the freedom to take more trips to places like Tahoe and Houston. In addition to the occasional vacation spots, I often got to go with Pamela when she attended trade shows for her new company. Sometimes these trade shows were overseas. One was in Birmingham, England, and I gladly accepted an invitation to accompany Pamela back to the country I loved. Birmingham was pretty far from Ipswich and Rochester, the towns where my English friends lived, but it was still in England.

Once in Birmingham, I rented a car and visited nearby Ironbridge where, just as the name would suggest, stood an impressive, black iron bridge that spanned a wide river. I think it was the first bridge of its kind ever built, but given my propensity to forget details, I could be wrong. I do know that I liked the town of Ironbridge though. I rented a room next to a pub on the main drag downtown. That evening I had a drink in the quiet pub, sitting in a booth in the back. Nobody spoke to me other than to ask what I'd have to drink. I spent the night in obscurity, alone in my own thoughts, not really aware of anything but the temperature and the hushed conversations around me.

The next morning, after walking across the iron bridge, I set off for Wales, with plans to catch a ferry from a town called Fishguard to Ireland. I'd always wanted to visit both Wales and Ireland. The ride through Wales was relaxing and pleasant, with lush, rolling green hills, enticing Sherwood Forest-like thickets, and rocky shoreline. It was how I pictured the quintessential United Kingdom. There were quaint pubs, of course, many overgrown with ivy and mystery. There was also a new language pervading my mind. It became apparent after I crossed another bridge over another of the many rivers. Suddenly, the voices on the radio stations and the words on the signs along the road took on a sort of other-worldly sound and look. It was my first introduction to Welsh and, as with any new language, it utterly confused me. But this distraction didn't matter too much since the fog was especially thick on that trip. I was already overcome with a sense of disorientation, so that my mind merely floated along with the words I couldn't even pronounce or repeat with any degree of success.

The itinerary was fairly straightforward in Wales. I drove all day, stopping only to eat, fill up the tiny rental car's gas tank, or look at something that caught my eye. More often than not, that something would be an archaic structure or a chilly, rock-covered beach. For some reason, oceans and their beaches have always had an especially strong pull on me, and I'm usually compelled to stop and explore them whenever I can.

As it approached evening in Wales, I'd begin to worry, just as I had on many other trips like that one, about whether or not I'd find a place to stay for the night. One way or another, I always did. Once I slept in a large college town that began with the letter A and was followed by a bunch of letters arranged in a way that left me baffled, but particularly intrigued me. The town's hotel, or bed and breakfast, or whatever it was with its many rooms, had a pub downstairs where I had dinner. I liked the pub because it was very old and small, and men were having conversations about sheep. The scene seemed like it had taken place five hundred years ago when civilizations were unconnected, and technology had yet to muddle a simpler time; a time when the fog and I would have fitted in a lot better.

Sometimes I think back to this pub in the town that begins with that letter A, the town I couldn't pronounce no matter how many times I heard its name pass my way. I almost wish it could have kidnapped me, understood I needed to live in a simple place doing simple things. Staring at the ocean, I wondered what lay on the other side and who sat there wondering about me. But nothing spectacular like that kidnapping happened, and I just got in my sterile rental car and drove to the next hard-to-spell place, passing by another field, another cow, another church. I knew I wouldn't recall much of it in a few months. Even the image of the pub with the sheep-talkers is just a dark, formless impression in my mind now. Only its essence remains with me; a prevailing mood or feeling, but nothing concrete.

I eventually found Fishguard, the one place I could pronounce. It proved that my map, with the little image of a ferry on it next to the town's name, was accurate. The ferry would sail across the immense brownish channel to Ireland. It seemed as though I'd soon be setting foot on the land of my father's father. I'd earned the chance since it had been an incredibly long drive to reach the little point on my pale map. But I didn't set sail that day, and it wasn't because of some sort of incredible turn of events such as the ferry breaking down or the channel drying up. It was because of something more mundane. I learned I would have had to leave my rental car behind. I don't recall why, since the ferry accommodated vehicles, but it was reason enough to deter me from boarding the ferry. I hadn't paid the full coverage insurance required on the car to give me the peace of mind needed in order to leave it behind. So it was with a deep regret that I turned the Metro around and traversed the same road that had brought me to Fishguard. The same road that would take me back to the modern Birmingham hotel, and ultimately back to a London airport and California.

Monkey on My Back

YOU'D THINK THAT an obsession with a tall, kind co-worker, a plethora of jobs, and a misty mind would have been enough to keep me busy before my marriage to Pamela, but it wasn't. When it rains, it pours. And when it pours, it pours whores. And just like the responsible mailman who makes his rounds so that the mail can get through in inclement weather, I made my rounds, so to speak. I could say my infatuation with picking up whores back in those sexually lean years prior to marriage was solely because I didn't have a lot of money and lacked a promising future, but it wasn't the only reason.

Still, it is true that women tend to be more prone to hand out sex when they know the men they're getting involved with have money and lives that are going somewhere worthwhile. One could also make the argument that I prowled the streets at night for prostitutes because I didn't have anything better to do; or that all those Harold Robbins books and hidden photos in my brother's pornography collection had contributed to my sexual appetite. But I know it was more than that too.

The fog was mature now and it needed grown-up sensual stimuli. A lucky feel in the back seat of a car wouldn't suffice. I needed to feed the fog and its craving with a certain adult outcome, and the only way I could reach this outcome was to pay for it. It went against the grain though. I've always considered myself good looking, and therefore as a good catch when it comes to the aesthetics of sharing flesh. I was fortunate enough to reach home plate with a few one-night stands without having to pay, but I could probably count these lucky rendezvous on one hand. No, when it came to getting laid, it was the prostitute who came to my rescue, or my demise, depending on how you look at it.

The prostitutes were women in every sense of the word, with all the parts and feminine wiles that heterosexual males want when needing a sexual experience, but they weren't the kind of women I wanted. Apart from the anatomical connections between pros and non-pros, the comparison ends. As with the pro I'd had sex with my first time, these women of the night were often dirty, smelly, nervous, and all business. Most of the whores had sex just so they could buy dope, and they didn't keep this fact secret. Looking back on things now, I shudder to think that I helped to keep many prostitutes' addictions alive and well, just so I could get my rocks off. Who knows what damage the money I paid them really did. I'm sure my financial assistance may have contributed to the deaths of a few empty women in filthy hotel rooms, a few longing, motherless children in foster homes; not to mention benefiting the drug trade and all its negative impact on the world.

But at the time I was paying for sex, the craving of my own addiction made it difficult to think of the consequences. A sexual addict's behavior is no different to a drug addict's. An addiction needs what it needs, when it needs it, and only deals with the consequences later. I was addicted to sex—and probably still am. I was so addicted back when I picked up prostitutes that, even though I wore a condom on my excursions—most of the time, thank God—I nonetheless threw caution to the wind when I felt the desire to have sex. I constantly went where prostitutes told me to go—without considering who might be lying in wait for me around the next corner.

Night after night, and sometimes during the day, I'd cruise the same stretch of El Camino I'd cruised years before during my first search for whores, looking for any woman who seemed as though she was doing more than trying to get some exercise or move from point A to point B. But there were some lines even I wouldn't cross. I wouldn't pick up anyone who looked sick, for example. Some of the women out there on the strip just looked too disgusting or near death. And I wouldn't pick up any women who looked as though they were crazy. Still, if the women I saw weren't too fat or skanky looking, I'd do my best to pick them up in whatever I was driving, either a work van, one of my many old beaters, or even my mother's ugly Pacer. All I needed was a set of wheels and a seat for my "date."

Sometimes we'd pull off the main drag to some deserted street and go at it right there, a quick nerve-wracking few minutes for both of us, the two of us wondering when the long arm of the law would pounce. Other times my temporary girlfriend would take me to her place, usually a seedy hotel room with shifty-looking males lurking in the shadows. But they weren't always lurking. I remember a time when a prostitute's husband was in the other room watching TV while I went at it with his wife. Another time, I had to crawl over a roomful of illegal aliens as my seventeen-year-old pro and I went into the bathroom where we did it on a cold tile floor.

We'd do it in the hills, next to fast food restaurants, behind walls, near railroad tracks, below giant mirrors, upstairs, downstairs, when it was quiet, when it was noisy, when cops were circling, when cops weren't anywhere in sight, and many other places I can't even recall. I didn't always pick up women on the street, however. One time I called an escort service and ordered a beautiful Hispanic woman sent out to my hotel room. The woman's skin was a lovely shade of chocolate, and I paid a lot more for her than the typical whore, though I ended up getting the same thing in the end. She was sweet, and she told me I shouldn't be paying for sex; that with my looks and personality I could probably find a legitimate girlfriend who would let me have sex for free.

In the end, all that mattered to these working women was that I had the usual twenty or sometimes forty dollars required to get what I wanted, and that we had someplace relatively safe to undress. Getting the money gave me all the more incentive for getting another one of the many jobs I held. I couldn't earn enough money to get out of my mother's duplex, but at least I could get laid.

As the john/pro scene played itself out with incredible regularity, I began to feel more and more guilty. Even though I continued to wear condoms, I also became more and more fearful of getting some God-awful disease that would stay with me for the rest of my life, or even worse, terminate it. I joked about all the prostitutes I'd had with my friend, Jake. He'd just laugh, shake his head, and say, "You better watch out." These were his words for: "The cops will get you, if you're not careful." I'd usually just laugh back and say something like "yeah." The fog hardly registered the seriousness of the situation.

My sexual addiction didn't stop at picking up prostitutes. When I wasn't looking for a purchased quickie somewhere, I spent my time in adult bookstores satisfying my hunger with film after film in the dingy, ejaculation-smeared booths where old men and other degenerates would congregate for a quick fix of porno before retiring to some lonely bed. I bought magazines that featured my many fantasies, and I'd take them home to dwell on every new scenario a twisted mind could think up.

But when you took away all the trappings of my perverted mind, the core of its sexual desire was simple: a fascination with women that transcended any other since I first began to obsess over coins on the living room floor as a child. Even today, when I see a woman, my thoughts are on each different body part, each different hair color, movement, and each seemingly insignificant idiosyncrasy that makes women what they are. Even when women are within my grasp, they seem untouchable. I don't think I've ever fully discovered all the secrets women possess, and I probably never will.

Each day is a struggle to go anywhere away from home without my mind going into a spin because some pleasing female walks within view. And as with my other obsessions, women are both a Godsend and a curse. Like music and driving, women can transport me to a friendlier place, but sometimes they can overwhelm me so much that I almost cease to function. After I've explored a woman visually, I then automatically consider all the possibilities of what it would be like to become intimate with her. When this happens, the fog takes me into an intense, sexually charged fantasy, as if my will is nothing but a feather trapped in a perpetually turning tornado.

The major difference between my life now and my life during the prostitute days is that it's not just sex that I'm looking for in a woman. I get to spend my time finding out what makes a woman tick, and there is a personal investment involved in marriage. Even back when I was cruising for prostitutes, I wanted more than just a quick physical connection. I wanted to be connected spiritually too, and I wanted to have a relationship that might lead to my becoming a father, so I could have more to look forward to in my old age. I wanted someone to talk to who shared my interests; someone I could get to know and who could get to know me. Back during my prostitute days I also wanted to get rid of the guilt over what I had become. In many ways, I saw that I was no different than the women I picked up. They were considered by many to be no more than predators who stalked the decent menfolk of society, and were looked down upon. I was no better. After all, even though prostitutes got paid for what they and I did, I still took advantage of their need to make a buck. In the end, I used them just as much as they used me. But my problem with hungering for prostitutes went further than this. I think the real reason I used them was so that I could control a woman for about ten minutes or so. So that I could imagine that I somehow possessed her. Maybe in some way, even though I did only know these women for such a short period of time, I had some unknown fantasy that they were closer to me than I realized; that on one level anyway I did possess them, and I was able forever to take something away from them. But in reality, of course, the only thing I really took from them was a sad reminder of who they were and who I was: two unfortunate victims who had been sentenced long ago to no other crime than that of their own need and the failure to somehow rise above it.

So it came as no small victory when I finally broke the cycle. Instead of being a social outcast when it came to my connection to women, I was a married man. Ultimately, marriage is a great experience, even though I often feel the stress of being limited to the terrain of just one woman's body and one person's predictable sexual behavior. I only wish I could have somehow found a wife, or at least a steady girlfriend, a lot sooner. Maybe then I wouldn't have run into the trouble I did as the result of participating in an illegal act.

Ironically, the trouble began only after my use of prostitutes had reached a point of saturation. I'd probably had sex with every hooker on the strip of El Camino. The area in question ran all the way from Fifth Avenue in Redwood City, right at the fringes of wealthy Atherton, (where getting lucky further south wasn't on the cards), to the Redwood City/San Carlos border, (where the hunt also went cold further north). I'd been in every hotel or motel on this strip of road, and I'd parked on most of the side streets that paralleled it.

It was only a matter of time before my luck ran out. It happened one night when I picked up a large-boned blonde hanging out in front of an out-of-business gas station. I should have known the woman looked too clean to be a pro, but I tested the waters by asking her if she was a cop. Someone had once told me a police officer had to identify herself, or any subsequent bust would be deemed entrapment by a court later. So what could go wrong?

What went wrong was that my source of information didn't hold true. I ended up in a hotel room and a bunch of sheriffs burst in as soon as I offered the undercover agent money for sex. When the female I had thought I would be getting on top of a few minutes after my payment showed me her shiny gold badge, an indescribable rush of fear came over me. My addiction had finally done me in. The idea that I was going to jail, the place I feared most, and the idea of the embarrassment the arrest would bring after my Christian mother found out that she was housing a degenerate son, raced through my mind. I kept thinking: why couldn't I have stopped earlier? Hadn't I had enough fun? But it was too late for that now. My life would be ruined.

Fortunately for me and my mother, I didn't go to jail that night. Yes, technically I had been arrested, but I found out that I'd just have to appear in court later and pay a small fine since it was my first arrest. My mother never found out about the shameful incident—as far as I know, anyway—and after a short probation, all that was left to show for my arrest was a new criminal record in some database listing some poor clown's misdemeanor for solicitation.

Even though the crime was rushed through the criminal court system without so much as a judgmental finger waving in my direction, I still felt a substantial amount of embarrassment, not to mention a consuming degree of guilt. All those cops in that hotel room the night of the bust knew that here was a man before them who had lowered himself to pay for sex, and it was enough to make me avert my eyes from theirs when my rights were read. I later appeared before a judge, a female clerk, and a handful of attendees in the gallery. The courtroom exit seemed miles away when I had to walk past all those gawkers about ten minutes after I'd entered their sight.

Still, all embarrassment, guilt, and my new criminal record aside, getting arrested for soliciting an alleged prostitute did one very important thing for me: it made me stop. Even though my sexual addiction was strong, my fear of going to jail was even stronger. The arrest had showed me how close I had come to serving a substantial amount of time behind bars. Because I had no prior record for picking up whores, I got a slap on the wrist. But since I was told by my new probation officer that I would go to jail if I was caught out there on El Camino trying to buy sex again, I hung up pursuing hookers for good. When I told the probation officer that I knew what I had been doing was illegal but I just couldn't stop, he gave me the number of a sex addicts' support group in Palo Alto.

The approach used to help someone with a sexual addiction is similar to the twelve-step program used by Alcoholics Anonymous. But the meetings didn't help me. In fact, they added new fantasies to my overfilled mental file cabinet. The stories women told in the church's meeting room were just too much of a turn-on, and I even had hopes of picking up some of the storytellers since they seemed as weak as I was. But even with my compromised judgment, I understood that this type of thinking was counterproductive to the goal of the meetings and the people trying to get a handle on their addictions.

So I stopped showing up at the sexually charged, Friday night get-togethers where everyone told about his or her deepest desires and frustrations. Instead, I spent the next lonely clump of years trying to get laid the legal way until I finally got lucky and met my wife. Of course, after that I didn't need to look for prostitutes anymore. But I still continued to lust after women just as I always had and probably always will, married or not. And I continued to try to get my wife to participate in a swinger lifestyle which she objected to. I guess once an addict, always an addict, as they say. You can probably say something like that about someone who has ADD too. Once an ADDer, always an ADDer, and I'm sure there's not much worse than a person with a sexual addiction and ADD. Thank goodness I have a new hobby to keep my mind off sex.

First Comes Love, Then Comes Marriage, Then Comes...

A GOOD PAYCHECK not only changes the way someone lives, but it changes the way he thinks too. Now that Pamela and I had moved up in the world and had more money and a roomier abode, we were ready for the next predictable step in a pampered western home.

After college, I landed a legal advertising job with a large Bay area newspaper in San Mateo. The job's pace was frenetic, and I barely kept up with my workload, but at least I had a job. Once my boss, Jane, had a chance to get to know me, I think she knew how my mind worked. Because of this, she gave me a lot of latitude. In fact, I think she had more patience with me than any boss I've ever had. It's lucky that she did, otherwise I'm sure I would have been fired early on.

One of the things that helped my boss get to know me was our banter and sharing of personal information during the course of the workday. Since the door that joined our offices was always open, we'd toss little tidbits back and forth about favorite pets or desires. I even got the inside scoop on Jane's love life. My pretty young boss was unmarried and didn't seem to have any hobbies to speak of. She focused most of her attention on a Basenji, a cute, little, shorthaired dog she had pictures of on of her office walls.

My dog-loving boss also had a thing for one of the sales reps in the back of the building. I really admired Jane because, no matter how much joking around or chitchat took place, she was always on top of her game and rarely,

if ever, made mistakes in her work. Even though I eventually came to understand my job duties and they became second nature, I still made a lot of
nagging little mistakes that irked me no end. I wanted to be like Jane in my
work, go about it without even a second thought and always come out right,
but it just wasn't on the cards.

Jane, however, was like one of those surgeons on the TV show *M.A.S.H*
who carried on a jovial conversation while performing some complex
medical procedure in someone's bowels. Unfortunately, I've never had the
luxury of being able to have my mind in one place with an adequate amount
of efficiency, let alone in two places at the same time. The fog is a methodical
beast and it likes to perform one task at a time. If it doesn't get its wish, it
becomes angry and overburdened and sometimes causes those nitpicky little
mistakes. In the case of my job at the paper, these mistakes took the form of
not making sure a legal ad got into the newspaper the way it was supposed
to, and if it did, maybe a few errors might sneak in with it, prompting Jane to
point them out to me. Of course, these weren't serious errors, and as I got
more familiar with my duties, they occurred less frequently, but that wasn't
the point. I wanted to be perfect, or as close to perfect as possible. If Jane and
those TV surgeons could do it, why couldn't I?

Though I sought to perfect my attention to detail, after a while even the
need to reach this unobtainable goal didn't seem so great. Ultimately I fell
into a routine that brought in paycheck after paycheck for close to a
year—much to Pamela's delight. Any extra income helped to pay off the
astronomical Stanford school loans and those exorbitant credit card bills
we'd incurred while in college.

In fact, our financial situation was looking so good to Pamela that she
brought up the next predictable step in our marriage. In short, my plotting
wife wanted a baby. Actually, the news hadn't caught me totally off guard.
We'd spoken about having children before. We both wanted them. But I also
knew Pamela's need to have a child was stronger than mine. So I went along
with her desire not to wait any longer. I wasn't opposed to the idea; in fact,
she was right again. It was an opportune time to have a child, and if my hope
for having a child who'd visit me in my old age was to become a reality, I had
to get started on the mission, too. After all, who else but my own child would
tend to a doddering old misfit who had few friends or other relatives left, if
any. Who else, but a man's children, would drop by some quiet nursing home
or musty room in the bowels of an arcane house somewhere? But this wasn't
my only reason for wanting to sire a child. I'd really wanted that child of

Susan's to be mine back in England. The fact that the child wasn't mine had left me feeling cheated somehow. With Pamela, I could now make up for that loss, and there would be no doubts as to the identity of this new baby's father.

So Pamela and the fog and I began to make all the necessary arrangements for a new baby's arrival. We also got to work planting the seed that would some day grow into our dream child. This planting was a welcome benefit since it meant lots of farming for my plow. But, oh, if I'd only known what would come a few months later, I don't know if even this pleasant pastime of mine could have lured me up that fertile path.

Still, once the seed is planted, all the farmer can do is wait for the harvest that follows. Meanwhile, there was still work to do away from the farm down at the newspaper. As was my usual modus operandi, I'd reached the point of disinterest there which had always led to my downfall with other jobs. To keep another travesty from happening, I tried to get a job as a reporter. I thought that at least if I had the chance to write, maybe the futility I felt with my legal advertising position would subside. Unfortunately, the paper's editor said I didn't have enough experience to write for the paper, so I continued scrutinizing the many boilerplate public notices that went into the paper's back pages, and I continued talking with Jane through our offices' adjoining open door.

The banter and joking around wasn't as common anymore, and I think Jane could sense that I wasn't as happy as I used to be. I frequently mentioned how I was getting bored with my routine, and how I needed a change, but I also told Jane I was trying to hang onto my job since I needed employment stability.

Nonetheless, the agitation and frustration of needing to get away from my nine-to-five world wouldn't leave me, and it began to wear on Jane. I could tell that she was getting upset and probably wished I would just quit. But even though my attitude made things unbearable at times, amazingly, she still wouldn't fire me. I think she wanted me to stay. After all, we were buddies, and our talks together were often more than just jovial in nature, they were heartfelt. We learned a lot about each other. Once, I even bared my soul to Jane, telling her that I thought I was a failure, that I'd failed at everything in life, but she told me I'd just created this fantasy, this lie. In fact, after examining my life bit by bit, Jane told me I hadn't failed at all, that I only thought I'd failed. This made me feel a lot better, and I looked at my life dif-

ferently (at least at that moment), but it still didn't alter the fact that I needed
a change.

As with Cooley, even though I actually had a lot more to keep me busy at
my present job with *The Times*, I started taking long walks away from the
building during breaks or lunch to get away from my work. Sometimes I'd
stop by the business reporter's office and shoot the breeze about my dream
of becoming a famous novelist. The reporter was a really nice guy and told
me that if I knew of any out-of-the-ordinary San Mateo County small businesses, to let him know, since at that time he was doing pieces on businesses
like these. He even said that I could submit some articles to him, and if they
were good enough he'd get them in the paper. Unfortunately, I didn't come
across any of the kinds of businesses the reporter was looking for, and even if
I had, I wouldn't have had the time to write about them given my other
duties at the paper.

Things were coming to a head both at home and work now. I'd reached
that pivotal time when staying put just wasn't an option anymore. Once I felt
this way, there was no possibility of change. Like a ship that has set its course
for some shore on the horizon, I had set my course too. But unlike the ship, I
had no destination, no ultimate end in sight. I just wanted to venture away
from the port in search of the unknown. Then I latched onto the idea that
someone would have to take care of our baby, who was now close to being
born. Since the idea of day care didn't sit well with me, I thought that that
someone should be me. Why not? If I stayed at the newspaper, my entire
salary would only go to pay for childcare to someone, or some business, that
didn't have the same incentive as I did to look after my child. And how hard
could it be to take care of a child? I'd be my own boss, set my own hours, and
maybe even get in a little time to write during the day. Okay, maybe that last
part was a little unrealistic, but I was naïve, someone who hadn't been around
children since I was a child myself. I'd definitely never taken care of a child.

Still, I had discovered a mysterious new land while in that open sea, and I
set off with a full head of steam for what soon would be called Stay-at-Home
Island. I cut through the fog in those uncharted waters with nothing more
than a made-up map to get me there. I knew nothing at all about diapers,
bottles, burp cloths, strollers, or any of the other kinds of provisions I'd need
for my Robinson Crusoe-like outpost on that unexplored island where I was
to land.

Nonetheless, I said goodbye to the predictable aspects of another
dead-end job, to the calm waters at the newspaper, to Jane, to the nine-to-five

grind, to everything that was remotely familiar to me, and for the next five years drifted away from the working world.

Kristina Rain Patterson was born on the morning of September 29, 1997, and I was there to witness her birth. I had planned to remain in the tiny hospital waiting room meant for nervous fathers and smiling grand-mothers. The truth is that it appeared as though I'd be even more removed from the delivery room than first thought. After checking Pamela in to her antiseptic room at Sequoia Hospital, I went home. I watched television and finally went to bed. The doctor told me the baby wouldn't be coming anytime soon so I'd be better off somewhere else. I had all the comforts of home and the family pets to keep me company. The next morning, after an unrestful night's sleep, I set off for the hospital since Pamela's doctor had induced labor.

Probably like a lot of fathers, I had secret thoughts that this day would be different somehow; that the most noteworthy event in my life was coming to pass, that my bloodline was being passed on. But the day wasn't different, maybe a little warm, but other than that nothing extraordinary. No flames were coming down from heaven, no mass societal changes of any kind. It was just another workday, and another baby was about to exit the wet and enter the dry, about to see the light and begin to experience the well-worn world I knew.

Even though the day showed no evidence of anything supernatural, it *was* the most important day of my life. It was true that I'd only added a little DNA to the mix for making a baby, and almost anybody was capable of doing the same, but in my mind Kristina would be the first thing in my life of value and uniqueness that I'd ever helped to create. I promised myself that I'd do my best from the day of her birth onward to invest the time needed to make sure our daughter would be an exceptional person and would have an exceptional life in every possible way.

Shortly after ten a.m., on a Monday, when Pamela's straining body could take no more, it finally happened: Kristina slipped into my world, and at last I was a father. For better or worse, that blue being before me was now a part of my cluttered life, and I had to shape up. And for some reason, just as I thought my daughter's arrival would somehow alter the day, I also thought it would alter me: that all the fog would somehow blow away, and I'd become like that *Leave It to Beaver* father who made all the right decisions. But there was no sudden insight, no incredible wisdom, no new clarity of mind bestowed upon me. I was still a man with ADD, grasping for answers and focus. If anything, the months ahead added to my confusion and lack of clarity and magnified my concerns about being a father.

I was beset with a barrage of banshee-like cries that would send my mind into a spin; cries that only someone who has spent days in close proximity to an infant can fathom. Sometimes Kristina's crying had so much of an effect on me that I wanted to run away from her, just so I could regain the composure necessary to perform the most rudimentary tasks associated with taking care of a baby. But I couldn't stay away from Kristina very long. It just didn't seem fair to her. It was my job to take care of my daughter, no matter how difficult the task seemed. I'd enlisted voluntarily for this duty and, just like a soldier who doesn't want to face an upcoming battle but in the end does, so too would I eventually have to re-enter the fray. Unfortunately, as with any sustained conflict, casualties are expected, and it would be no different on my isolated front lines.

I was hit hard by the daily bombardment of screaming that left me wounded and shell-shocked. Each morning, Pamela would go off to work, and I'd be left alone with Kristina in what used to be a peaceful setting in the hills. Each time Kristina began to cry, my mind felt like it would begin to separate into tiny chaotic fragments. At first, I'd try to console my daughter with milk or lullabies so she'd go to sleep, but most of the time this wouldn't help and Kristina would continue to scream until I couldn't think straight. I literally began to shake, and I thought I would go mad if the screaming didn't stop. Then, when I couldn't take any more, I'd walk out onto the deck and scream without making a sound. Sometimes, I'd pound my fist on the deck's railing, or call out "Why? What happened to my life?" Other times, I'd merely utter words of profanity or try to cry, but I never could. There were times when I even cursed my Kristina for causing me such anguish. Of course, later on when she was silent and looking up at me with a smile on her face, I'd feel extremely guilty for ever holding my daughter responsible for her behavior.

Ultimately, I'd leave the deck and head back into the room where my screaming daughter lay and pick her up, but I'd still be shaking. I'd beg her to stop crying, but most of the time this didn't work. I learned early on that there is no such thing as a rational baby. I also learned that almost nothing would help to bring calm into my world. It soon became clear that I couldn't handle the situation by myself. In fact, I became so compromised as a result of engaging the baby front lines that I occasionally had to call for reinforcement. Pamela began to take time off from work just so I could take some well-needed R&R—at least until I could deal with the screaming a little better. Eventually, I was able to control myself enough to face the racket that came from Kristina's tiny mouth, so that I could be in the same room with her. Either I became conditioned to handle it or the crying lessened. Pamela started coming home less often, and I fell into a routine that helped to get me through the day.

I soon got used to taking care of a baby, learning the ropes just as well as the most seasoned mother: the important stuff like diapers which seemed to leak the least, which formula to use, when to heat up bottles of Pamela's breastmilk, how many burp cloths to take on an outing; all the rituals that stay-at-home moms had been taking for granted for years. But even though I found that the basics of caring for a baby weren't that complex, I soon discovered that the boredom and monotony of being at home with a small child were almost more unbearable than the screaming I'd had to deal with. I also found that I watched the clock while engaged in this latest job more than in any of the others I'd had. Each day I silently begged for five-thirty p.m. to arrive, so that Pamela would walk through the door, and I could literally hand off tiny Kristina to her mommy. It was only then that I was free.

When all was said and done, this was the biggest shortcoming of my new job: a lack of freedom. At least with all those out-of-the-home jobs I could occasionally leave my work behind for a walk, or coffee break, some diversion to take me away from my work for a short period of time, or in some cases—a long period. I seldom had this luxury while taking care of Kristina. From the time Pamela went off to work in the morning until the time she came home in the late afternoon, I was stuck with my work no matter what. And I do mean no matter what. Once I even had to take care of Kristina when I had a high fever and could get no more than about six feet from a toilet without throwing up. It was days like these that I cursed the world, God, Pamela, and anything or anybody else I could think of. If Pamela had to work late, or attend one of her out-of-town business assignments, leaving Kristina and me alone for a few days, I nearly lost my mind. Sometimes, my little girl and I were lucky enough to accompany Pamela on a business trip. A trip of note was when Kristina turned one, and the three of us went to Paris for a trade show. It not only sums up what it was like for me to be abroad while carrying out the duties of my newest and latest job to date, but also the gist of my state of mind at its most extreme and fragile moments while caring for Kristina when she was a baby.

I'd never been to Paris, so I was looking forward to the experience, even though that meant toting around a demanding baby. In some fated way, however, this pairing seemed appropriately balanced. On the one hand, there was the oblivious one-year-old unable to properly communicate her needs, and on the other hand there was the oblivious adult in a fog who spoke very little French.

The two of us holed up with Pamela in a lavish little hotel in the Latin Quarter, and each day my successful working wife walked a few blocks to a subway where experienced pickpockets secretly waited for the next victim, and uniformed men carrying machine guns walked freely with the rest of the Parisian commuters. While Pamela busied herself with her trade show, Kristina and I explored Paris. Every minute in the so-called "City of Lights" was even more of a struggle than the one at home. Not only did I long for Pamela's working day to end, but I also ached for a fluent understanding of the French language and an expedient ride to the American Airlines jet that would fly us back to California.

But even though the language barrier caused me continual problems, aggravated by extremely rude and unhelpful Parisians and the fact that I was in a hurry to leave France, strangely, I began to feel a sort of freedom I'd never experienced before. It was as though I could walk through the city as if nothing mattered anymore. So what if Paris had few ramps for strollers or highly sought after high chairs for needy babies? And so what if restaurants didn't cater to the needs of parents with children, or if there was no such thing as half-and-half for my morning coffee? I laughed at it all and endeavored to become even ruder than any of those who served me with the typical condescending expressions and unintelligible nasal voices that were clearly meant to mock my lack of understanding their native tongue. These Frenchies just didn't know with whom they were dealing. I'd never been able to understand much of anything before—in my own country, in my own surroundings, or under the best of conditions. What made these people think they could rattle me?

I matched their cold stares, and I even grumbled when they smiled at me. "Je voudre!" quickly became a favorite phrase of mine. Everywhere I went I would command "Je voudre!" this and "Je voudre!" that—"I want! I want!" This command was always followed with one of the few nouns I could muster. The three most common nouns I seemed to use were bread, milk, and butter, three foods the French seem to live on. I also managed to mimic the facial expressions and rude hand gestures exhibited by locals as I wheeled my cumbersome American Kmart stroller with the extra large wheels through streets that were often strewn with dog faeces or other detestable substances that I'd ultimately have to clean off the wheels with a babywipe as I swore under my breath that I would survive whatever was thrown at me.

When I got tired of trying to use French or find an interpreter to convey my intentions, I'd point. Not just a casual finger in the direction of the object of my desire but a mean-spirited je voudre finger that told them I was a man with a cranky baby and I didn't have time for language barriers or rudeness; not in the Baby Gaps where I needed to buy thicker clothing for a shivering little American, and certainly not at Disneyland Paris while demanding that our seafood be cooked and not served raw straight from the icy Atlantic.

We *would* survive Paris, I continually said to myself, even when Kristina had a high fever after first setting foot on French soil. That's all that seemed to matter: to survive. Even if I understood nothing else, we had to eat, to drink, and to get back to that hotel at the end of our four- or five-hour walks around the city. Survival often meant merely to keep moving: climbing the Eiffel Tower, controlled by attendants who wouldn't allow me to leave my stroller at its base; floating down the Seine on a boat toward Notre Dame; or rambling the wide corridors of the Louvre where I took a picture of the Mona Lisa behind its thick sheet of unfriendly plastic. The final movement in Paris took place as we hastily sped through the now far-off foreign streets in a cab toward the airport, where we boarded a plane, which flew us over the enormous Atlantic and back to our familiar home.

It was good to be home again, even if my life still lacked the excitement or freedom it needed. At least people spoke English, and Kristina and I could watch *Teletubbies* or *Sesame Street* in the comfort of our living room, and I could appease my daughter's demanding attention for an hour with the aid of America's favorite babysitter. Just as we had done in Paris, Kristina and I resumed our long daily walks; walks that took us from city to city, thrift shop to thrift shop, bookstore to bookstore, and park to park; all the places where a man and a baby could pass the time until it was the man's turn to have his life back again.

With all the turbulence and boredom, I grew to love Kristina even more. When she wasn't with me, I felt a loss, even though I longed for time for myself, to write, to read, or just to think without being interrupted. Now that Kristina is five and able to discuss just about anything with me, and also able to attend certain children's activities like My First Gym for five hours a day, two times a week, much of my free time has returned, and I don't remember much of the previous five years.

I continue to be a stay-at-home dad, but taking care of Kristina isn't as hard as it used to be. All those days pushing strollers or warming bottles, all those diapers I changed, are now as lost to me as all those minutes I held her everywhere we went, or all the times I wiped food from her dirty face and fingers. I think parenting must be like this even for people without ADD. How can you recall the routine of days that don't differ very much from one another? All those days the fog just tried to cope with another banal few hours while caring for the most precious treasure in its life. In the end, when people reminisce about raising their children, it isn't changing diapers or feeding them that they remember, it's the overall joy of bonding with irreplaceable family members as they grow to maturity. It is a joy that transcends even the clinging fog of ADD.

Epilogue

IN THREE MONTHS I'll be forty-one. No longer am I the bewildered child awakened by the sound of his brother's bed tapping on the wall, or the disillusioned eighteen-year-old embarking on a military career. Instead, I'm a man who's been married ten years with a predictable day-to-day existence and few surprises. Thanks to the efforts of a well-educated and business-savvy wife, I've staved off my need to enter the workforce. I can also thank my wife for helping me to overcome a plethora of problems that would have been difficult to solve on my own.

Even so, I've struggled and continue to struggle with a number of seemingly trivial hurdles, like deciphering a grocery receipt while shopping, or taking much too long to read a clump of pages in a novel. The fog has continued to keep me from that wonderful clarity and peace that I assume everyone else takes for granted.

My life hasn't been all storminess and catastrophe, however. There have been a few moments of clear direction and calm. After all, I have two college degrees, four literary awards for four different pieces of fiction, a wonderful wife I've just barely managed to hang on to, a precious five-year-old, and now a son named Dustin—A little boy who I'm taking care of here in Texas: a boy with the cutest smile I've ever seen; a boy I love dearly and whose interests I will nurture carefully. My one and only hope is that both my children find themselves far from the tribulations associated with ADD, and far from the fog that clouds my mind even now, as I look into their probing young eyes.